# MANAGING
# INNOVATION
# FOR
# GROWTH AND PROFIT

# MANAGING
# INNOVATION
# FOR
# GROWTH AND PROFIT

By

**BEN MILLER**

1970 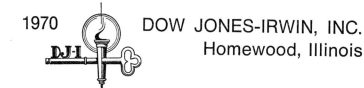 DOW JONES-IRWIN, INC.
Homewood, Illinois

*First Printing, January, 1970*

Library of Congress Catalog Card No. 77–98256

Printed in the United States of America

# WHY THIS BOOK WAS WRITTEN

This book was designed to develop a greater awareness among executives—in business, hospitals, and colleges—of the threat as well as the opportunity presented by an accelerating rate of change in our society. Too often, managers possessing the most advanced skills are either overwhelmed by the forces of change or assume a posture of rigid defiance toward them. Such a manager ceases to be of value to his organization. He is not only obsolete—he is archaic.

What the executive needs in dealing with the forces of change (from both inside and outside his organization) is a force even more powerful. He has that available to him in innovation— planned, purposeful, profit-oriented change. In effect, the manager needs to develop his capacity to manage the *future* just as effectively as he manages the *present*.

I conceive of the job of managing as consisting of two vital roles. One role is that of a caretaker and the other that of an innovator. On the one hand, the manager performs as a caretaker in the sense that he concentrates on achieving day-to-day operating targets. That is, he effectively maintains the status quo. At the same time, the manager assumes the role of an innovator by improving upon day-to-day operations through planned, purposeful, profit-oriented change.

It is the manager's failure to fill the role of innovator which may be his most conspicuous shortcoming, no matter how fine his managerial skills may be. In effect, he is doing half a job when he deals only with day-to-day operations; such a manager may truly be considered archaic.

v

The test of a manager's value is in the results he gets, not merely the skills he may possess. To achieve growth for himself and for his organization, the manager has to be an innovator in addition to meeting current operating targets.

It is the purpose of this book to help managers develop the attitude and skills necessary for innovating. More than that, *Managing Innovation* attempts to provide the manager with guidelines for implementing successful, profitable change, and thus showing the *results* of his upgrading in managerial skills. The focus is narrowed on how to innovate by providing a conceptual framework as well as practical examples of actual innovations by managers in a variety of organizations. The concern is, therefore, for the manager's *performance* in using his innovating skills.

I might add that the need for managers to deal effectively with the forces of change—to innovate—is not confined to business organizations. Hospital executives and college administrators have been rudely confronted with the fact that they too must develop a capability for innovating. Otherwise, they will be unable to cope with the conflicts as greater pressures for more education and better medical care give rise to financial crises.

It is the point of this book to emphasize the *"purpose* of innovation in terms of management objectives so that the results of innovation are measured against the objectives established by the company." (Taken from this volume, pages 4–5.)

Finally, it is hoped that this book can help managers avoid doing half a job and so prevent their own and their organization's decline. They must fulfill their day-to-day operating obligations *as well as* improve on the status quo by innovating.

Great Neck, New York
*December, 1969*

BEN MILLER

# CONTENTS

tions to Facilitate Change. Community Problems Facing the Manager. Problem of Maintaining Growth through Innovating. Problems over the Risks of Innovating. The Problem of Foreign Competition. The Problem of Obstacles to Innovation. The Individual Company and Innovation. The Need for Leadership.

## III. Human Problems of Innovating

## Appendixes

INTRODUCTION

# THE MEANING AND
# IMPORTANCE OF INNOVATION

### The Challenge of Change

One of the greatest challenges facing our society today is how to cope with the accelerating pace of change. Regarding the immensity of change, our time has been described as the "age of multiple revolution," stressing the fact that we do not yet comprehend the size and speed of change.

Some of these revolutions and their reactions upon one another could change human life. People must accept these immense changes, intellectually and even spiritually, in order to be able to master them.

Our society's dynamism has been characterized in dramatic fashion by calling our present time an "era of radical change."

The challenge of change that is taking place has an impact upon every area of our economy. What is happening is at so fast a pace that a *new* method is needed to successfully harness change. This method is available in the form of the process of *innovation*.

### The Meaning of Innovation

To many people the term innovation is simply the equivalent of anything that is new. To others it seems to involve something more

1

complex that is somehow mixed with research and invention. Innovation does have some of each of these characteristics but it goes far deeper, embodying as it does a refreshing new spirit as well as an array of new techniques. It has grown out of an environment that is different from anything known before: an environment which can be described as a restless dissatisfaction with the status quo. This "feeling" is quite different from that which is generated by other kinds of change that are the typical outcome of sporadic and unpredictable events.

The excitement that pervades innovation is brilliantly captured by Peter Drucker:

> Innovation, as we now use the term, is based on the systematic, organized leap into the unknown. Its aim is to give us new power for action through a new capacity to see, a new vision. Its tools are scientific; but its process is of the imagination. . . . Innovation views change as controlled, directed and purposeful human activity. **(1)**

As incisive as this definition is, it still does not provide enough of a working guide on how actually to harness this new process—innovation.

### The Process of Innovation

There has been a considerable amount of analysis of the nature of planned, purposeful change in all areas of our society. Perhaps the least amount has been in the area of business.

Let us examine the nature, principles, and techniques of innovation or, as it is used interchangeably in the literature, planned change. It involves the collaboration between the one who directs the change and the system being changed, and it employs a valid body of knowledge which is growingly scientific.

Innovation thus involves three distinct ingredients. The idea of *deliberate* and *conscious* effort towards innovation is boldly distinct from spontaneous changes that may occur in a company. It is also different from evolutionary changes that seem to develop over a period of time. Innovation (or planned change) is also different from changes that may occur in a company. None of these latter types of change—spontaneous, evolutionary, or externally caused —is within the purview of this discussion. Rather, we will deal with innovation, which is *planned change that originates with a decision to make a deliberate effort to improve the system,* or to accomplish a specific objective. This involves the collaboration of the change director (any professional who can help in research, training, or consulting to bring about the innovation) and the client in achieving the declared objective. The change director (or group) is not necessarily to be considered as coming from outside. The *client or client system* may be thought of as any organization or enterprise that is being helped towards improvement.

Any planned change attempt relies to a great extent on the rapport between the helper and the client—their joint understanding of the factors essential to this relationship and their mutual goals. Above all, underlying the relationship to be established between change director and client should be the feeling of confidence or trust that will create a give-and-take climate between the two parties.

## Innovating—The Manager's Basic Functions

Perhaps the greatest significance that lies in understanding the nature and implications of our present "era of radical change" is that it adds a totally *new* dimension to the job of managing. The burden of this challenge is placed squarely on managers, who must develop it effectively so as to assure the health and even survival of their own companies, as well as their own careers. Indeed, it leads to designating innovating—the process of developing innovations —as a *fundamental* and ongoing part of every manager's responsibilities, injecting the dynamic ingredient which makes the manager's functions of planning, organizing, and controlling "go."

Thus, not only is innovation a new approach towards change, it is new as a basic function of managing. Indeed, this is increasingly being recognized by management thinkers. A recent symposium of seven leading American managers stressed the importance of innovation as they predicted a greater need for it among American companies. This is so because we are increasingly aware that for a manager to perform planning, organizing, and controlling tasks he must deal largely with day-to-day operating conditions in which he is concerned with maintaining a norm, a standard, or, quite simply, the status quo. In an earlier, less dynamic age the type of manager who was in greatest demand was the one who had a bureaucratic mind. He was then a necessary ingredient for the economic success of the firm. Today he is a distinct liability.

However, by injecting the substance as well as the form of innovating, the emphasis upon *improving* present operations is clearly established. The net effect will be to establish programs of change (innovating) that, in themselves, require application of the skills of planning, organizing, and controlling.

Indeed, not only is innovation *now* a necessity, but a manager must continually extend his capacity to absorb innovation so that it keeps pace with his own expanded capacity to innovate.

In essence, then, there will be two major objectives in this book: to develop in the reader, *first,* an understanding of innovation, and *second,* a capacity to manage innovation. By the latter I mean how to plan, organize, control, and *innovate* company resources in order to achieve greater profits on invested capital.

A brilliant commentary will drive home this essential point:

The central figure—on the capitalist stage—is concerned not with the administration of existing industrial plant and equipment but with the incessant *creation* of new plant and equipment, embodying new technologies that revolutionize existing industrial structures. **(2)**

Let us add three ingredients which serve to adapt the general concept of innovation to a specific application of its use by a manager in company operations. The first of these is the recognition that, in business, any change from the status quo involves risk; the second item is that the very purpose of a business is to satisfy economic wants; and the third is that innovation results in greater profit to the business. In toto, then,

Innovation is risk-taking change introduced for the purpose of satisfying economic wants and resulting in increased profitability. **(3)**

A significant ingredient that I would add to the above definition is one designed to emphasize the particular importance of innovation to the individual manager and his company. This has to do with underscoring innovation as directed towards the particular objectives that are identified by the management of a particular firm as representing its unique goals. It is this orientation which integrates the *purpose* of innovation in terms of management objectives so that the results of innovation are measured against the objectives established by the company.

Unfortunately, there is a tendency to delay in setting specific objectives that are to be accomplished by innovation, in contrast to operating objectives, because there is no apparent urgency with innovating like that which usually prevails with day-to-day operations.

Another reason for putting off the setting of innovation objectives is that they are, frankly, much more difficult to establish than operating objectives. It has been pointed out that "the problem in setting innovation objectives is the difficulty of measuring the relative impact and importance of various innovations." **(4)**

Incorporating all of the ideas expressed above, I view innovation for business as: *purposeful, planned, and profitable change.*

It is *purposeful* in that it is directed towards the accomplishment of specific goals prevailing within a specific company.

It is *planned* to the extent that it is developed according to prescribed discipline and through the organization of material, human, and financial resources.

It is *profitable* in that it must achieve definite profit objectives that will clearly lead to a greater profit return on invested resources.

## Types of Innovation

Two broad categories of innovation that are applicable to a business are technological innovation and administrative innovation.

*Technological* innovation involves the development of planned, purposeful, and profitable change in a wide range of technically oriented areas such as products, services, or processes.

In contrast, *administrative* innovation deals with changes in the methods of operating a business that make more effective *use* of its resources: technical, human, and financial. These may include changes in organization structure, policies, work methods, and any procedure for making, financing, or marketing a product or service.

A parallel to the dual view of innovation I have developed above is found in the observation that "there are two kinds of innovation in every business: innovation in product or service, and innovation in the various skills and activities needed to supply them." **(5)** In another comment those business innovations are pointed out which have had the greatest impact in recent years in the area of administrative innovation: "innovations in marketing, innovations in measurement of the managerial job, innovation in the development of competence and skill among managers, and innovations in the management of workers and in the organization of work." **(6)**

## Relationship of Innovation to Other Types of Change

Innovation is different from other kinds of change, first of all, because it has developed out of an environment that is different from anything known before. It has grown out of an environment of accelerated change that has engendered a spirit of innovation which can be described as a restless dissatisfaction with the status quo. This "feeling" is quite different from that which is generated by other kinds of change that are typical outcomes of sporadic and unpredictable events. Indeed, with regard to these latter types of change, the reaction is often a fatalistic shrug.

Innovation is characterized not only by a spirit but by a form through which this enthusiasm for change will be translated into specific acts of purposeful, planned, and profitable change. It further represents a conscious and deliberate marshaling of company resources specifically designed to achieve greater profits.

## Misconceptions about Innovation

Even after a full examination of the meaning of innovation, there still remains the possibility of misconceptions about the term innovation simply because we are constantly exposed to variations on the word as well as variations in its meaning.

The term that is most commonly used today, and often as a synonym for innovations, is automation. Aside from conflicting uses of the term automation, it is further plagued by distortions because it has taken on an emotional quality that stimulates a whole range of personal reactions.

Before developing what automation *is,* we can be quite certain of what it is *not*. It certainly is not synonymous with innovation in its broad designation as purposeful, planned, profitable change of any kind. However, automation generally would be considered an example of one of the two basic types of innovation, that is, techno-logical innovation. Even known authorities, however, are in basic disagreement as to the nature of automation. One authority believes that automation is the "relegation to a machine of the function of performing operations previously performed manually." **(7)** This description of automation is completely inadequate, for all it does is to provide us with a definition of mechanization, which is a far cry from automation.

Another authority states that the word automation "represents technological change, which surely is nothing new." **(8)** A colossal failure to grasp the immensity of this major example of innovation —rebutted sharply by a former chairman of the council of eco-nomic advisors: "Automation has its roots in mechanization, to be sure, but something new was added when electronic devices made possible the widespread application of the feedback principle." **(9)**

To fully crystallize the basic concept of automation it is only fair that we draw upon the ideas of the two people who, operating independently from one another, are responsible for adding this word to our language: M. S. Harder of Ford Motor, and John Diebold. Harder has used the word automation to describe the significant development of automatic handling of materials and parts that allows the continuous manufacture of items, like engines. Diebold contributes to the concept of automation the emphasis that "the theory of communication and control are combined with ma-chine technology to form a total system." **(10)**

Thus, automation is an important example *of* innovation, not a synonym *for* it.

# PART I

# Conflicting Pressures on Innovation—Implication for Managers

# CHAPTER 1

# THE BROADER SETTING

Our introduction has served to bring out the issues confronting our society in terms of the challenge that innovation presents. It has provided some insight into the nature of innovation and its two areas, technological and administrative, that are of particular interest to the business enterprise. We will now examine the unique role of the manager with particular emphasis upon his potential of fostering innovations in his company.

The manager views the crises that periodically arise over planned change with unusual concern because it is he who is faced with the decision to implement an innovation. At the same time that these pressures for change have been increasing there has been a dramatic, if not revolutionary, increase in the influence of managers over the resources of the business enterprise.

Thus, within the larger context of increasing managerial power, the responsibilities confronting a manager have also been increasing. On all levels, he must serve the demands of current operations while at the same time coping with the task of planning, installing, and controlling technological and administrative innovations. Before examining some of the factors and consequences of a manager's involvement in innovation, let's review the broader setting which may influence his approach towards innovation.

## Institutional Effects on Innovation

The underlying conditions that create the framework which surrounds the manager's efforts with innovation grow out of the basic

11

social, economic, and political institutions in our society. These institutions have a stabilizing effect and yet themselves are subject to revision—at times gradual, at other times sudden. It is particularly important to examine the forces that are pressing for alterations in our institutional way of life so that an assessment can be made of the conditions and attitudes that exist now and are likely to continue in the future.

*The manager in transition.* The classic view of the manager as an entrepreneur who marshals the business resources and is engaged in business risks involving their use has undergone a significant change. In a mature industrial society members of the managerial group rarely engage in planning innovations that directly involve their own financial interests. Their approach toward planned change would tend to differ from that of the owner manager. The growth of the professional managerial class therefore has significance in its manner of handling innovation. The importance of this condition is magnified when we realize that this group is rising in numbers and influence in our society. The control of productive forces without ownership of the resources is of social interest in its effect upon innovating—itself a risk-taking proposition.

The emergence of this managerial class has been heralded as a powerful change in our economic and social institutions:

Certain individuals: the operating executives, production managers, plant superintendents, and their associates, have charge of the actual technical process of producing. It is their job to organize the materials, tools, machines, plant facilities, equipment and labor. (1)

This vast group of hired professionals, as distinguished from the owners, actually controls the substance of business enterprise. One authority supports this assessment of the change that has taken place with a biting comment that:

Owner operators were replaced by professional executives whose behavior reflected their scientific management hired-hand role—the risk-taking owner operator of the nineteenth century was replaced by the general manager surrounded by technical staff and advertising men. (2)

This distinction between the hired-hand manager and the owner manager goes well beyond the separation of ownership and control.

Indeed, the typical corporate "owner" or shareholder has abdicated all his power, including his right to vote, creating a vacuum that the professional manager has filled.

An example of managerial power without property is the operation of Standard Oil of New Jersey:

"The directors run the company"—for the power of stockholders is only potential and has not recently been wielded in sufficient concentration to bother management at all. **(3)**

It has been said that the emergence of management as an essential, a distinctive, and a leading institution is a pivotal event in social history. Rarely, if ever, has a new basic institution, a new leading group, emerged as fast as has management since the turn of this century. Rarely in human history has a new institution proven indispensable so quickly; and even less often has a new institution arrived with so little opposition, so little disturbance, so little controversy. Management will remain a basic and dominant institution perhaps as long as Western civilization itself survives. **(4)**

The significance of the manager's current status in innovation is twofold. First, he tends to risk his position in the company hierarchy rather than his personal wealth when he proposes innovations. Second, since he is part of a larger group of managers, any innovation he encourages will usually require the cooperation of other managers. Rarely will he "go it alone." It is apparent that the manager's present role in planned change is bound to be far different from the time when he existed as an owner manager.

**The economic climate.**  Let us now examine some effects of the nature and changes in our economic institutions upon the manager's role in innovation. In exploring the economic climate, consideration will be given merely to the level or state of the economy. The prevailing economic thought as well as the particular economic level will be considered in the light of their effect upon a manager's ability and willingness to advance innovations.

Just as the change in position of the manager from owner to professional has completely changed the institution of management, a fundamental change has gradually occurred in the economic institutions of our society. The classical concept of economic thought with its cornerstone of free competition and the rational economic man is no longer tenable—if ever it did exist as a picture of the real economic world. The theories which more nearly describe today's dominant economic thought lie much closer to Keynes' thinking than to classical theory.

Because the manager—rather than the owner—has control of the resources and investments that are employed as the *result* of innovations, this *newer* view of economic forces reinforces the image of a growingly important influence upon innovation in our society. This contrasts sharply with the manager's position in the previous era and denotes the disappearance of an era of "free enterprise" by the beginning of World War I.

Another evidence of a revision in our economic institutions in its effect on the role of a manager in innovation is reflected in the level of economic activity. In the recent decade, and even more sharply today, we have been giving greater attention to this question in terms of national growth rates. In itself this is a departure because formerly our preoccupation has been with the business cycle of depression and recession, or "boom and bust." The examination of growth rate for any period has been compared to our own rates of previous periods in contrast to the growth rates of other nations.

Changes in national fiscal policy and in the operating policies of managers have concentrated more and more upon means of developing growth in business *in addition* to the concern for the unsettling effects of recurring expansions and contractions in business activity. Whereas formerly a manager may have waited for the signs of "recovery" to introduce an innovation, there is an increasing tendency to disregard the level of business activity as the critical factor in encouraging innovation. It is necessary to create an awareness in the individual manager that the success of his administrative or technological innovation will be dependent on the timing of its introduction as well as on its inherent merits. But because innovations are developed largely on a noncyclical plan, a condition often results where many of the projects completed in any boom come in too late to be of much benefit before the following recession.

However, whereas until very recently business felt itself at the mercy of the business cycle, today *individual* managers are making daily operating decisions which serve to *influence,* and indeed serve to *restrict,* the extreme economic fluctuations of the past. This has been made possible, in no small measure, by technological and administrative innovations, which in turn develop and create faith in the power of further innovations to foster growth and minimize harmful economic fluctuations. The two innovations that have contributed most to the present restraints on cyclical behavior are the computer (a technological innovation) and improved executive control techniques.

The computer has provided faster and more accurate information on sales, inventory, product acceptance, profits, and a whole range of data vital to business operations. Improvement in control techniques has led to utilization of data that has resulted in an amazing picture in the business prosperity we are now experiencing. For the first time in history, expansion of facilities, inventory, and other resources has *not* outstripped growth in sales. The evil that led to precipitous decline in the past, namely, excess inventory and productive capacity, is being more effectively controlled. This is a major reason for the longest and steadiest period of business expansion in our nation's history.

The consequences of this are twofold. Firstly, managers are becoming more aware of the need for a continued emphasis on the pursuit of innovation—in good times or bad. Secondly, the "stabilization" of our economy in the emphasis upon national growth has made it more respectable to take the offense rather than the defense in pursuing decisions on innovation.

***Shift in economic classes.***  The long-term trend of advancing technology is revealed by census figures which show that the majority of employed persons are in white-collar positions. This category includes professional, managerial, sales, and service groups. Production employees, in both farming and industry, are now a minority and destined to continue their relative decline in future years.

Also of importance is the way incomes are distributed among various groups in our society. The long-term trend towards equality of income has been leveling off, if it hasn't actually begun to reverse itself towards a greater disparity of income and wealth. The poorest class is becoming smaller. This has been accompanied by an increase in the number of persons in the highest income bracket. As a result all groups have been moving up the income ladder.

Before World War II each of the groups below the topmost income level was obtaining a greater share of the total income at the expense of the highest income bracket. The New Deal era produced social legislation as well as tax changes which had a direct effect upon the redistribution of income. During the war, the lower income groups continued to raise their share via higher wage levels, particularly due to the availability of employment for persons accustomed to employment.

Immediately after the war the trend towards a more equal share of income was halted. The underlying cause of the swingback in distribution is illuminating. Since the lowest income group generally consists of people with the least skills and the least education, the increased pace of innovation, since World War II, has hit this group sharply because new methods and techniques generally place higher demands upon human beings. It is the increasing gap between the demands of the new innovations and the inability to provide the skills and education necessary for employment that has resulted in a sharp separation of occupational income levels. During the decade of the 1950's, professional and managerial workers raised their incomes at a much faster rate than semiskilled workers and laborers. Moreover, though the median wage of most working groups continues to rise (particularly in the professional and managerial categories), the wages of laborers and service workers are at a continuing decelerated rate.

## Social Values and Innovation

Our social values provide a fundamental and pervasive influence upon innovations. The kind of influence they exert is so subtle and ill-defined that it may appear of no consequence. However, to pretend that centuries of our social heritage can fail to influence our attitudes towards planned change is unrealistic. To examine the effects of social values upon innovation, two viewpoints will be considered. One will be that of an outsider, Father Bruckberger, who like his countryman of an earlier day, de Tocqueville, attempts to assess (with a sympathetic attitude) the characteristics that contributed to the growth of our society. The other view will be drawn from "insiders," Reisman *et al.,* who present a somewhat biting view of some character types that appear in our society, and whose values greatly affect the issue of innovation.

In his *Image of America,* (5) Bruckberger probes the development of our nation to determine the basic special values that were fundamental to our progress. He identifies three characteristics that are peculiar to our social institutions. They are: our regard for the individual as a nonabstract living human being; our optimism; and an essentially experimental attitude.

The effects of the basic social values—our heritage—upon innovation may have been more intense in the frontier days than at present. Nonetheless, they still form a significant motivating force to planned change. The regard for the individual will probably continue to encourage the spirit in which it is acceptable, even in the atomic age, and will continue to spur attempts to make this a better world. Lastly, the experimental approach has given our people a sense of delight in discovery born of observation and experience. All three of these ingredients would tend to provide encouragement of individuals to innovate.

In contrast to Bruckberger's view of America, as providing a social climate sympathetic to innovation, is the analysis found in *The Lonely Crowd,* by Reisman and his associates. (6) The essence of their view is the classification of social characters into three groups. The first such classification is what they describe as the "tradition-directed" type whose actions are rigidly codified for him. He is typically completely devoid of initiative and is often described as a classic member of a feudal society. The second type is called the "inner-directed" person, whose development grew out of the spirit of the Renaissance and the Reformation. With traditions being suddenly eroded there emerged the independent soul who in our day might be called a self-directed person. It is this type which is portrayed in the picture of the pioneer of frontier days and the entrepreneur of our industrial expansion. The same type is presumably to be found in the emerging nations that are seeking to develop a society that will release them from a feudal way of life.

The last character type is called by Reisman the "other-directed" type, and has been popularized as the "organization man," whose mode of living is strict conformity. To the extent that this attitude prevails, there is little doubt that it produces an almost complete barrier to innovation. Moreover, it is certainly true that in many companies this atmosphere of conformity is imposed upon the manager as well as other employees. However, in the decade since

Reisman's work there has been a revival of the "independent spirit" amid a recognition that it is a necessary ingredient to company prosperity.

## Industry Characteristics Affecting Innovation

There are seven classes of industry that have features so unique that they may require distinctly different approaches by managers seeking to advance technological and administrative innovations. These industry classes are: (1) the mass production assembly industry; (2) the process industries and (3) the unique product (made to order) industry; (4) the program-oriented industry; (5) the multicraft-oriented industry; (6) the clerical industry; and (7) the public service industry (such as hospitals or schools, subject to public scrutiny).

In every one of these types of industries the kinds of growth, and therefore their innovation characteristics, are quite distinct. It is for these reasons as well as their distinctive operating methods that in each case there may be unique considerations arising when confronted with planning and implementing an innovation. Let us take a look at the features of each industry group and note the challenge a manager faces in considering an innovation.

*Mass production assembly industry.* The characteristic that is peculiar to the mass production assembly industry is that each assembled part is standardized to achieve uniformity. Our folklore generates an aura around this type of industry as symbolic of America's growth into a world leader. Indeed, our fascination with this type of industry as the "end-all" may tend to make us overlook a particularly limiting feature. It is the nature of this industry that long runs of essentially similar products are necessary to achieve economical operations. Innovations in technology and administration must be so geared as to result in economic long runs.

*Process industry.* This type of industry is unique in that it centers around the arrangement in fixed positions of distinct major processes which fabricate large volumes of a uniform (usually bulk) product. Normally, production takes place in batch stages, with a specific quantity of goods processed at each stage and then moved to a subsequent stage. Should a movement or handling system link each of these processes together, the ideal would be achieved in the form of continuous processing. It therefore is in this type of industry that automation has the greatest potential application, resulting in considerable pressure for technological and administrative innovation. Moreover, innovation in this area may be particularly complex and challenging to implement.

*Unique product industry.*   The unique product industry (custom-made) has a number of peculiar features, including a great variety of fabricating equipment; and in particular, no production proceeds without a customer's unique order. The last is not entirely true, for usually there are some features of the product that occur with many of the items produced. However, because there are usually relatively small quantities of goods produced and the procedures require a great deal of flexibility, the area has not been marked by significant innovations. It is interesting to note that the former attitude of managers in this area, namely, "Oh, our production is too unpredictable to do much planning and innovation," is gradually disappearing. Managers are becoming less defensive and instead are becoming aware of the potential for their industry of planned purposeful change.

*Program-oriented industry.*   An example of a program-oriented industry is one in which large weapons systems are designed and produced for national defense. This type of industry has a number of unique qualities with regard to management's role and the impact of innovation. First, the completion of such a program is typically measured in terms of years. Second, at the inception of the program what is generally known is the function to be performed by the system, rather than its exact nature. In other words, research and design is the *only* activity pursued in the early stages of work and continues to some extent throughout the program until after the system is completed. As a result, projections of the final product that is to be produced are faced with three alternatives. These are: the final system may be produced essentially in the original form conceived at the inception of the program; it may be revised substantially during the research and early production; or the project may be abandoned completely because it has become obsolete or it has failed to realize the expectations originally held for it.

The characteristics of this industry have created extreme pressures for technological innovations. But interestingly, the administrative innovations have been as significant, as in the example of the development of the PERT (Program Evaluation and Review Technique) concept, which is an invaluable tool in planning and controlling these programs. Because of the consequences to our national welfare, manufacturers in a program-oriented industry are probably confronted with the greatest of pressures for innovation.

**Multicraft-oriented industry.** Historically, the classic forms of production centered largely around the application of skills along well-defined craft lines. In many of these crafts the practices have passed down through the centuries essentially devoid of innovation. Due to this condition and because there is the need to utilize many crafts in varying combinations, the manager in a craft-oriented industry has a particularly difficult task in encouraging innovation. In addition, these managers face conditions similar to those in unique product industries in that each "job" is essentially made to a customer's specific requirements. They are also confronted with problems similar to the program-oriented industry in that their projects may, at times, also require years to complete.

Ancient civilization produced structures that even today are marvels of advanced technological and administrative capacity, in addition to their architectural beauty. Over 50 years ago, Frank Gilbreth, a construction executive, developed administrative innovations (methods improvements) that promised revolutionary advances in the industry. Yet, at this time, most construction companies have failed to apply the changes he recommended. The task confronting the manager in this industry is a dual one. He is faced with the challenge of encouraging innovations in each of the numerous crafts while at the same time seeking changes in practices that can more effectively *combine* the energies of these distinct skills.

**Clerical industry.** Every enterprise has a portion of energy devoted to what may also be called white-collar tasks. However, some of them, like insurance companies, have the major share of their work centered around clerical activities. Census figures each decade continue to show a rise in the absolute and relative number of clerical workers as well as an increase in the number and size of companies with a high percentage of office employees. Technological advances in this area have been dramatic in the last few years as machines have been devised that have kept pace with the sharp rise in clerical activity.

In addition, a whole range of administrative innovations has been developed to increase the effectiveness of office work while reducing its cost. Notwithstanding these advances, there are two issues that tend to cloud this progress. First, in a great many cases where the symbols of office innovation have been adopted in the form of the computer, there has been little if any administrative innovation accompanying the installation of the machine. In many cases, technological innovation has proved unworkable when combined with archaic administrative practices. Mere acquisition of an advanced machine is not enough to achieve innovation. Many computers have, therefore, failed to achieve their purpose and have failed to prove an economic advance.

Second, there are a great many medium- and small-sized companies that are heavily clerical which still have not been exposed to significant innovation. Managers in this type of industry are, therefore, faced with the challenge of selecting among many mechanical and electronic devices available to them. In addition, they are confronted with the need to devise administrative innovations that can be made compatible with technological advances in their field.

***Public service industry.***   This group includes a vast array of enterprises or institutions that are either devoted to public service or are publicly owned. Two major groups are schools and hospitals. In both these cases there has been a growing emphasis upon increasing the quality of service to the public. The peculiar condition facing these institutions is that they are continually subject to public reaction (whether positive or negative). Thus, when a question arises involving the implementation of an innovation, many groups may express their concern in very decided fashion, either in support of or opposition to the change. For example, many elementary and secondary schools (whether public or private) tend to involve students, parents, and community groups in their school's affairs. In turn, colleges are inextricably tied to their alumni for moral as well as financial support for innovations in programs and facilities.

The hospital is perhaps the most trying example of this type of industry in terms of the difficulties facing the manager who will foster innovations. In the last decade alone, advances in medical science and technology have confronted hospital administrators with the opportunity of providing far superior patient care than had ever been possible. To exploit the amazing progress in science and equipment it has become necessary to greatly improve administrative techniques. This is vital in order to avoid any waste of professional and technical resources that are committed to the improvement of patient care. While these innovations in technology and administration have proceeded, a growing array of professional groups have been gathered together outside the institution in the cooperative effort for patient care. Among these have been groups of accrediting agencies and prepaid insurance companies, all of which have exerted influence to raise standards of professional and administrative practices. In addition, the involvement of local, state, and federal governments in medical care, coupled with community civic groups, has provided funds and guidance to raise the level of hospital practices. The managers of hospitals on all levels, in planning future innovation, will be confronted with an even intensified involvement of those groups. Not the least of the reasons for this "pressure" will be the intensified economic squeeze that hospitals will face.

### The Worldwide Setting

As part of the broader issues which impinge on the manager in this era of accelerating change, the manager should become aware of, and sensitive to, economic events in the international arena. This sensitivity is important for two reasons.

In the first place, much of the pressure for change is now emanating from areas of the world that have been, until recently, economically dormant. The other reason is that the rise in political and economic "appetites" among peoples throughout the world has led to markets for goods and services that would have been unthinkable just a few years ago. Thus, the manager should realize that international events provide twin facets of economic rivalry on the one hand and an ever-increasing economic opportunity on the other.

In terms of rivalry, there are four main sources from which it derives. The first source of rivalry is the nations of the Western world; the second, those nations occupied by the victorious Allies in World War II; the third, the Communist bloc nations; and the fourth source is that group of nations that have recently achieved statehood and are attempting to achieve status among the older nations.

The first group consists of Western European nations that have seen fit to enter into economic cooperation, which (in spite of de Gaulle) has tended to foster an innovative state of mind. The second group of nations consists of Germany and Japan, who have undergone massive rehabilitation—supported by subsidies from the United States—that has seen them grow at such a fast pace that they are among the economic leaders of the world. This is especially true in Germany where the director general of Volkswagenwerk stated that "our problem at Volkswagenwerk is the labor shortage . . . It is virtually impossible to hire workers in our country because there are more jobs than there are workers." (7) This is evidence that in these nations their economic advance has proceeded at such a dramatic pace as to create manpower shortages.

Pressure for rapid growth in the Communist nations, with its attendant emphasis on innovating, is spurred largely by the ideological battle and is a consuming issue among them. For example, Russia has shaped her goal of innovating in terms of a basic determination to lay the material foundation for Communism and to surpass the United States in the per capita production of goods in the shortest possible time. (8)

The last group—nations that are intensely active in spurring innovation—are the ones who have the longest distance to go in their economic climb. This group consists largely of underdeveloped, newly emerging nations that are particularly anxious to foster change.

The reason it is important to understand the forces propelling these four groups of nations in search of innovation is that, to a large extent, they share a common motivation: to achieve the living standards that exist in the United States. American managers must come to realize that the international challenge to our leadership must be met by us in equally determined fashion.

Just as these groups pose a challenge—and in some cases, a threat—to American managers to acclerate the pace of innovating, they also provide a vast opportunity in the form of expanding markets for our goods and services. This circumstance is another valid reason for American managers to develop an awareness and interest in economic world affairs as reflected in the rate of innovation among these nations.

Our auto industry is typical of the dynamic spirit in fostering innovation. It is not surprising, therefore, to note that the leading car makers in America have fully recognized the opportunity that lies in foreign markets. One example of this international consciousness among American managers is revealed by the announcement that when Arjay Miller was selected as president of Ford Motor Company he revealed his plans for an immediate trip to explore the markets of Central America and South America. **(9)**

## American Values and Their Effect on Innovation

A most significant reason for examining the broader setting in which innovation takes place is for the purpose of assessing the effect our society's values may have on the rate of innovating. Understanding these values, or social norms, will be of help to managers and may help determine the effectiveness of their efforts in planning and implementing innovations.

As the pace of change and innovation keeps rising, our real task will be to make judgments as to the worth—to us—of these changes. This may be difficult to do, for we have become oblivious to the *pace* of change and come to fully and passively accept its inevitability. We, therefore, will have to become more fully involved in "making sense" of change, as Max Ways puts it, and of judging progress as "how good" rather than "how much." **(10)**

One of the significant and gratifying effects of the current emphasis upon innovation is that corporations are tending to stress, more and more, the need for individual creativity and initiative. It would seem that in a fast paced, highly organized society just the opposite would occur; that is, a deemphasis of the individual's contribution to industry. A bit of reflection, however, would make us realize that in an innovative society there develops a greater demand for highly trained people with greater breadth of knowledge. To survive and grow, the newer structure of corporations is thus designed to provide greater authority to act in each area of the firm. This growing emphasis on the importance of the individual is, therefore, a most important value that persists in our society and is indeed consistent with a greater stress being placed throughout the world on the role of the individual. Moreover, there has been a greater recognition that in building an innovative society, Americans place a high price on maintaining "an order of freedom in a world of change." **(11)**

Regardless of which values seem to be changing and which are dominant at any time, the basic challenge to managers is to persist in developing innovations. At the same time, they must relate this innovative system of ideas to the values of our society so as not to sacrifice, in the political or social arena, the potential benefits created by innovations that may serve man's needs and wants.

CHAPTER **2**

# LABOR-MANAGEMENT ISSUES

As one aspect of exploring the conflicting pressures on innovation, the relations between management and labor have a subtle but telling effect upon the success of innovation. At one extreme will be found bitter conflict between management and labor. Under those conditions, even the most elementary attempts at innovation may be foredoomed. At the other end of the spectrum is the condition where a spirit of good will and common purpose prevails between management and labor—a contributing factor to the success of an innovation.

The innovative manager should be sensitive to those features which may contribute to the creation of a positive or a negative position between labor and management. In a great many companies long years of positive dealings between management and labor have led to a stable and peaceful atmosphere that has been a boon to innovation. In contrast, some companies have compiled a history of discord that has led to an inhibiting effect on innovation. More often, the current attitude towards change among company personnel is found to exist largely as an outgrowth of the specific company's experiences in making changes. The quality of these experiences with change is influenced greatly by the conditions that place a strain on the process of innovating.

One of these conditions breeding conflict grows out of the difficulties that arise in an industry or occupation that is threatened with decline or even extinction; the other condition that contains seeds of conflict develops over the *manner* in which management has prepared and implemented innovations. It is necessary to distinguish these two situations. In the first example conditions of conflict exist because of the inherent threat to the people affected by it; while in the second there is no implicit threat, but rather, potential conflict which may arise from the characteristics of the change itself.

In the case of a declining industry with shrinking employment opportunities, the most conspicuous evidence of conflict over implementing innovation is to be found in the strike, used to prevent the installation of the change. The forces that are brought to play often obscure the real issues and tend to make it difficult to create an atmosphere conducive to change.

The printing industry is a particularly apt example of this situation. Among newspaper publishers in Cleveland and New York, recurrent strikes have damaged the potential of innovations. A crucial issue in each case was the threat posed to typesetters in being replaced by electronic typesetters. What is interesting about this example of conflict is that electronic typesetting has been in use for more than a decade, but only recently has it loomed as a major threat to continued employment.

It has been suggested that a committee consisting of printers and publishers study the effect of the use of tape, with payments to be made to the union by any publisher who uses the tape. Still, the union is afraid that the change would be a step toward the use of computers to eliminate the use of Linotype operators.

Where are the men with imagination, drive, or, quite simply, with the innovative spirit? They are rarely, if ever, to be found in labor, because the political infighting that characterizes union affairs has tended to breed strong leaders who are apparently more concerned with perpetuating that position than in coping with the multiplying problems of innovation in themselves and among their subordinates.

The manager should develop an awareness of the shortcomings of many labor leaders he may have to deal with on day-to-day issues, as well as on complex discussions in contract negotiations. He must learn to push even harder in dealing with the realities of an accelerated era of change and thus be able to cope with the problems that often accompany technological and administrative innovation.

The issues that point up the conflicting pressures in the labor-management area which have a bearing on the prospects for successful innovation include the following: First, a basic lack of emphasis by most union leaders in labor-management deliberations concerning innovation that seeks imaginative and new ways of overcoming its potentially dislocating effects. This is driven home by the capricious use of the strike weapon in the steel, railroad, newspaper, and coal mining industries, and among flight engineers, civil service, and white-collar personnel.

Second, government officials on a local, state, and federal level will be called upon to help prevent crippilng disputes that inhibit the advance of innovation.

And finally, the manager is faced with the challenge of motivating employees in his department or section to achieve an accommodation with innovations. The manager is also faced with the task of influencing union and government officials to take positions that will encourage rather than inhibit the introduction of innovations.

Quite a tall order for the manager. On each of these issues the manager, on every level, has a specific role to play that will result in having him more effectively perform his managerial function: innovation.

It becomes apparent that, because of the faster pace of innovation, a new examination will have to be started of those questions affecting labor-management relations in the United States.

A paradox exists in the industrial relations system in this country. It is the same prime mover that makes American workers the best paid in the world that is causing the most difficult situations at bargaining sessions. Technological changes are pushing the American laborer's productivity upward. It is this increased output per man-hour that is the main factor that permits American employers to pay their employees more and yet keep their prices within limit.

However, the United States is now going through a railroad dispute which is an instance of the problems that technological innovations cause at the bargaining table. The railroads' problems arise from a combination of factors. Technological improvements and competition from other means of transportation have greatly reduced their need for so many employees. The number of employed has been sliced in half—from 1.4 million to less than 700,000—since World War II. The future appears to be bringing more reductions.

With the change from steam to diesel locomotives came the present work rules dispute which involves the diesel firemen in freight and yard operations. There are 37,000 such men who, the railroad industry says, are no longer needed since there are no more coal-burning engines.

Since management demands more efficient and profitable operation, while labor demands job security, a conflict was inevitable, because each faction was thinking solely about itself. The railroads want to eliminate old work rules that inhibit their taking full advantage of the available technological innovations. There seems to be developing slowly between the two extremes of labor and management a workable middle ground, but it is nothing to rave about. It boils down to the employers' buying out the workers' resistance to technological change.

To the Kennedy administration, this dispute had significance far beyond the railroad industry and involved, it was hoped, private and not governmental negotiation. "It should be possible to find a solution that permits termination of jobs which are not justified and that protects the equities of the men involved," said the late John F. Kennedy. **(1)**

It is easy to see how this featherbedding problem came into existence. The introduction of more efficient equipment or systems often creates unnecessary employees. But what occurs next stays unsolved. Should employees fire these excess workers, who probably have spent most of their lifetime acquiring their specialized skills? Should the employees be kept on to perform unnecessary tasks that undermine their spirit and initiative and add significantly to production costs? Should the government retrain and relocate displaced workers?

The stand of the railroads has been that these employees are expendable and create an unnecessary financial burden. With an 8–0 decision, the Supreme Court supported a previous Circuit Court of Appeals ruling that held that $600 million a year was spent "for unneeded employees . . . for time not worked . . . compensation commensurate with the value of services rendered, and the cost of owning and maintaining equipment and facilities that would not be required . . . apart from the restrictions placed upon the efficiency and economy of operations. . . ." **(2)**

The five railroad brotherhoods, on the contrary, argue that the present work rules and the jobs that are performed are necessary for safe and efficient operation of the trains. By using safety as their rationale for featherbedding, the railroad unions are making use of an argument offered in both the airline and newspaper fields to protect their interests. However, a significant difference is that while the railroads have actively opposed featherbedding, the airlines and publishers have often silently accepted it when it seemed to their advantage.

March 16, 1963, was a very historical day for the railroad industry. For the first time a railroad dispute was solved on the principle that workers to be displaced by technological innovation would lose their jobs only by normal attrition: retirement, resignation, death. This solution came about as a result of never-ending pressure from the federal government. Furthermore, it was agreed that if a worker is displaced for any other reason than those mentioned above, he will be retrained for another job with the company under a program to be formulated by the government, the railroad, and the union. **(3)**

"The presiding fact in our time . . . is the fact of change," Labor Secretary Willard Wirtz said, and went on to state that a man used to expect to keep his job all his life and still expects to do so—even though a job today cannot be expected to last a lifetime. Change is inevitable. **(4)**

Basically, this is the situation confronting the railroads as their operations and equipment change as a result of technological innovations in order to keep up with competition. With these changes problems have arisen, most of them focused on the impact the improvements have on the human factor in the railroad industry—the employees.

It would be an injustice to the railroads if no mention were to be made of the fact that the railroad employees are protected against loss of income to a greater degree than workers in most other industries. During the past several decades various agreements have been drawn up and signed by both the railroad industry and the unions.

Workers in the railroad industry also have the protection of an unemployment insurance plan, which is financed completely by the railroads. The Railroad Retirement Board reports that in recent years jobs were found, both in and outside the railroad industry, for more than 43,000 unemployment insurance claimants. This was accomplished through the combined efforts of railroad and union officials and the board's staff.

Our American way of life is complex and is becoming progressively more so. The needs and desires of tomorrow will call for the utilization of the most advanced technological and scientific knowledge in implementing successful innovation. This is true in the transportation field as well as in countless other areas.

# CHAPTER 3

# GOVERNMENT IMPACT

Of great significance in its impact on innovation—and destined to be even greater in the years ahead—is the effort by government to influence the rate of innovation by direct, as well as indirect, means. With the government resources available on the national level it is not surprising that the greatest impact is from Washington. However, both state and local agencies are increasingly exerting an influence upon innovation.

It should be made perfectly clear that the government's impact upon innovation consists of negative as well as positive actions. The challenge is for the manager to become well aware of the government obstructions to innovation, as well as of the ways in which government tends to foster it. In this way, he can minimize the frustrations of coping with the obstacles and instead concentrate on exploiting those government actions which are of benefit to the manager and his company in spurring innovations.

The primary motive behind state and local efforts to foster innovation is usually to raise the economic level of inhabitants. The federal government shares this objective, but its reasons for encouraging innovation are far more varied. Certainly a prime consideration for federal support of innovation is economic advancement, but it may also seek economic stability or social advances. Such diverse factors were behind the programs of massive tax reduction and reform in 1964, as well as sponsorship of innovation projects to increase our water supply in the same year.

The federal role in supporting innovations takes on a broader significance because of its concern with the international role as well as the domestic one. Another important basis for federal support of innovation is the government's desire to maintain its military and economic strength in the face of the challenge of the Communist bloc nations.

It is therefore most important that we examine the means used by government, especially on the national level, to spur innovation, so that the manager will be enabled to assess more intelligently how these government programs may help to advance specific innovation projects in his own company.

## Types of Federal Innovation Projects

The means used by the federal government to encourage individual company innovation are expressed in two distinct ways. One is the *direct* commitment of government resources that results in specific innovations that are subsequently shared with private industry. The other type of support is by *indirect* means, either in the form of congressional legislation or by the actions of federal agencies that offer aid or encouragement to companies for innovating. The direct support or sponsored type of innovation typically involves designing and implementation of an innovation by private industry with the direct support of a government agency. The indirect approach finds the federal government involved either in providing some form of assistance or in removing some obstacles (real or imagined) to company pursuit of innovation. One agency that acts to remove such obstacles is the National Commission on Automation and Technological Progress.

*Government direct support of company innovation.*   Under the heading of government-sponsored innovations are those for which federal agencies organize and direct specific projects. These include programs directed by the Department of Defense, the National Aeronautics and Space Administration, and the Atomic Energy Commission. Though these three agencies represent the overwhelming proportion of Washington's direct sponsorship of innovation, others that are active in these areas include the Department of Agriculture, the National Institute of Health, and the Federal Communications Commission. The major portion of our federal commitment to innovations is for defense purposes or half of last year's research expenditures, amounting to $7.5 billion. **(1)** What is of particular interest to the manager is that over 65 percent of *all* federal research and development funds are assigned to private industry.

It is important for managers to become more fully aware of the government's role in this area, for two reasons. The more apparent one is the possibility of having their companies participate directly in government sponsorship of innovations, and in turn sparking the individual companies' pursuit of innovations. **(2)** The second reason for interest is that managers should be aware of the impact these government programs have in sharing *results* of innovations with private industry. For example, technological innovations in such government-supported areas as electronics, atomic energy, and space utilization not only have spawned new industries and products but have had the catalytic effect of speeding up the rate of change among stable and even declining industries.

An example of a significant government-sponsored project that does not have the glamour of military weaponry or an orbiting satellite is the program of innovating post office operation via the model of the "turnkey" post office. The achievements acquired include technological innovations as well as innovations that evolved out of efforts to improve the handling of vast quantities of mail. In addition a great deal was learned—largely of what *not* to do—about managing the implementation of a complex innovation.

The turnkey post office at Providence, Rhode Island, was dedicated in October, 1960 and was designed to handle a daily volume of mail 50 percent greater than the facility it replaced. Moreover, it was fully expected that substantial economies would accrue from the expected reduction in personnel needs for a given volume of mail. These hopes and expectations were never realized. The new post office was a failure on both counts: it neither handled more mail than the old post office nor did it achieve any reduction in labor costs. **(3)**

Perhaps the reason for the faillure of this innovation in mail processing is that the administrative innovations that were necessary to supplement the technological innovations were not forthcoming, and without them the project collapsed. However, underlying this specific shortcoming was the overall lack of management capability in handling the innovation. That is, the innovation was poorly planned, organized, and controlled. This was evident when the startup day for the turnkey was arbitrarily moved up (for political reasons) so that it was placed into operation before the facility had even been fully completed. Moreover, no provision was made for adequate training of personnel; there was faulty (sometimes nonexistent) communication between the designers of the turnkey, the supervisors, and the employees; and a slipshod process was used to evaluate operations after the changeover took place.

The federal government's direct sponsorship of innovations is not confined merely to the technological variety. Government investment in administrative innovations is typified by sponsorship of many projects that seek improved means of making policy, decision making, and changes in long-range planning and strategy technique. Indeed, government investment has helped to form whole companies devoted entirely to what is popularly called the "think factory." Some of the more widely known of these groups are the Aerospace Company, the Rand Corporation, and the Institute of Defense Analysis. The energies of these groups are largely devoted to nonscientific aspects of national defense. One such group concentrates largely on policy implication of the cold war and the strategy implications of the use—or nonuse—of nuclear weapons. **(4)**

Although the specific findings and recommendations of these groups may have little application to private industry, the techniques that are developed may have a vast potential in improving the rate of administrative innovation in a particular company.

The developments in both technological and administrative innovations sponsored by the government and performed by a host of private organizations represent a vast storehouse of innovation opportunities for the individual manager to apply to his own department or company. There has been a growing tendency for the government to "spin off" these innovations. Some of the most dramatic have been technological innovations, but the government is prone to stress the business applications of an array of administrative innovations.

Two examples that are particularly deserving of mention will show how managers are exploiting the "spin-off" of such administrative innovations and a growing interest by the management profession in the results achieved. One of these innovations is the "zero defects" approach to quality control which was spurred by the demands of the space program for higher quality of parts produced for space vehicles. This program, adopted by a contractor, is spreading at a fast pace in private industry, with amazing results.

Another government-sponsored administrative innovation that bids fair to making the widely heralded PERT seem modest is the development of RAND research efforts called "program budgeting." Every indication is that the concepts evolved from this innovation have so enthused managers, accountants, scientists, and government personnel that it will "trickle down" to use in private industry very quickly.

***Support of company innovation by indirect means.*** A whole range of federal activities is designed to encourage the individual manager to increase his company's rate of technological and administrative innovation. These activities result from special congressional legislation as well as from the work of dozens of government agencies and departments. The motivation for innovation is provided by both positive and negative stimuli. The positive incentives include both general and specific economic assistance, as well as government efforts in removing obstacles that may inhibit a company's progress with innovation. The negative incentives vary from such pressures as imposing restrictions on vendors' dealings with the government to pressure in the form of moral suasion to encourage investment in domestic innovations rather than sending dollars abroad.

***Economic incentives.*** For a large part of our history the government has engaged in providing financial benefits to companies for pursuing innovations. At one time this took the form of grants to railroads to extend their lines and also to spur technological advances in railroad equipment. The forms of support have changed measurably and so have the industries affected by them.

1. SUBSIDIES. One form of support that is widely used today are subsidies that have been awarded to the farm, maritime, and airline industries. In each case a fundamental rationale for this has been to maintain the stability of these industries should their resources be necessary for national defense. However, there have been other valid reasons for this support, including the need to support such a basic industry as farming for fear of inflicting social and economic

decline in vast areas of our country. These financial payments have presently become a significant portion of our national budget, with the farm subsidy remaining the largest of these. It is because of the size attained by the farm subsidy that Congress has made new efforts to add controls to farm subsidies that give strong hope of reducing this government outlay. **(5)**

2. FASTER DEPRECIATION.    A significant boon to spurring industry investment in innovations is the government's ruling to allow faster depreciation of company equipment and other fixed assets. The result of this action has been to increase the cash flow of companies that has been turned to use in greater capital spending.

3. TAX REDUCTION AND REFORM.    Tax reform, and particularly tax reduction, can have a marked impact upon industry's investment in innovation. This was made evident by the boost provided by the federal action of 1964 in reforming the laws and reducing the level of corporate and personal taxes. In the case of corporations it has made more funds available for investment. In addition, the increased consumer spending resulting from the tax reduction has further encouraged managers to seek innovations that would effectively increase productive capacity.

**Government aid in removing barriers to innovation.**    Another means used by the government to indirectly boost the rate of business innovation is to remove barriers or difficulties that tend to discourage managers from pursuing innovations. These facilitating measures are one of the fastest growing methods for government support of innovation. They result from the recognition that a climate of enthusiasm for innovation is a necessary ingredient for its success. The removal of social, political, economic, and procedural barriers can result in achieving such an atmosphere. Following are some examples.

1. PATENT OFFICE.    Many users of the services of the United States patent office were briskly reminded of the role this agency plays during congressional deliberations over changes in patent fees. **(6)** It is this office which offers protection and advice to those who have developed innovations of immediate or potential value.

2. RETRAINING TO PREVENT DISLOCATIONS FROM CHANGE. One of the frustrating problems facing managers results from personnel dislocations caused by an innovation. Often it is found that surplus employees are unsuited for the newer tasks that result

from change. Unless these persons are substantially retrained and even reeducated, they represent a serious challenge to the successful operation of the innovation. The federal government has embarked on a major program in the area of retraining that may help to overcome this barrier to innovation.

In April, 1961, the Office of Manpower, Automation and Training was established and given the responsibility to develop programs to:

*a*) Provide an early warning system of impending changes in automation technology and their impact on employment and jobs.

*b*) Communicate this information to labor, management, government, and educational and training institutions so that they may take necessary action.

*c*) Mitigate the impact of changing technology on the labor force, especially through programs of training and retraining of unemployed workers and through effective guidance and placement work by employment services.

*d*) Prevent the impact of these changes as far as possible through training of employed workers threatened with the obsolescence of their skills and through guidance and career counseling of young persons in the light of changing technology. **(7)**

Today, government is moving into areas separate from the traditional kinds of intervention and aid in labor-management relations. Large investments are being made in educational and vocational training to meet the rapidly increasing skilled and technical manpower requirements of our age of technological advancements. Many industries are approached by government to partake more strenuously in the development of training and educational progress. There is a high correlation between unemployment and lack of education and skill. This means that those people who suffer from the impact of unemployment in our society are those with the lowest educational and skill achievements.

Let us now examine those steps the United States government has taken or plans to take in order to ease the human consequences of technological innovation. Have they created new employment opportunities? Have they been retraining the labor force? Have they given aid for labor mobility?

One of the major steps thus far taken by our federal government has been the Manpower Development and Training Act of 1962. Labor Secretary W. Willard Wirtz said that this act:

. . . reflects the growing awareness by American people of the basic fact of scientific and technological change—change which is having lasting effects upon the Nation's economy and labor force. Change—involving automated and manufacturing processes, the complex world of computers, the creation of brand new industries and jobs, new means of world-wide communications and transportation—has contributed to our Nation's general prosperity and high standard of living. Change has also created hardship for many of our working people. Jobs have become obsolete. Demand for unskilled and semiskilled workers has decreased, and demand for well educated and highly trained skilled workers has increased.

In our battle against unemployment, one of our most important tasks is to prepare our youth who are about to enter the labor force, and the unemployed and underemployed who are already in the labor force, for jobs that are now available or will be available in the future. The Manpower Development and Training Act, through research and training, is an attempt to meet this problem. It is a program which accepts automation and technological change as a challenge, rather than as a curse, and attempts to prepare the American labor force to meet that challenge. **(8)**

With the great complexity of the American economy today, it is not logical to expect either labor, management, or government alone to resolve the numerous economic and social problems that may arise. Through joint cooperation, more effective results can be achieved. Many of the trouble spots are of such magnitude that it is inconceivable that any one organization could adequately achieve success. It is not even right to place the burden on the shoulders of any one agency. After all, many industries have achieved outstanding technological innovations, and these advancements not only benefit the industry or company but our nation as a whole. Therefore, our country en masse should try to handle any of the social and economic problems that might be part of these technological advancements. It would be wrong to ask that technological innovations be curtailed because a group of people will be out of work. By the same token, however, these innovations should not be instituted helter-skelter. They should be thoroughly thought through and carefully planned, so that the impact on the workers will not be devastating. It is not right to discard these people as one would discard a useless pair of shoes. They can, if given the opportunity and needed retraining, become productive elements in our economy.

**Government assistance.**    The railroad industry hassles within the past five years seem to have aroused the government's thinking. Government would prefer to see labor and management work out their own problems—an understandable position. If government were to step into every dispute, many quarters would accuse it of dominating. However, in instances where the common good is in jeopardy it is the government's duty to assist in formulating a solution.

From a combination of business and technological innovations, employment has been cut appreciably in the railroad industry. The government is sure that similar cuts will appear in industry after industry if more is not done to stimulate the economy, creating more jobs, and to evolve methods to handle the specific problems of the individual people who are displaced. If the impact of an advancing technology is not eased, their resistance will mount, with the outcome that the initiating of new equipment and methods will be slowed down. This would be extremely detrimental to our economy, national defense, and competitive position.

Mr. Ralph Cordiner, the former chairman of the board of General Electric, put it this way:

> If, in spite of the best planning we corporate management can do, some people are temporarily unemployed because of technological change, both industry and government have a recognized responsibility to help families through any such periods of transition. **(9)**

What we must recognize in viewing the joint responsibility of industry *and* government is the balance that is required between the need to spur the pace of innovation and the need to minimize its dislocating effects. The two sides of the dilemma are that on the one hand, if government protects the workers too much, it will slow down innovation; on the other hand, if government and industry do nothing to protect jobs, then labor will tend to obstruct innovation.

The manager should recognize, therefore, that what is needed is to maintain a delicate balance so as to foster innovation.

*Facilitating labor movement peace.*   Another obstacle to innovation that government may help to remove is that represented by labor-management conflict. One of the consequences that often attends the installation of innovation is open conflict between labor and management. Indeed, in anticipation of the effects of innovations, many unions have shifted their bargaining emphasis from higher wages to safeguards against the impact on employees of innovation.

Crises have arisen in the steel, coal, printing, airline, and other industries over the question of technological and administrative innovations. The most difficult situation to solve has been in the railroad industry, as we have seen. Federal officials recognize the importance of this case in terms of indicating the future role of government in reducing conflict over innovations. A sound resolution of the problems in this kind of situation, with the help of government, will be a significant forerunner of future attempts to remove the threatening impact of conflict when managers seek to install innovations. Indeed, with the federal mediation service active in railroads, steel, newspapers, airlines, and other industries, it is evident that the government will continue to seek an active role in removing labor-management conflict as a barrier to innovation.

*Support of education as an aid to innovation.*   Another important aid that facilitates innovation is the government's further extension in support of educational facilities. This is a recognition that one barrier to advancing innovation is an uneducated citizenry. It is worthy of note that those states in our country with the highest commitment to educational facilities lead the nation in producing innovations.

## Negative Incentives for Innovation

The federal government has had its greatest impact upon business innovation by using positive measures of motivating innovation, both by direct and indirect means. This could be characterized as the "carrot" approach. However, under certain conditions, the obstacles to innovation represent management inactivity that requires a negative incentive or prod to motivate change.

These government pressures to spur innovations are sometimes gentle but at other times take rather harsh form. They range from a specific ruling by a government agency on the acceptability of a company's innovation for public sale, to a more subtle suggestion that certain innovations by the company would bring them more favorable consideration as a vendor to the government. Following are some examples of the federal government's "pressure" to induce innovations, in some cases of a technological nature and in others leading to dramatic administrative innovations in individual companies. The net effect has been to raise the general level of capability in private industry of managing innovations (planning, organizing, and controlling them).

*1. Innovation by edict.*  This is a type of spur to innovation in which a government agency (or Congress) decides that as of a certain time, specific innovations are to be implemented by companies in a specific industry or group of industries. An example of this action was the requirement of the FCC that, as of May 1965, all television receivers sold in this country must be able to receive ultrahigh frequency broadcasts. This was one of those actions that benefited both the consuming public and industry, for there is no doubt that the production of UHF receivers lagged until the FCC edict.

*2. Pressure for innovation on potential vendors.*  Another important influence government has exerted on business innovations is to establish requirements for all potential government vendors. The interesting aspect of these actions is that they very often have demanded administrative innovations in individual companies. For example, in soliciting bidders for certain classes of contracts involving complex program design, the government has required that any company asking to be considered for contracts have the PERT system installed. This administrative innovation has proved immensely valuable in reducing both the time and cost of programs, with the Polaris missile system representing one of its early achievements. Though private industry has been improving PERT in nongovernment activities, a large part of the impetus for its use resulted from government pressure.

Another example of government prodding of business innovations is revealed in the Air Force pamphlet distributed to its prospective vendors. One passage places great stress on the benefits of incorporating a cost reduction program in the company's procedures. This program is identified as one of the criteria to be used in evaluating the capacity of a vendor to perform its contract properly. Having taken the hint, many companies have launched a systems study which leads to even greater benefits than just a cost reduction program.

An instance of federal pressure to achieve technological innovations was the requirement by the General Services Administration that all automobiles sold to the agency would henceforth come equipped with advanced safety features. Coupled with the pressure of congressional hearings on auto safety and suits against manufacturers for auto accident injuries, significant changes in safety equipment were made by the auto industry. The effect was to increase the rate of innovation in the area of safety equipment.

**3. Antitrust pressure for innovation.**  The antitrust law is designed to prevent serious restraints on competition. The threat of prosecution by the Justice Department has resulted, in a subtle way, in a greater emphasis on developing innovations as an acceptable way of achieving a competitive advantage.

**4. Pressure of appeal to patriotism.**  Another government inducement that has had an effect on the domestic rate of innovation has been the moral suasion used by the President to curtail investment overseas. Industry is encouraged to invest in innovations in this country instead. The basis for this request was an appeal to the patriotism of managers to help improve our balance of payments position. The Secretary of Commerce has clearly indicated that this appeal has been heeded by industry. **(10)**

## State and Local Government Influence on Innovation

In recent decades there has been a running debate between the side that sees the federal government extending its role at the expense of state and local government, and the group that feels that the growth of federal government is in proportion to the growing complexity and size of our society. Indeed, these latter people stress that a large part of federal growth results from local inaction.

There is little doubt that in spurring innovation, as in other fields, the federal government will continue to have a large role. However, in recent years a number of state and local agencies have taken dramatic steps to increase their influence on the rate of innovation. Very often this has come in response to political or economic pressures. Of the two situations to be explored, one will reflect the desire for economic development of a state and the other will reveal the reaction to political pressure from Washington.

**New York State development.**   The Office of Regional Development has prepared for New York State a program which gives recognition to the future changes in population, innovations, industrialization, and urbanization. Even the title of the report, which summarizes the state's approach as, "Change, Challenge, Response," fully captures the spirit of encouraging innovation. The essential ingredients include:

CHANGE.   The explosion of the world's population, and the matching explosion of human knowledge and technology, are the pressing realities of our time.

CHALLENGE.   To meet needs of our future citizens requires hard thinking and careful planning by all local and state government agencies.

RESPONSE.   To build in great scale and with great sensitivity is our free society's response to the challenge of change. **(11)**

**Local government influence on innovation.**   An example of political pressure by the federal government that has fostered innovation is reflected in the present emphasis on developing water resources. The pressure grows out of a distinct threat of congressional action if no steps are taken on the state and local levels. A most striking case is the involvement of various communities in the pollution of Lake Erie. For a long time local government took no action and even disclaimed any responsibility for contributing to the contamination of the lake. Now it is apparent that in the years ahead greater effort will be made by local governments throughout the country in sponsoring innovation projects that will help solve such problems. **(12)**

### Government Obstacles to Innovation

The previous discussion of the ways in which government (local, state, and federal) can foster innovation for the manager has meaning only insofar as he can envision their applicability to his efforts in advancing innovations. In this regard, we have tried to point out the ways in which a manager can get direct and indirect government support for his aspirations to innovate. An assessment of the government's role in innovation would be inadequate, however, unless we also examine those areas in which the government tends to inhibit innovation. With this in mind, let's examine some of the pitfalls that the government generates that the manager must guard against—or work around.

*Antitrust obstacles to innovation.* A growing menace that pervades corporate discussions is the increasing emphasis by the courts and regulating agencies in prohibiting increased size and combinations of business firms. This situation not only concerns the top echelons, but has a direct influence on the thinking of individual managers who may advocate innovative programs that have vast potential in improving departmental as well as corporate effectiveness.

The barriers to innovation erected by the FTC and the courts have been in the form of prohibitions of an increased scale, or mere change that may have resulted from an administrative innovation such as reorganization, consolidation, or the development of a new marketing program. Restrictions have also been placed on technological innovations, such as new products or processes that have won wide acceptance by customers and have achieved greater profit.

To label these *legitimate* efforts of innovation—in our free competitive society—as against the public interest is sheer folly. Moreover, to suggest that these achievements, per se, are in restraint of trade is simply dead wrong.

As Max Ways has said, in advocating the *Fortune* proposition to amend the antitrust statutes so as to encourage competition by spurring innovation, "In short, what we know of the next twenty years is that corporations will need the utmost flexibility because in each year the economy will be more and more involved with innovation."

It behooves every manager to recognize this state of affairs and to participate in bringing about changes in legislation rather than to leave these deliberations to the corporate counsel and the inhabitants of the board room. The reason this awareness on the part of manager is necessary is that he should realize that "We are moving, year by year into a more truly competitive and more innovative society in which we will not need and cannot afford the restrictive side of antitrust." **(13)**

***The patent system obstacles to innovation.***  In many ways, as discussed earlier in this chapter, the operation of the patent office tends to spur innovation. However, it is necessary for the manager to be aware of how the patent process may tend to restrict innovation. One of the greatest obstacles to implementing innovation is the delay incurred in processing patent applications. Typically there is a backlog of a quarter of a million patent applications. These await processing by an undermanned staff housed in quarters that are crowded and inefficient. Another obstacle is that the procedure and criteria for evaluating potential patents is in need of revision after many years of use.

Still another obstruction to innovation generated by the patent process is that facing the individual innovator lacking extensive financial and corporate support. The reasons these obstacles confront the individual are the cost burdens, delays of up to four years on a patent decision, and the need to bring suit to prevent patent infringement. Another obstacle is that the patent office as well as the courts stress patent production for technological innovations but tend to ignore administrative innovations.

***Obstacles to innovation from progressive taxes.***  Aside from the social and fiscal consequences of the progressive income tax which may make it a just and efficient tax, it tends to have a restraining influence upon innovation. Individuals as well as corporate groups realize that the additional profit advantage that may acrrue from a particular technological or administrative innovation is largely nullified because of a tax *rate* increase as income levels rise. The effect is to produce a hesitancy towards innovating.

***Obstacles to innovation by regulatory agencies.***  The restraints placed upon publicly regulated companies in limiting their profits tends to dull the enthusiasm for innovation and even makes it financially difficult to achieve. The classic case of regulating profits that may diminish innovations is the large-scale examination of A.T.&T. by the Federal Communications Commission. The key response of A.T.&T. to this investigation of its profit and rate structure has been its insistence that to spur its rate of innovation, in keeping with the future needs of our nation for growth in communication, the profit rate of the Bell System would have to be increased. Individual managers in all companies are watching these events closely to determine whether restrictive practices of administrative agencies of the government will tend to dampen future innovation and restrict the manager's desire to seek more efficient ways of operating.

In Part I there has been an emphasis on the role that managers, above all, must play in innovation with regard to dealings with labor and in appreciating the negative as well as the positive impact of government. In this way managers may minimize the obstacles and take advantage of the supports provided in these areas so that they can foster the adoption of innovations they have conceived or those conceived by others and affecting their own area of responsibility.

# PART II

# Developing and Implementing Company Innovations

# CHAPTER 4

# MANAGEMENT PROBLEMS IN AN ERA OF CHANGE

The previous chapters have served to present the meaning of innovation and to reveal to the manager the forces that are exerting an influence—both positively and negatively—on the process of innovating. It is the manager who is the central figure in the events of change and, want it or not, he has the central position in America's industrial future.

Let's now take a look somewhat deeper to learn more of what the issues explored in Part I mean in terms of how the manager performs his job. If innovation represents opposing conditions of threat and opportunity, it is fruitful to examine a little more deeply, first, the threat in terms of the problems that innovation presents to the manager—which may be of a far more urgent nature than ever before.

An incisive comment on the dilemma presented by change—threat or opportunity—was made at a symposium which projected management into 1985, pointing out that reactions to the challenge might be "defensive and conserving, or offensive and innovative." (1)

And here we have the essential way out of the dilemma managers face in change. The *threats* that it harbors may be very real, but the way in which a manager reacts to these threats—indeed, whether he

51

views them as threats at all—will determine whether they become unbearable or, instead, are converted into opportunities. The way, then, is clearly by innovating in substance as well as form, or by "taking the initiative against the future." (2) Bright sees innovating as "far and away the most important force for management to consider." (3)

It is necessary to recognize the immensity of the challenge of change before the manager examines the problems growing out of innovating. Perhaps the most succinct comment on the task facing managers is one made by Robert W. Reneker, president of Swift & Co., who has said, "Providing goods or services is an unbelievably complicated job today because the market is constantly moving, shifting and changing." (4) This comment brings the immensity of the problem of innovation right down to the day-to-day corporate operations. With this as our context, let's take a look at how the manager might view the problems of innovation.

### The Personal Challenge Facing the Manager

The most significant management problems arising in this era of accelerated change are the personal challenges confronting the manager in performing his role. On the one hand there is the growing fear among some executives that their skills may be becoming obsolete. They are aware of the real possibility that their jobs will be contracted or eliminated entirely.

Far worse off are other managers who completely blind themselves to the possibility that they are becoming unnecessary. The pity of this latter group is that they will be caught off guard, for they are not developing the capabilities to survive in a world of accelerated change.

Borrowing from the diagnostic process of the physician, the best way to determine whether there is a danger of being tossed aside due to executive obsolescence is to search for symptoms of the disease. These symptoms of obsolescence include: "A negative attitude, inflexibility, excessive egotism, indecisiveness and over-concern about fellow officials." (5) Admittedly, if these attitudes are deep-rooted in the manager, he may be in danger of being supplanted. On the other hand, the greatest assurance of being able to confront the challenge of change with success is for the manager to develop flexibility and to adapt to change, and at the same time to be imaginative and innovating.

The personal challenge to a manager today is the contrast between the manager of a former age who may have dealt with day-to-day operations in the nature of a caretaker, and that of today's manager who must emphasize innovating more than caretaking. The hardening of the wrong attitude—caretaking—can happen to any manager after a few years in the same job. As Weigle puts it: "After that time he isn't innovating; he's minding the store." (6)

The real shocker is that the manager, in order to avoid obsolescence, is not required to *replace* the caretaking with innovating, but must *add on* the burdens of innovating to his caretaking responsibilities.

Another personal pressure confronting the manager is the competition he faces in the process of decision making. At the 15th annual meeting of the Systems and Procedures Association, participants examined the role of automatic data processing in decisions typically made by managers. (7) While it was emphasized that jobs at the top of the corporate ladder would continue to grow in scope and number, it was made equally clear that a whole group of middle managers who formerly made operating decisions in the areas of sales, inventory, finance, and production was being replaced.

Even more pessimistic for middle managers is the prediction that "by 1985 we will possess the technical capability required to handle most managerial jobs by machine" and that "computers will be capable of taking over practically all of the familiar managerial functions and of doing many of them better than human managers." (8)

A word of caution may be in order about this prophecy of doom. It may well be true that, in a sense, computers can think, learn, and make decisions. It may also be true that many managerial tasks can be performed equally well by computers. But it will generally be found that these managerial tasks of the "caretaking" variety are *not* of the innovative type. A lot of them are relatively routine and repetitive.

Barbara Ward, the economist, brilliantly crystallized both aspects of the computer, as a threat and as an opportunity for the manager. She accepts the "forecast of the machine's ability to solve the familiar and defined problems," but goes on to insist that:

The truly challenging and important problems for any organization are those that have no precedent. These are the problems that arise because something completely new has occurred, to which the appropriate managerial response must be innovative and for which relevant information is lacking or must be developed from sources outside existing records. **(9)**

In essence, it is true that the ranks of middle management are thinning from the impact of both technological and administrative innovations. However, the kind of manager that is *not* being replaced, during this period of accelerated change, is the one who has developed the *skills* and *attitudes* of the innovating manager.

## Skill in Managing

To develop a capacity to manage change, it is *first* necessary to concentrate on how to *manage*. Training in management skills should follow the format I (and my associates) have used, with dramatic success, in improving manager performance for in-company training programs:

*a*) The manager's functions—planning, organizing, leading, controlling, and innovating.
*b*) Managing of work—methods analysis, work standards systems, work schedules, setting performance standards.
*c*) Managing the worker—selecting, training, disciplining, evaluating, and so on.
*d*) Human problems of managing—motivating, communications, adjusting to change, morale, and so on.

***Understanding the process of innovating.*** After concentrating on increasing the managers' and supervisors' sensitivity and skill in managing, it is necessary to develop, in managers, a greater understanding of the innovation process. This exposure to the nature of innovating should include:

*a*) Principles and techniques of creative thinking—how to generate more and better innovative ideas.

*b*) Learning the manager's role in innovating—developing proposals for innovations; facilitating innovations proposed by others; how to evaluate the potential of an innovation; techniques for programming an innovation; and techniques for implementing an innovation.

**Handling of change.**  The manager's skill in handling a change which involves his department or affects him in some way is vital during the transition to the change. The manager, therefore, needs greater sensitivity and skill in handling change, including: human problems of change; resistance to change; and means of facilitating individual adjustment to change. It is important to recognize the ingredients that are necessary for the manager-to-be or the student of business in developing an educational philosophy that will prepare him for an era of accelerating change. A particularly effective job has been done, for a number of years, in the Bell system, through their course for managers on "The Handling of Change." Other companies would do well to duplicate it.

We need to help students to learn to work more effectively, flexibly, and creatively in a world of continuous and rapid change. We need to help them to develop analytical tools and skills widely applicable, even to problems unknown today. We must encourage an intellectual attitude that is open-minded and imaginative in its visualization of dynamic business institutions operating in dynamic environment. We need creative skepticism in the assessment of the manager's future role in a democratic society and in the definition of the corporation's future role in the national and world economy. **(10)**

## Problem of Motivating in an Era of Change

Still another challenge of a personal nature facing the manager is in effectively motivating his subordinates in the face of conflicting forces that are unleashed in this age of radical change. Two sharply different situations may help to make this clearer. One case is of what has been called the major part of the "knowledge" industry, or a university. The other is of a life insurance company. Both are characterized by an unusual rate of expansion in recent years. In the case of universities the challenge to higher management has resulted from demands for a shifting role of both faculty and students in the affairs of the institution. The forces underlying these pressures for change should be assessed and fully appreciated by a manager.

An example of a life insurance company faced with complications resulting from change involved its top management's efforts to change operations and personnel in dramatic fashion. These events were capsuled into a short period of time and involved the shifts of great numbers of people. The effect of this management action was to evoke dismay and then dissension among employees. The tension created led to the introduction of an outside force—a union—in an attempt to redress some real and some imagined grievances.

Both these cases describe conditions which resulted in a revolt against constituted authority, and, in turn, widespread replacement of top management personnel. This is not merely a question of obedience to constituted authority, but rather of how a manager—by an awareness of the turbulent forces that occur on the *fringes* of change—can effectively motivate his subordinates to support the goals of the organization in the face of pressures generated by rival forces. The manager must learn to understand, cope with, and then *lead* these forces underlying change, in addition to managing the change itself.

### Communications to Facilitate Change

Another personal problem confronting the manager in this era of change concerns the difficulties that arise in communications during the implementation of a change. These arise in the form of "barriers" between the manager and the people who design the technical aspects of the change. Mere lip service for a program of communications will not maintain the communications links that are vital during change. The program should be developed using every means available and including particularly face-to-face exchange of ideas involving *all* individuals and groups affected by the change. Some issues to cover might be:

1. Announcing plans for developing the innovation.
2. Keeping people informed of the change—including reasons.
3. Maintaining effective communication during changeover.
4. Preventing communications barriers after the change.
5. Using communications to facilitate individual and group adjustment to the change as it continues in operation.

A recent survey by McKinsey and Company, to find out the factors that lead to successful innovation and what conditions tend to obstruct success, found that the managers who overcame communication difficulties between themselves and scientific or "idea" people were distinctly successful in managing innovations in their companies. On the other hand, where such communications difficulties led to frustration on the part of managers, the innovations tended to meet with failure.

***Developing new managerial skills.***   One of the personal difficulties confronting managers is the painful realization that their personal skills seem inadequate to the task of innovating. The manager may come to the further awareness that he must acquire new skills and sharpen old ones—posthaste—to cope with the challenge facing him in an era of change.

The demands placed upon the manager not only grow out of the fact that situations surrounding him are far more complex than ever before, but also because the people around him are more highly educated and more knowledgeable about a vast array of techniques and concepts. The new, innovative manager must be equipped with the "new knowledge" whereby he can discriminate between the useful and the impractical recommendations submitted to him. **(11)** He does not have to master every detail known by the specialist, but does need to know what can be expected from mathematics, from computers, from organizational theory, from science, etc. Necessary and possible, though not easy to do.

In addition to these knowledge skills it is necessary for a manager to reexamine his use of the managerial functions of planning, organizing, and controlling, to attune his approach more toward innovating than merely toward caretaking.

Another important additional skill the manager should develop is the skill in creating attitudes among his subordinates that view change as a positive phenomenon—that welcome change as an opportunity and not a burden. **(12)**

### Community Problems Facing the Manager

The quickening pace of innovation in our economic society has had its effects in areas outside of company operations in the surrounding communities. Moreover, these changes have produced problems which inevitably require the involvement of managers in community issues. Many times these community changes affect the physical, social, and economic characteristics of the community. It is virtually impossible for the manager to ignore these changes, since they may have a direct effect upon his company's operation of its plant or office in that community.

*Area redevelopment.*    One of the significant changes in communities leading to problems for the manager lies in the physical redevelopment of a neighborhood, area, or region. The factors that may make necessary the "bulldozer approach" to redevelopment may run anywhere from physical decay of the structures, shifts in population, movement of industry, to the need for a higher economic use of property. More and more, the innovative manager faces up to the challenges these changes induce and participates fully in them. Successful redevelopment, resulting in a higher tax base, has taken place in such cities as Hartford, Pittsburgh, and Detroit. The achievements were due, in large measure, to the involvement and leadership of corporate managers. The benefits to the companies whose managers participated were immense.

Increasingly, managers in urban as well as rural communities are recognizing that redevelopment is not confined to a few urban areas. As a result of this awakening to the potential of community change these managers are becoming avid supporters of community planning on the local level.

*Social problems.*    One of the most compelling pressures facing the manager is that which arises from social changes in the community, especially when it generates conflict between opposing groups. The manager's problem is to prevent harm to his company's day-to-day operations. He must also prevent these conflicts from retarding the adoption of innovations that produce economic benefits to his company. He finds it increasingly difficult to assume the pose, "this is not my company's problem," to avoid involvement in controversy.

Of vital interest, in recent years, have been disputes over racial integration in a community, whether it involves conflicts over existing conditions of *de facto* or legal segregation, and regardless of what aspect of the community it may involve (employment, community services, government, education, or recreation).

The experience of the Crown Zellerbach Company has provided a dramatic example of one company's attempt at first to ignore, and finally to come to grips with, a problem that has rocked Bogalusa, Louisiana, and has led to a complete reshaping of the company managers' roles in the midst of significant social change in the communities in which it operates. **(13)**

The stress of community involvement has been particularly strong in the case of two of Crown's managers, Read O. Hunt, chairman, who is located in headquarters at San Francisco, and Roy R. Ferguson, manager of the company's plant at Bogalusa. This experience has led managers like Hunt and Ferguson to painfully examine what their role should be in conflicts of this type. The problem at the local scene involved Ferguson's attempt, at first, to maintain the delicate balance of avoiding directives to the community, on the one hand, and encouraging the attitude that company employees should participate in community affairs, on the other. At its headquarters office in San Francisco, Crown and Hunt were pressured with demonstrations by civil rights groups. Coupled with these pressures were harassments and criticisms from the public at large to the effect that Crown was indifferent to events or, at the other extreme, that they were engaged in duplicity with both sides.

Something had to "give," and it did. Though there may never be a completely satisfactory solution to the problems in this community, the shift in the role of Crown's managers may provide insight that could guide managers in other companies. To begin with, Ferguson, the local manager, emphasized to the citizens of Bogalusa his company's support for the national policy of nondiscrimination in hiring. He added, however, that Crown did not intend to impose these standards to achieve social reform in the rest of the community. Ferguson and other managers in the plant have also taken part in the discussions with community leaders designed to cope with some ongoing problems. On a national level, chairman Hunt has explored with the Department of Labor the possibility of obtaining Manpower Training and Development funds to attack community problems on the educational level. In essence, Crown's managers have accepted their role as peacemakers in what is a noncompany dispute. They realized that this role was essential in attaining a peaceful atmosphere that is vital for successful operations in Bogalusa.

### Problem of Maintaining Growth Through Innovating

A peculiarly sensitive problem facing a manager in an atmosphere of change is that, once having achieved the momentum of growth that results from innovating, it becomes difficult to maintain company growth because of forces it generates. Many companies achieve a growth peak but are unaware that the seeds of potential decline may arise from the very process of growth.

This condition was brilliantly revealed in a Dun's Review article which analyzed the history of a number of "growth companies" to determine what had caused them to "run out of gas." **(14)** The cases of Brunswick, Raytheon, Lily Tulip, and American Photocopy all depicted a dramatic pace of innovating that led to sharply higher earnings in the late 1950s. It was revealed how each of these companies went through the first stage of growth through innovation, but have, so far, failed to achieve the vital second stage of growth. The first stage usually begins with an innovation or series of innovations that provide expanding opportunities. Once this stage ripens, managers must reckon with the creation of potential evils that accompany these innovations. The dangers are threefold:

1. Being dynamic and highly profitable, the product or process invites new competition, which the originating company must be prepared to resist.
2. For the same reason, the product invites accelerated technological developments by other companies.
3. Even without competition, management may have made no provision to broaden the market, and eventually saturates it.

As a result of the forces unleashed, the manager who has gone through the first phase of growth by innovation must marshal the resources to embark on the second phase of growth or else face possible collapse. There are now two alternatives facing the manager. They are: either to continue innovating an improved family of products, services, and processes; or to go the route of acquisition. The latter may be considered the technique of "buying" innovations, and is sometimes an extremely costly proposition.

The immensity of this problem of maintaining and even accelerating the pace of innovation to continue company growth can be emphasized by noting that a "one-shot" approach to innovating not only will not work; it may leave the company in a far worse position than if it never pursued innovation in the first place. Managers, beware this trap of innovating.

Finally, another peripheral problem associated with maintaining the innovating momentum is that a large investment in the process of change builds in a kind of rigidity that results from developing excess amounts of production capacity. Knowing when to discard a no-longer-profitable innovation and embarking on a bolder innovation demands a lot of fortitude. There is often the tendency to put off the decision until it is too late. Moreover, some of these innovations generate large sums of cash which, too often, "burn a hole" in the corporate pocket. Recent economic difficulties in the paper and in the oil industries may well represent this condition.

## Problems over the Risks of Innovating

One of the problems that plagues the manager is that the pursuit of innovation generates certain risks. Unfortunately, the blithe spirit who plunges into this era of change without an awareness of these risks is due for a shock. Indeed, a lack of sensitivity to these risks may invite disaster.

In addition to the purely commercial risks there are subtler ones which seem more remote but nonetheless can become pitfalls for innovation projects.

*Risk incurred by wrong motives.*   Very often there is a risk incurred in entering a program of innovation for the wrong reasons. This tends to compound the risks of innovating because there are no clear motives established for the project and thus no possibility of measuring accomplishment. These "wrong" motives are usually variations of caprice. In referring to such ill-considered bases for embarking upon innovations, Robert Cannon of Cannon Electric disparages these warped motives by indicating that they are basically the motives of the status seeker. "It seems to be the O.K. thing now to join the club." **(15)**

*Risk of innovating by acquisition.*   A popular approach to innovating for some companies, and an absolute must for "catching up" in the innovation race for others, is to use the acquisition route, or "buying" innovations. However, the basis risk apparent in this approach is magnified by the astigmatism associated with the typical "paper" analysis of a going business. This short-cut is so enticing to some managers that they overrate the chances for success. A call for caution was very aptly sounded by the late John I. Snyder, who as chairman of U.S. Industries made that company one of the most innovative and profitable companies in the last decade, having transformed it from the point of bankruptcy. He warned that in outright acquisition you have to be careful. You can't simply look over a company's books, walk through its plants, talk to your lawyers about the financial details, and then, having come to your decision, assume that everything will turn out all right. If this is your attitude, you're in trouble before you start. **(16)**

***Risk of going too deep with a poor innovation.***    For an innovation to be a success it *must* produce a profit. It is important to stress that an inherent risk of a commitment to innovation is that the company will go *too far* investing in an innovation that is doomed to failure. These risks are multiplied as the innovation passes through stages from the conception of the idea, its evaluation, and then its actual operation.

The minimal risk is incurred at the first stage, in which a preliminary assessment is made of potential profit. To minimize investment in a faulty innovation, it is desirable to stop in this early stage. The second crisis point is reached just before a heavy commitment is made in fixed investment. The risk of continuing a poor innovation is immense. Finally, if it is a new product or service, the third stage of risk is in the market test of acceptability. A thorough and early review of customer response is essential to minimize investment—and risk—at this point. **(17)**

***Ethical risks of innovation.***    Quite apart from what may be called commercial risks are ethical risks of innovating that may conflict with, or even negate, the commercial success of an innovation. It is hoped that in weighing the profit potential of an innovation, the manager also develops an awareness of ethical considerations surrounding an innovation. There is a strong need for establishing ethical norms for economic innovations or else, failing this, "Law and other instruments of community decisions—outside of markets—must be evolved rapidly enough to set bounds upon innovation." **(18)**

A poignant example of the upsetting, though unforeseen, evil result of one of the most significant examples of modern innovation is the development of insecticides. An expected side effect of these chemicals is that they destroy useful as well as destructive insects. Indeed, they may threaten not only plants, trees, and animals, but, via the pollution of drinking water, man himself. Drucker's assessment of the ethical risks is summed up as he declares:

Innovation is thus not only opportunity. It is not only risk. It is first and foremost responsibility. No one is responsible for change; no one can do anything about it. One can only welcome inevitable progress or bemoan it; at most one can attempt to delay it. But innovation is deliberate choice, and we are responsible for its consequences. (19)

The three essential risks of innovation are: the risk of exposure —the risk, once having committed the company to innovation and expansion of innovation, that it may become obsolete overnight because of international upheavals or any number of incidents; the risk of failure which may occur, at times, through no weakness of the innovation but from a host of unfortunate circumstances; and finally the risk of success, in which unknown rival forces may be unleashed as a result.

## The Problem of Foreign Competition

A growing problem the domestic manager must face is the intense and spreading competition offered by foreign companies in the innovating arena. The concepts of innovating are taking hold around the world. The rate of accelerated change is even steeper in a great many nations than it is in our own country. This is true in Western Europe as well as in the Far East, and someday soon the emerging nations of Africa, Asia, and Latin America may offer the competitive challenge.

The problem facing managers in terms of marketing goods and services is one example. The organization of facilities into multinational groups such as the European Economic Community has had a dramatic impact on the innovation rate among American companies. The effect of this competition will present additional pressures for change, such as altering products, reorienting marketing strategy, and revising manufacturing techniques and methods. Managers must always be on the alert to meet and solve these problems.

## The Problem of Obstacles to Innovation

A very compelling problem facing the manager who accepts the challenge of innovating is in the form of obstructions to development and implementation. One of the key obstacles to the success of innovating is in developing ideas for innovation. Another is in the form of human resistance offered by the people affected by the change.

## The Individual Company and Innovation

The previous sections have examined the "Atmosphere" outside the individual company that exerts an influence upon the way a manager approaches innovation. It has included an assessment of the institutional, social and industrial conditions that inevitably shape a manager's decision to innovate. From this view of the outside forces, let us examine the role of the manager inside the company to help determine those factors which influence his role in innovation. This will include a consideration of the company's past experience with planned change, the various roles a manager may have in innovating; the different groups who may take part in change; and the range of attitudes a manager may adopt towards innovation.

*Company experience with innovation.* A first step in determining a company's ability to innovate is to review the changes that have taken place in order to analyze and classify them. It is desirable to distinguish first between technological and administrative innovations. Under administrative changes it is desirable to identify those that have had a companywide impact, such as changes in company organization structure or policies. In addition, administrative changes should be linked to each major functional subdivision of the company as well as distinct operating divisions. Under technological innovations, past changes may be separated into those involving the development of new product lines or changes in old ones, development of new or improved processing equipment, and changes that lead to improved plant and office structures and facilities.

For each significant company experience it might be desirable to analyze the events and actions that indicate the *approach* taken by managers responsible for implementing the innovation. It would be of interest to note, for example, the activities that took place to plan and implement the change and how these duties were shared among the various persons involved in the change.

Another aspect of the company approach worthy of note is the manner in which the participating groups became involved in the change. It would also be useful to accumulate information on the steps planned to install the change as well as the manner in which they were scheduled. Whether the change was gradual or introduced all at once is also important. By far the best critical aspect of reviewing past innovations is to determine the results achieved and the reactions to the events that took place.

The measurement of the degree of success should be based upon qualitative as well as quantitative criteria. A true innovation—a profitable change—must achieve a purpose and be economic. Quantitative measurements are valid, but may not reveal the whole picture. They should be supplemented by an evaluation in terms of qualitative criteria, too.

The phase of the assessment dealing with the impact of the innovation upon people may provide clues as to the employees' reactions to future innovations. Inevitably, changes have a dislocating effect upon company personnel. In those situations where major shifts occur, the jobs of many employees may be eliminated. On the other hand, the change may involve only the transfer of persons on a departmental level. In still other situations, a considerable amount of training is required before employees can assume newer tasks that result from the change.

Of considerable importance is the record kept of side effects and how the company has dealt with them. Also forming part of the institutional background on innovation is the record of policies and precedents on such issues as dismissal, transfers, and training of employees. The direction these policies take is of considerable importance in terms of future employee reactions to company innovations.

*The groups involved in innovations.*   It is worth noting that the persons who are affected by innovations fall into distinct categories. Their identity in terms of the primary group has a considerable influence upon their view of the innovation. These groups may at times be in conflict with one another, because of what they may perceive as diverse interests in the outcome of change. The two broad classes into which they fit may be considered groups inside the company and groups outside the company.

*A manager's view of innovation.*   The key role in implementing a planned change falls to the manager. A great many managers are positively inclined towards innovations—or, in the popular view, *should* be. To recognize the importance of the manager's role in innovation, we must realistically examine the many ways in which he may view innovation. Only in that way is it possible to properly determine whether the heavy responsibility he assumes in planned change is likely to be fulfilled. Put another way, many of today's managers are decidedly unreceptive to the idea of change, and they are the ones who create the greatest obstacles to a successful change in organizational structure and methods. Obviously, the higher a man's position in the organizational hierarchy, the greater is his ability to obstruct changes. There's little an individual employee can do to resist a change that management really wants to put into effect; but an individual executive is often in a position to thwart needed changes—or at least to impede their application to the point of reducing their effectiveness to a minimum.

### The Need for Leadership

It is of vital importance for managers to become leaders of change. In his book, *Big Business and Free Men,* James C. Worthy emphasizes the need for executive leadership on a broad level:

As members of a leadership group businessmen must assist in developing policies that will deal effectively with emerging problems, many of which are created by advances within business itself. Not to do so, or merely to resist change, is to abdicate and through default allow others to exercise the initiative.

Even within their own companies, there is evidence that many managers fail to accept change as an essential characteristic of their jobs. A 1962 research study found that over half of the participating companies encountered difficulties in making major changes— difficulties that were directly attributable to the actions or inactions of top or line management. **(20)** Such resistance presents a most serious obstacle to a company's progress.

CHAPTER **5**

# MANAGEMENT OPPORTUNITIES FOR INNOVATION

It is easy to sympathize with a manager who might blanch at the prospects of innovation after surveying the problems examined in the last chapter. However, just as there are immense problems created by innovation, there are boundless opportunities for achievement via innovating. If only he can tap this potential, the manager can find personal as well as company benefits.

Merely being aware, in broad terms, that there are prospects in innovation is not enough to evoke enthusiasm. Rather, a process of exploration must be undertaken. The manager, first, seeks ways of discovering new opportunities for profit through innovation; and, second, he must select from the vast gamut of opportunities the very best for early exploitation.

Though we have categorized innovation in two distinct types, technological and administrative, the underlying rationale for a fruitful search of *any* business innovation lies in the basic objective of business itself—serving the customer. It is with this emphasis upon customer-oriented innovation that the manager may find the most ready route to his company's innovation, prosperity and growth.

### Ingredients for Company Growth

With the objective of increasing company profitability and growth clearly established, combined with a customer-oriented search for innovations, let us examine the ingredients necessary for company growth before uncovering opportunities for innovation that will achieve that growth.

In one of the most brilliant analyses of "formulas for company success," Jack Weiner of *Dun's Review* has held up to full view the 13 top growth companies in the United States. In so doing, he has isolated those ingredients which, apparently, have had a direct bearing upon their amazing success. Weiner cautions against projecting the six rules developed as foolproof. However, he does indicate that the *underlying* reason why these rules *have* worked for these companies is attributable to their universal acceptance of the attitude that—*the only* constant in business is change itself.

Following are the six basic rules that lie beneath the successful innovating and growth of each of the 13 companies. In effect they offer guidelines for identifying and exploiting the opportunities for innovation. These rules for growth through innovating in an era of accelerated change include:

1. The difficult task of starting long-range planning at the grass-roots level of management and the involvement of even lower level employees in the job of looking into the future.
2. A truly dynamic corporate structure that enables the company to seize a profit opportunity whenever or wherever one appears.
3. An active, viable program to encourage employee innovation and creativity.
4. An infallible sense of timing, of being equally adept at knowing when to launch a new product or close down an old plant.
5. Above-average investment acumen, a particularly challenging capability that few corporations can really master.
6. An integrated line, with a program of product development and acquisition designed to avoid both risk and merely temporary gain. **(1)**

The heart of the message to be found in these capsuled "rules for success" is that growth is dependent upon an innovative attitude among a company's managers. This attitude is embodied in two ingredients: the capability of developing innovative ideas; and the "guts" to proceed with their installation in the face of problems generated by innovation.

The Weiner study also dramatically reveals that companywide programs of innovation, to be successful, demand the involvement of *all* people on *all* levels, from the planning stage to the actual implementation of change. Implicit in this approach is the clear understanding that each person, on his own level, has the creative capacity to make a contribution to the growth and prosperity of "his" company. With managers leading the way, each employee develops a proprietary interest in seeking the "optimal entrepreneurial environment."

Chairman William C. Norris of Control Data expresses his company's philosophy, stating that: "Our people are to be in an environment where they are not only free to exercise their individual drive and ingenuity but are encouraged and expected to do so—corporate initiative being the sum of all individual initiatives." This philosophy is echoed by "Tex" Thornton of Litton, who says about his company, "If we create change we don't have to adjust to it—but the other fellow does, and he has to follow it."

### Establishing Targets for Innovating Opportunities

Another preliminary to examination of potential areas of innovation is for the manager to help choose the directions innovation will take, or rather to establish targets that will guide his search for innovation opportunities. In this way a search procedure may be developed that will avoid overlooking likely innovation prospects.

One helpful source for developing such a "classified directory" is provided by Bright, with the limitation that his search is limited to technological innovations. (2) However, his approach in pinpointing broad targets for innovation is readily applicable to administering innovation as well. Bright's analysis grows out of his highlighting a series of trends in change affecting various segments of our society. The six trends he reviews—with their consequences for technological change—are: increased transportation capability; increased ability to extend and control the life of animate and inanimate things; increased ability to alter characteristics of materials; extension of man's sensory capabilities; growing mechanization of physical activities; and growing mechanization of intellectual processes.

Developing such categories to help pinpoint the directions in which to seek innovation opportunities is a helpful preliminary to the actual search for specific areas of innovation potential. Perhaps the most thought-provoking examination of this kind is provided by

Peter Drucker. He not only highlights broad areas of innovation for possible investigation but he singles out the few areas that are destined to provide the most likely avenues for innovations in the coming years.

With his belief that the only valid function of a business is "to create a customer," Drucker conceives of innovation as oriented to that customer by providing better and more economic goods and services. With this emphasis on the compelling nature of innovating, Drucker advocates some broad directions in which innovation opportunities should lie. In effect he provides innovation goals for a typical business:

1. New products and services that are needed to attain marketing objectives.
2. New products or services that will be needed because of technological changes that may make present products obsolete.
3. Product improvements needed both to attain market objectives and to anticipate expected technological changes.
4. New processes and improvements in old processes needed to satisfy market goals—for instance, manufacturing improvements to make possible the attainment of pricing objectives.
5. Innovations and improvements in all major areas of activity—in accounting or design, office management or labor relations—so as to keep up with advances in knowledge and skill. (3)

What is of greater significance, in terms of prospects for innovation opportunities, is Drucker's highlighting of what he regards as the areas of greatest opportunity for future innovations. The general direction in which he feels the greatest profit opportunity exists for innovation is in what may be called nontechnological innovation. I use the term administrative innovation. This is in sharp contrast to Bright's emphasis upon technological innovation to the exclusion of all others. In fact, though, neither type should be pursued alone. Rather, a manager should seek innovative opportunities for his company wherever they may lie.

Nonetheless, Drucker proposes that "the greatest need for innovation seems more likely to lie ahead in the social rather than in the technological area." His use of "social" is akin to what I have called "administrative" innovation. He further crystallizes the greatest potential as lying in four areas: innovation in marketing; innovation in methods, tools, and measurements for performing the manager's job; innovation in the management of workers; and finally, innovation in the organization of work. **(4)**

This brief examination of the need to define broad areas of innovative opportunity before seeking individual prospects has, at least, given some indication of the immense possibility that lies ahead in innovating. Moreover, for most managers, the opportunity for personal career growth as well as company prosperity is so huge that it readily dwarfs the view that innovation is a threat. Let's now move closer to examining where these opportunities lie by reviewing the role of adequate planning in searching out innovations.

### Planning as the Basis for Innovation Opportunities

For a manager to go off in search of innovative opportunities without relating his quest to companywide, integrated planning is sure to prove frustrating. It is even more discouraging for the manager to learn that *no* company planning exists. Should this be the case, a search for innovative opportunities is almost senseless. It is company planning which will form the guide for sound exploration of innovation opportunities.

A magnificent outline of the planning process, to be used as the preliminary to an innovation search, was developed at a conference sponsored by the President's Association of the American Management Association. **(5)** The most vital part of this planning process is the group of four steps that may be considered the preliminary to taking action in formulating plans. Put in the form of probe questions, the planning stages that are vital to developing innovations are:

1. Where are we, the total business, as of now? This, the first step, involves self-assessment of the current position in terms of company strengths and weaknesses.
2. Where are we going as we now are? Here is an appraisal of company momentum along the course it is steering, assuming no fundamental policy changes or shifts in direction.
3. Where do we *want* to go? What business or businesses should we be in? The answers, though tentative, may well end up as the basic goals to be reached by the company plan.

4. What may get us there? The broad and general strategic plan for the corporation as a whole, toward which the foregoing questions have been directed, is mapped out at this point.

At this conference of top company planners the final stage of planning that was described involved the pinpointing of specific means and responsibility for achieving the planning goals that were being established. The sequence was described as a vital "base" from which to start a search for innovation opportunities.

A second preliminary to identifying opportunities is to collect the available published materials that may help generate ideas for the search. For example, there are a number of books on new product ideas that may prove helpful. A fuller development of how to generate innovative ideas will be presented in the next chapter.

Now let us identify some of the areas in which lie great opportunities for profitable innovations.

## Close-to-Home Opportunities for Innovation

In addition to the opportunities discussed above that tend to have a companywide emphasis, there are many opportunities that present themselves to the manager which have a more immediate limited impact but are more directly under the control of the manager. Whatever kind of section or department is involved, or whatever the function performed, these day-to-day and close-at-hand opportunities arise. What's more, they have a more significant impact on the manager's *own* progress and performance.

It is up to the individual manager to be alert to these innovation opportunities and to exploit them in his area of responsibility. A ready type of opportunity the manager will likely find is in administrative innovation. For example, a tremendous potential exists for methods or systems for performing individual or group tasks. Closely similar to these methods changes are improvements in small appliances, tools, or other equipment that can be developed for office or plant use or converted from other known uses. The manager can readily adapt these to improve his department operations. Depending upon the specialized function of his area of responsibility, the manager can encourage his subordinates to propose innovative ideas that will improve departmental efficiency. There are also countless opportunities to seek to deal with subordinates (personnel relations) and to better organize the effort of his department for administrative and technological innovations that are "close to home." The essential attitude is for the manager to develop a "mental set" in looking for innovative possibilities, coupled with the goal of expecting a given number for any time period.

## Opportunities for Product Innovations

Still one of the most fruitful and glamorous areas for innovation is in additions and improvements in products or services. With change proceeding at a phenomenal rate, the race which makes today's product obsolete tomorrow is a major factor in contributing to the pace of change. This is a far cry from the day in 1845 when the U.S. patent commissioner recommended that the patent office be closed because he seriously thought that everything useful to man had already been invented.

The pressure for product innovation has developed to such a pitch that a product may become obsolete simply because the consumer has become accustomed to continually seeking something new. In such an atmosphere, the resources of companies are being harnessed to achieve the greatest possible return for their investment in product development.

In a study by the National Industrial Conference Board of techniques used by companies to turn new product ideas into commercial success, a picture was presented of the immense effort involved in harnessing the company's energies for product innovations. Moreover, to help companies organize a program for product planning, the report recommends the approach to each of five critical steps in product innovation: "Ideas, development, production, marketing, and finance and control." **(6)**

One of the most effective aids available to guide product planning was culled from the suggestions of leading executives who covered every aspect under the title, *New Products/New Profits*. **(7)** As in the case of the NICB report, this book analyzes the major phases of a program but also examines many of the problems that arise in its use.

The key to the potential of product innovation is the recognition of its urgency, because, five years from now, the major portion of corporate profit will likely be derived from products that do not even exist now. There is little question of the vast opportunity that lies ahead. What is in doubt is any *one* company's ability to *economically* tap this potential. Some guidelines for doing just this will be developed in later chapters.

## Opportunities for Process Innovation

If the potential for product innovation is vast, the certainty of opportunities for innovating the processes to make these products is no less so. Often, this follows, since there is a tendency to innovate processes as new products are developed. But the intensity of process innovation is motivated by far more than the need to keep pace with new products.

Process innovations are often the result of developing new industries and also result from a manager's search for greater productive capacity at reduced cost. The greatest drive for process innovation, therefore, comes from the desire to achieve greater operating economy for increased company profits. Two trends that govern process innovations are: first, to seek an extension of the continuous process concept which links each of the processing steps into a continuum; and second, to reach for automation which represents the establishment of self-correcting controls at each stage in the processing.

The continued competitive pressures for accelerating the rate of change in processing will continue to provide increasing opportunities for innovation in processes.

## Opportunities for Innovation in the Organization of Work

A most fundamental part of a manager's work—organizing—involves: identifying activities to be performed and arranging them in logical relationship; determining how the work will be performed; assigning people to those tasks; and evaluating performance. The function of organizing is becoming more difficult as the work becomes more complex and as the education and training of people becomes more intense and diverse. The result has been a growing search for innovations that will more effectively aid the manager in organizing work. A review of some of the innovations developed recently in this area will give some hint of the vast need, and growing opportunity, for innovating in the organization of work.

**The functional team company.**  A recent development of Gerald Fisch, called the functional team, is an organizational innovation that is designed to more effectively utilize the talents that abound in a company. **(8)** Referring to what he considers unrealistic and outdated approaches to organizing a manufacturing company, Fisch suggests that, "We abandon this arbitrary division of functions and realize that the accomplishments of manufacturing are the result of *team work.*"

The functional team idea rejects the compartmentalization of activities peculiar to other organization forms, and instead emphasizes the relatedness and the interdependence of these heretofore *isolated* activities in the company. It advocates that concrete recognition should be given to this interdependence of functional activities, by bringing them closer—organizationwise—together under the same wing. For example, Fisch proposes that in a manufacturing company there should be only three major groupings of activities, called resources, operations, and relations. Within each of these three categories tradition should be upset by bringing together those activities that must "work together" to accomplish a certain goal. A typical situation is what Fisch suggests should be included under the functional team for operations. This unit should include the three activities of engineering: manufacturing, sales, and distribution. In this way all groups responsible for providing the product or service to the customer, namely, design, manufacture and distribution of a product, are "teamed" together in that goal rather than considering themselves as functional *rivals.*

**PERT.**  One of the most dramatic and widely used recent innovations in work organization and progress analysis is the Program Evaluation and Review Technique. The basic concept underlying PERT is the network analysis technique. In this respect, it is derived from two remarkable innovations of a few decades ago: the flow chart, as developed by Frank Gilbreth, and the production scheduling chart devised by Gantt. The Navy began using PERT as part of the Polaris program in 1939 and a large part of the success of this program is attributable to PERT.

The significance of PERT, in terms of organizing work, is that it provides a strong incentive for the planning and the controlling of work. By requiring intense concentration, in advance, upon the many problems that may arise in the completion of a program, PERT makes its most important contribution by forcing logical thinking in organizing work expectations and commitments. Its further impact on work organization is that it more clearly defines the relationships and interdependence among various activities, functions, and skills. Moreover, it enables the manager to pinpoint responsibility for results with great precision.

The whole future of network analysis is one area of vast potential for innovation in the organization of work, for, as company systems become more complex, the demands of the techniques of network analysis (of which PERT is a leading example) will grow stronger.

*Industrial dynamics.*    One example of innovation in the organization of work that is also used as a diagnostic tool in identifying operating problems is Jay Forrester's "industrial dynamics." Though Forrester's technique has practical use in spotting company weak points, the underlying approach is based upon an innovation in the concept of organizing work. Continuing the work of Fisch's functional team concept, with its grouping of interdependent functions, Forrester views the entire complex of company functions as a *single* system of interdependent parts. With this configuration (organization) of work to be performed, his technique helps to identify which part of this system is malfunctioning and, therefore, requires correction. **(9)**

This technique has already been of benefit to a number of companies in solving pressing problems. However, the opportunity that lies ahead as a result of further organization innovations of this type is potentially enormous. Testifying to the future prospects and stressing the need for further exploration in the area of work organization is Chairman Robert C. Sprague of Sprague Electric, whose company has received significant benefits from "industrial dynamics." He states that:

Millions are being spent for electronic research and practically nothing for management research. We feel there is a need for both. That's why we have spent $100,000 on Forrester's industrial dynamics.

Industrial dynamics is based on an analysis of six major ingredients in the organization of work, namely: orders, materials, manpower, capital equipment, money, and information.

### Innovation in the Organization of Work through Job Enlargement

A most significant trend in recent years, based on innovation in work organization, moves in the opposite direction from one of the hallowed principles of scientific management—specialization of task. Specialization seeks to make the job as small and simple as possible so that the repetition of the task will quickly achieve worker proficiency. Instead, job enlargement reaches in the direction of organizing work so that a *greater* number of different tasks is performed by a single worker.

Heretofore, the organization of work in both plant and office has been along the lines of almost complete specialization of task. Some common characteristics of such jobs are: "the small repetitive increments of work, minimum skill requirements, mechanical pacing of work, operator difficulty in relating the task to the finished product, and adherence to a rigid time cycle." More and more managers have become convinced that to presume that specialization results in economy is no longer true. Moreover, the negative impact upon employee attitudes that through specialization they become a mere "cog in the wheel" has become a compelling reason for organizing work on a basis where the employee can view his own contribution to the end product, or job enlargement.

Irwin Rose, vice president of manufacturing at Maytag sees the multiple objectives of job enlargement in the following way:

Originally it was our concern for the quality and the cost of our product that prompted our interest in job enlargement. At the same time, however, we are intensely interested in employee job satisfaction. **(10)**

What is of additional importance in terms of further innovation in organization is that, in addition to the change in the nature and relationships that took place in the workers' jobs, what occurred at Maytag was that the organization of the supervisors' work also changed. This change involved a shift from the role of "oversupervisor" to the development of the working foreman who became part of the work team.

Job enlargement, as an innovation in organization of work, has been successfully used also at IBM. In that company, production work organization not only combines many different skilled operating tasks, but even extends to setup tasks and inspection of the workers' own output. To an increasing extent the worker and his foreman are also given the task (formerly reserved entirely for the industrial engineer) of determining their own production norms.

The results of this innovation in the organization of work at IBM have been impressive.

This approach has not only resulted in a constant increase in productivity at IBM, but has also significantly affected the attitudes of company workers. In fact, many observers both inside and outside the company think that the increase in the worker's pride in the job he is doing is the most important gain.

## Opportunities for Innovation in Marketing

A vast array of opportunities in all areas of marketing lie ahead in the years to come. Part of the reason is found in the fact that for many decades many managers stressed innovations in production with the presumption that there was little need for change in marketing. Moreover, our productive capacity is increasing at such a pace that greater effort must be applied to marketing of an increasing volume of goods. There is universal awakening to the fact that the customer must be served better through expanding emphasis on innovations in marketing.

The spirit of challenge and opportunity are highlighted in Levitt's formula for grasping the opportunity to serve the customer via marketing innovations:

One thing we know for sure about society and consumers is that they are constantly changing in ways that are extremely important to every business. The trick is to anticipate and act on these changes before the competitor does, and to do it at the right time and in the right way. (11)

Vast opportunities have developed in marketing at a faster rate than ever before because of the growing acceptance of the need to develop the emphasis on the *customer*-oriented business rather than a *product*-oriented business. The meaning of customer orientation is brilliantly crystallized by Ferrell:

The awareness of and fulfillment of the concept that a business enterprise's profitable growth depends upon its future ability to serve selected customer needs rather than to sell particular products or services. (12)

To give some idea of the many opportunities that are ahead in marketing innovation, let us examine just a few recent innovations to note the spirit of change that prevails in the marketing area.

**Opportunities in marketing diversification.**    Companies that have long been confined to serving customers in a narrow marketing area have recently taken to diversifying the customer appeal. This may have been designed to enhance company growth as a protection against decline due to concentration in a narrow market area. Pet Milk is an example of a company that in recent years has decided to overcome its dependence upon a single product grouping (in Pet's case, dairy products, with an emphasis on canned milk) and, instead, has switched to the status of a fully diversified food company.

What is apparent from Pet's case is that a major marketing innovation (for this company) requires administrative innovations in other areas of the business. Its effect was a complete reversal of declining profits.

**Opportunities in distribution methods.**    The fact that innovation opportunities abound in methods of distribution was never more clearly, or brutally, revealed than by the clamor by retailers that has greeted the extension of dual distribution.

Dual distribution is the means by which a manufacturer of a product who sells to a particular distributor or retailer opens his own outlet and competes directly with the independent dealer. **(13)** There is nothing new about dual distribution, per se, for it has been with us for a long time in such examples as the oil and paint industries. What is new, however, is the rate of growth of this practice and its introduction into new industries with novel forms. Moreover, the practice is sparking marketing innovations by retailers as a means of responding to the competitive threat. These have included attempts at cooperative approaches to distribution and legislative pressures that might result in congressional restrictions on the practice of dual distribution. In addition, these practices have led to responses that include intensification of older marketing techniques which may result in further innovations in distribution.

For example, Maytag Vice President of Marketing Claire G. Ely flatly condemns dual distribution by declaring that,

I'm enough of a businessman to know that my future is wrapped up in the sale of my products through normal distributive channels—by sales through dealers to the ultimate consumer. I know I can't serve two causes at the same time. I can't forever work both sides of the street.

***Opportunities for merchandising innovation.***   Perhaps the most dramatic innovation in merchandising since the supermarket has been the emergence of the discount house. This technique has received some jolts from the shake-out of the early successes in discount operation, but it remains today a fixture and a distinct challenge to the traditional department store. Moreover, the discount merchandising technique has produced pressure for innovation among department stores. Richard Bond, president of John Wanamaker, recently pinpointed the reason why discount stores remain competition to them. He suggests that department stores follow the discounters who have adopted a more flexible management concept, catering more and more to customer wishes.

New techniques of inventory control, data processing, and simple, old-fashioned good service to the customer, are providing the basis for future dramatic innovations in merchandising that may become even more important than the supermarket or discount approach. A typical example of merchandise innovation is the rise of the "convenience" store in recent years. Its attraction is based upon the fact that the profit rate prospects are up to five times that of the typical supermarket.

***Opportunities in international marketing.***   Innovations in domestic marketing techniques certainly abound. However, they may someday be dwarfed by the possibilities that are ahead in terms of world markets.

In spite of current pressures that tend to restrict investment abroad, American companies have shown such dramatic investment returns from foreign markets that the desire is very strong for developing innovations in marketing and distribution that will exploit foreign profit opportunities. About the only region where investment interest seems to be lagging is in South America.

## Opportunities for Innovation in Manager's Performance

It used to be considered taboo to measure the performance of managers, even though such judgments were made of all other employees. This is no longer the case, and instead, there is a growing awareness that in the manager's job there lies a potentially valuable area for improvement through innovation. This trend has been a consequence of the great emphasis, in recent years, on raising the productivity of office employees.

The effort in improving managerial performance stresses developing innovations in setting performance standards and in techniques of appraising the manager's performance. This activity has been fostered by the greater demands for outstanding managers—those that are creative and innovative rather than tied to the status quo. What is of interest to note is that although the criteria for top management performance were always high, the burden on middle and even lower managers has been sharply increased. Indeed, the picture that is emerging of the middle and lower manager is in sharp contrast to the legendary "organization" man. This new type of manager is best described as the "dis-organization" man. In spirit he resembles the old-style entrepreneur. In method he tends to be unorthodox. In outlook, he has little patience with tradition and no ready acceptance of the order of things. "He is the man," says Paul H. Kiernan, managing director of the recruiting firm Kiernan & Co., "with vision and enough guts to change things." **(14)**

In a recent series of articles on the young executive, *Fortune* characterizes this "new breed" that is raising the level of manager performance in the following way, describing how the young executives react to situations:

> We have seen the young executive dealing with the delicate network of business situations; the renewal of obsolete facilities, the making of a president, the sale of an ebbing company, the need to adjust to the frenetically accelerated change of the space age. But in none of these situations was the man cast in the corporate mold. **(15)**

Within this setting of increasing demands upon the manager, let us examine some strides made in techniques for improving executive performance. These will merely serve to *hint* at the future possibility that exists in the area of improving manager performance.

**Setting performance standards.**  In order to achieve an improvement in the manager's performance it is vital to develop standards against which his performance will be judged. One of the keenest minds in the area of management development (with an emphasis upon *improvement*) is Virgil K. Rowland of the Detroit

Edison Company. He has been the source of many innovations for improving manager performance and has provided the spark for the work of others. He states, in convincing terms, how performance standards are "to help the management person improve his performance on his present job."

Designing performance standards has come under close scrutiny in recent years and well-organized procedures are being prepared and undergoing continual revision. In developing a standard program for manager performance there are three guidelines that have proved very helpful in assuring sound standards. These are:

1. To direct attention primarily to results on the job rather than to sensitive, hard-to-change personality factors.
2. To work out clearer and more specific check-points or standards for on-the-job results for each executive.
3. To provide for participation of the subordinate in setting the check-points, so that the standards will be as realistic as possible. **(16)**

There is growing significance and interest in improving managerial performing of many innovations in a field that is gradually taking shape as the field of *work control*. These innovations include even the use of computers in designing and applying standards, as in the following description: "Right now, computers probably handle most of the clerical chores of matching job performance with job expectations."

**Performance appraisal.**   Just as there have been important innovations applied to established performance standards, there is a great deal of effort on the other hand in improving the manager's performance. The opportunities for innovations are considerable, and companies are supporting a search for better appraisal methods, as revealed in a recent Booz-Allen study of managerial appraisal plans. They found that "An accelerated interest in better ways to evaluate executives is rising among managements of leading companies." **(17)**

In terms of the total effort towards improving managerial performance, Rowland provides valuable guidelines as to which innovations should be taken in extending the boundaries of manager performance. As he describes them:

First, the effort should be directed primarily toward increasing skill in the direction of others. This does not mean that the development work should be confined to "human relations." The manager may need more technical knowledge to make the best possible decisions about what his subordinates may be doing and how they should be doing it. He may need counsel on and practice in coordinating, planning his work, and organizing his department. "Human relations," in the sense of tactful handling of subordinates, is only a part of the management of people, though it is of course important.

Second, the primary responsibility for the development of any manager rests on his immediate superior. The latter can get help from the staff departments, others on his own level and above him, but he himself must be the prime mover in the development process.

Third, the superior's own boss must inspect what he is doing in this and evaluate the results. **(18)**

### Opportunities for Innovation in Personal Relations

The nature of innovation as well as its impact, the problems it induces, and opportunities it affords have all been explored in the previous pages. All of these considerations have had, and will continue to have, a startling effect upon people in an era of accelerated change. Vast shifts have taken place in the composition of employee groups, with expansion of jobs among managerial, professional, and technical ranks and a decline in routine and production tasks. These changes have resulted largely from the implementation of technological and administrative innovation in business. There has also been a shift in the size and makeup of unions vis-à-vis companies.

With the pace of innovation continuing to rise, it is inevitable that there will be further changes in the role of all persons affected by these innovations. Let's examine just a few aspects of the impact of innovation on people, so that we can reveal a need for innovating in the techniques of personal relations.

*Manpower planning.* Some companies have developed new approaches to the analysis and planning of future employment needs. However, most companies have failed to recognize the tremendous impact that a further acceleration in the rate of change will have on their personal needs. Research at Princeton University has revealed that companies "are baffled by the question of what to do about manpower development and confused about how to go about it in this century of rapid and unprecedented change." **(19)**

*Recruiting and selecting.*    New demands for higher levels of training and education of personnel will mean demands for new approaches in recruiting and hiring of personnel. Moreover, as salary structures are strained, adjustments and reevaluation of contribution to the company of managerial and professional personnel will demand new approaches.

*Union relations.*    The decline of union membership in industry, coupled with the rise of new industries and new working groups, will mean further developments in dealings with unions in a period of accelerated change. The approaches used in a static economy are not appropriate today. Effects of innovation, conflicts that damage the public interest and safety, programs for achieving adjustment to innovations, all will demand innovations in principles and techniques of union-management relations.

*Employee motivation.*    Vast insight has developed in our understanding of human motivation since the Hawthorne Studies. We are more aware of the nature of motivation, morale attitudes, and their interrelationship than ever before. The results of this knowledge have been applied to such innovations as team management and job enlargement. These developments are recent, but already they are producing such intense and enthusiastic reactions that we may be on the threshold of many dramatic innovations in techniques of motivating people.

*Innovations through personnel research and experimentation.* The disciplines of organizational behavior and "scientific management" are joining forces in search of ways of managing workers. It is interesting to note that companies are turning more to personnel research experiment, and then to the actual application of research as a means of developing innovations in personal relations.

# CHAPTER 6

# CREATIVITY—THE KEY
# TO INNOVATING

Having just explored the vast gamut of innovation opportunities that exist it is necessary to reflect that enthusiasm for these opportunities is not enough. We can easily flounder if the search for them is misdirected or uncertain. It is necessary to develop a deliberate approach to this selection—to develop an awareness that in the creative capacity of man lies the seed of future innovation. Drucker has brilliantly cast the spirit in which the innovation search should go on and also indicates the general method needed to develop innovations:

Innovation, as we now use the term, is based on the systematic, organized leap into the unknown. Its aim is to give us new power for action through a new capacity to see, a new vision. Its tools are scientific, but its process is of the imagination, its method the organization of ignorance rather than that of known facts. **(1)**

It is clear, then, that the starting point of the innovation process is to tap the full power of man's innovativeness; that is, to develop the creative aspects of the man—the use of imagination.

By far the greatest potential source of innovation lies in exploiting the creative talents with which each person is endowed. In addition to university creative education courses that are available, hundreds of companies have embarked upon employee training in creativity. The obligation of universities to extend this area of education is clear-cut according to Harvard's President Pusey, who said that universities and colleges should "nurture that all-important creative spark which is the difference between the first and the third rate." (2)

At General Electric, which has the oldest program of creative education, a two-year course is provided for incoming engineers. In addition, experienced scientific staff members are given a 16-session course. The results of this effort are truly amazing, as revealed by the fact that graduates of this course obtained about three times the number of patents as did engineers who did not go through the training. A great many companies, including General Motors, International Business Machines, United States Steel and Minnesota Mining and Manufacturing, have been providing employee education in creativity for years.

Of particular importance to realistic development is that the benefits are not merely for hand-picked superior candidates or for special classes of employees. Rather, *any* individual can increase the number of his creative ideas as a result of this training. The person thus trained in the creative process has a greater chance of developing worthwhile innovations than a person without such specialized training.

Indeed, intensive research by Dr. Arnold Meadon and Dr. Sidney J. Paines at the University of Buffalo has revealed that the creative capacity of individuals can be almost doubled as a result of a course in creative problem solving. What's more, the subjects tested could be classed as average. The fact that the average person can show improvement is strong support for extending training to the majority of a company's employees.

### A Preview of the Creative Person

More and more emphasis is being placed upon attracting and holding creative individuals as the best means of devising innovations that will assure continued success for an enterprise. There is a trend towards recognition of the creative person on all levels, who has little patience with tradition and no ready acceptance of the order of things.

It is in this atmosphere that the following comment is appropriate:

In IBM we frequently refer to our need for "wild ducks." We are convinced that any business needs its wild ducks. In IBM we try not to tame them. (3)

This trend is expressed also in the criteria used to judge performance evaluation as a basis for selecting candidates for promotion. When asked to identify those skills which are the basis for promoting young executives, Edward J. Hekman, president of United Biscuit, emphasized imagination, creativity and resourcefulness. (4) The president of a large rubber company names these same qualities as the criteria for promotion and considers as of the greatest significance a "capacity for change."

The selection of persons with creative ability—those who are innovators, and those who are dissatisfied with the status quo—represents more than just a shift in personnel standards. It reflects the impact of hundreds of major upheavals among some of the largest companies, such as Westinghouse. Weiner's study of these upheavals reveals reorganizations that have swept the entire ranks of top and middle management. Although shakeups generally result from a sharp drop in earnings, it is of particular interest to note that the prime cause of these shakeups was a companywide inability to "ride with weather and take advantage of change." (5)

### The Essentials of Creative Decision Making

It is apparent from the growing emphasis on creativity that more companies are becoming aware that great rewards lie in unleashing the creative talents of their employees. A program that could result in greater and more valuable innovations should be carefully designed. Such a program would include the following categories:

1. Overcoming the forces inhibiting creative decision making.
2. Principles of creative decision making.
3. Techniques for generating creative ideas.
4. The steps in the creative decision making process.
5. Determining the innovation potential of an idea.
6. Gaining acceptance of ideas as a basis for decision.

**1. Overcoming the forces inhibiting creative decision making.**
Many of us look upon the creative person, whether he be in the arts, sciences, or the world of business, as blessed with unique and rare capabilities. In many cases, of course, this is undoubtedly true. However, by far the greater number of people who apply their creative talents do so largely because they have been able to remove the restrictions that they and society have imposed upon their creative imaginations. Many people in our society are reluctant to use their initiative; they feel silly in giving their imaginations free rein and are quite hesitant to express their originality.

In the fifties we believed that the way to success was in avoiding any disruption in the smooth sailing of the company ship, rather than in contributing to its more determined propulsion through competitive seas. This attitude is often expressed as "work well with the group," "don't rock the boat," and an adoption of the "yes man" pose. Such attitudes are in direct conflict with individual creativity.

Just as conformity has contributed to the inhibition of creativity, so has fear. The fears that are the greatest barriers to creativity include: the fear of having a new idea challenged by others; the fear of being "different"; the fear of losing "peace of mind"; the fear of loss of status and the approval of the group as a result of challenging what is orthodox.

A special kind of courage is required to overcome these fears. It grows out of the fact that the inevitable end product of creating an idea is its implementation. This stage often demands a personal "hardening process" that is necessary to withstand criticism, delay, and even outright attempts of sabotage.

Another barrier to creativity is the educational process that most of us have experienced. For the most part our educational system stresses the development of the absorptive mind rather than the imaginative one. From the primary grades to college the emphasis is overwhelmingly upon the intake and retention of data, or just simple cramming. This is a sterile concept when we realize that the last decade has produced more new information than in all of mankind's history. Moreover, the technological advances have provided our society ample sources for storing and making available this vast amount of knowledge. The digesting of facts for their own sake is now completely obsolete. It is distressing to note that for the most part higher education does *not* increase the individual's creative abilities.

Personal habits, another barrier to creativity, are by their very nature designed to avoid a search for new ideas in reaching a particular goal. If we recognize that attitudes and habits become relatively fixed ways of responding to situations in our environment, they can be valuable in helping us to cope with situations that have repeatedly appeared. When we have available a satisfactory solution to a problem that has occurred and has been solved before, habits prove a decided advantage. But when habits tend to provide old solutions which are not suitable to new conditions, they stultify the generating of ideas that might find a proper solution. If we rely upon habit for the "pat" solution, we fail to use our creative capacities.

By far the greatest and most common barrier to creativity is the tendency of others to judge, too quickly, a new idea—to react with a negative comment. Perhaps it is competitiveness or a feeling of inadequacy that brings forth the comment: "Oh, that won't work!" Unless an atmosphere is created in which no idea is rejected as being unworthy, the flow of ideas may be halted and be prevented from developing.

Our minds operate in two basic ways. One facet is the judicial mind, which analyzes, evaluates, and determines values. The other facet is the creative mind, which generates ideas through the use of imagination. It is essential that both these processes be used in solving a problem. However, they cannot be used at the same time. The creative mind is used first in searching for ideas. The imagination must work freely, without judging as to whether the ideas are good or bad. Once the ideas are produced, the judicial mind accepts the good ideas and sets aside the unworthy ones.

Unless the burdens to creative thinking are removed, the principles and techniques of developing ideas cannot be employed with any degree of success.

**2. Principles of creative decision making.**    There is growing recognition that valuable alternatives for reaching a goal—an essential prerequisite of effective decision making—can be developed by applying the principles of creative thinking. Four of these principles are:

*a*) EXTENDED EFFORT.    This is a willingness to apply intense concentration to develop additional ideas when one thinks he is drained creatively.

The distinction the creative decision maker holds is that the information he uses for making his decision is to be found in his imagination rather than in some body of statistical data. To extract this information demands a mental effort that is demanding in terms of quality and duration. Extended effort is needed for two reasons. In the first place, only by applying extra concentration is it possible to shut out the distractions that abound internally and externally. Once the flow of ideas is begun, mental effort is necessary to provide a continued flow that will produce large volumes of ideas. Secondly, some of the best ideas are produced toward the end of a period of concentration. Popular notions consider the mind as tired after a period of creativity, but actually the prior ideas form the "spark" for later ideas, thus providing a base upon which to build.

*b*) SUSPENDED JUDGMENT.    Any individual can generate a continued stream of ideas, provided judgment is suspended until a large number of ideas has been added to the decision-making process.

As previously stated, the greatest deterrent to creative ideas is the too early application of judgment. Positive as well as negative judgment can stop ideation. It is easy to see that negative comments are an alarming challenge to thinking creatively. However, reacting positively will also halt or slow thinking, because once we've come up with a "good idea" there seems little incentive to search for better ones.

*c*) VOLUME OF IDEAS.    The greatest number of ideas is to be sought as a basis for achieving the greatest quality of ideas.

In the matter of ideas, as well as in other things, quantity breeds quality. For example: a contest to name a public structure will produce a greater variety of ideas. Encouraging a great volume of ideas for developing new products, new services or brand names is vital for better results. A large list of ideas can form the springboard for thinking: "What further possibilities are there?"

*d*) INCUBATION.    Ideas have a way of blossoming during a period when one's mind is apparently at rest. This usually results in a new and better idea after one has "slept on it."

Some people, including the writer, develop many of their best ideas in those few minutes before falling asleep or at the time of awakening the next morning. These may be "new" ideas or, more often, elaborations of ideas generated the previous day. To exploit this principle, a list of ideas prepared the day before can be examined to start the generating of additional ideas. After a day's incubation period, creative thinking proceeds with renewed vigor.

**3. Techniques for generating creative ideas.** Despite the fact that creativity development is an art, a body of techniques has evolved for producing ideas that are certain to spur the imagination. The four techniques that will be examined here are: the laws of association, sector analysis, freewheeling, and creative questioning.

LAWS OF ASSOCIATION TECHNIQUES. From the time of the ancient Greeks we have known three laws of association: contiguity, similarity, and contrast.

*a*) *Contiguity* refers to closeness or nearness, as when an item of children's clothing in a store window in a strange city reminds one of a son who wears clothing of a similar nature. In this way someone with a fluid imagination may bring forth ideas suggesetd by objects or phrases.

*b*) *Similarity* is by far the most useful law of association in producing valuable ideas. Inevitably we turn to expressions of similarity when we describe some thing or event. Another fruitful use of association is to use a word list to generate ideas based upon similarity.

*c*) *Contrast* can many times achieve amazing ideas by association. Contrasting or opposite associations will often result in avenues of thought that we might not ordinarily explore.

Association produces greater rewards for persons whose imaginative *skill* has been heightened by training. Many have the impression that ideas developed by association are merely chance events. Its real value occurs when association is used in a deliberate fashion to induce the continued outpouring of ideas. A practical use is in developing ideas for sales promotion, starting with the product, its uses and characteristics in terms of contiguity, similarity, and contrast.

SECTOR ANALYSIS. Most problems cover so wide an area that it is often difficult to direct the development of ideas into practical channels. We can compare the total problem to an open umbrella which covers a large surface divided into many sectors by the ribs. Were we to separate a problem into sectors, like the umbrella, we might then concentrate idea finding into a smaller area. These ideas might even provide such a wealth of alternatives that the solution to the subproblem would lead directly to a solution of the wider problem.

FREEWHEELING TECHNIQUE. This technique involves a group effort in idea finding designed to bring forth a large volume of alternative proposals for a solution. Under prescribed conditions this technique has immense value. Freewheeling, or brainstorming, became popular as the result of success in advertising. However, many companies that tried and later discarded this technique approached it as a panacea and failed to abide by its ground rules. The conditions required for successful freewheeling are:

*a*) Proper facilities—the participants should be grouped around a large conference table so that they can confront each other. The room should be completely isolated from distractions of any kind. In addition, there should be provision for recording the ideas produced.

*b*) Judgment must be withheld—any comment of criticism or praise must be avoided during the conference session. No sneering or sarcasm should be permitted.

*c*) Release inhibitions—the participants should be made aware that "nutty" or "way out" ideas are welcome. These so-called impractical ideas can evoke in others immensely valuable and novel ideas.

*d*) Volume to be sought—it should be made clear that there is no "best" idea that is being sought. It follows that a search for a volume of ideas is necessary to continually find *better* ideas.

*e*) Problem limitation—it is important to establish the boundary for ideas by identifying a single goal or problem that will be the subject for freewheeling.

The first step in freewheeling is to be certain that a creative climate has been prepared to prevent inhibitions of the participants. Immediately in advance of the meeting the conference leader should send a memorandum to each of the expected participants, clearly describing the problem to be brainstormed and its background. There might also be a suggestion on the kind of ideas that might be sought and the possibility of having each participant note a few ideas in advance of the meeting.

At the creative conference, ideas are brought forth in keeping with requirements of successful freewheeling. Immediately after the conference the secretary should summarize the ideas and incorporate them in a note to each participant from the leader, accompanied by a request that any additional ideas that occur should be presented the following morning. Under the principle of extended effort, combined with incubation, the participants might be encouraged to suggest how the group ideas could be combined to form new ideas.

To avoid disappointing results, careful preparation is in order, and too much should not be expected. Freewheeling only supplements other means of developing ideas, and the best results are achieved where the members of the group have received training in creativity development.

CREATIVE QUESTION TECHNIQUE.   The question is an excellent spur to the thinking process. For this reason the use of checklists of questions is widespread. A classic example is the one prepared for use by the Army in World War II that produced ideas that resulted in saving $10 million. The six questions are:

*a*) Why is it necessary? (Maybe it can be eliminated.)
*b*) Where should we do this? (Can we do it somewhere else?)
*c*) When should it be done? (Maybe it can wait.)
*d*) Who should do it? (Pick the right person.)
*e*) What should be done?
*f*) How should it be done?

For his creative engineering classes at M.I.T., Professor John Arnold has developed nine idea-spurring questions. They are: Can we (1) Put to other uses? (2) Adapt? (3) Modify? (4) Magnify? (5) Minify? (6) Substitute? (7) Rearrange? (8) Revise? and (9) Combine?

As an alternative or in addition to the use of checklists it is possible to develop one's own idea-spurring or creative questions. Creative questions are the kind that demand a multiplicity of ideas. In contrast, a fact-finding question can be answered by a single reply, and a judicial question requires an answer based on judgment or comparison, rather than new ideas. A creative question usually begins with, "In what ways . . . ?"

Derek Castle, a leader in creativity development, describes a creative question as:

One with a multiplicity of answers with varying degrees of acceptability, ranging from total acceptability to total unacceptability. No idea is ever rejected completely because once an idea is created it exists for all times.

To improve a familiar product like a toothbrush, the creative question designed to spur ideas is: "In what ways would you improve the toothbrush?" An adequate reply requires multiple answers.

**4. The steps in the creative decision-making process.** In the decision-making process, alternative proposals are analyzed and from this one course of action is selected as the decision. Often, creative thinking is ignored as a means of developing alternate proposals. It is this addition of creative thinking which distinguishes creative decision making from ordinary and often ineffective decision making. To distinguish creative decision making, there follows a description of its four basic steps:

*a*) GOAL OR PROBLEM SELECTION.   This involves the deliberate process of first finding a problem and then rephrasing, dissecting, and amplifying it to sharpen the problem areas for which ideas may be developed.

*b*) GENERATING IDEAS.   The principles and techniques of creative thinking are directed towards the problem areas identified. The greatest variety and number of ideas are sought.

*c*) USING CREATIVITY TO SELECT EVALUATION CRITERIA. For the ideas generated in the above step to have any meaning, they must be judged in terms of how practical they are. Valid criteria for making this evaluation can best be determined by intense use of one's imagination to select a whole range of criteria for the application of judicial thinking. These criteria can then be intensely applied to the whole range of alternate ideas.

*d*) DECIDING THE SELECTION OF IDEAS AS ALTERNATIVE SOLUTIONS TO A PROBLEM.   The processes of selecting the appropriate alternatives for problem solving involves applying the criteria of selection to each idea developed in stage (*b*) above. During this step the ideas are tested critically for their practicality. All "stargazing" ideas are thus set aside. Only in this way can decisions be made, by proving their applicability to the real world. Professor John Arnold firmly supports this process of discriminating among ideas by stating:

Few ideas are in themselves practical. It is for want of active imagination in their application rather than in their means of acquisition that they fail of success. The creative process does not end with an idea—it only starts with it.

**5. *Determining the innovation potential of an idea.*** If the starting phase of creativity is an idea, then the end of the creative process is the evaluation of its potential for becoming an innovation. Indeed, the evaluation or judicial phase is equal in importance to generating the idea in the first place. Unfortunately, the evaluation step is often performed in a cursory manner. This results either in implementing impractical ideas or in discarding potentially valuable ones. The judicial process should be no less intense than the original search for new ideas.

A particularly apt method that could be used for evaluating ideas includes the following:

I. Collect Ideas. As the first step in the judicial process, it is desirable to line up the alternate ideas to highlight those that are overlapping or duplicated. Visual inspection would indicate those that should be rephrased for greater clarity or which could be arranged into separate categories. What results from this early screening still remains but a tentative list of ideas that are now suitable for evaluation as potential problem solutions.

II. Selection of Evaluation Criteria. This stage demands creative thinking in developing ideas that are themselves potential criteria for determining the feasibility of each of the ideas previously generated and arrayed. The evaluative criteria can be statements of individual qualities that are desirable, or they may be phrased in the form of questions (singly or in groups) that reveal the degree of desirability of the idea. At this point judgment is suspended, to allow complete freedom to develop multiple criteria. One example of a criterion is a group of questions the author has found useful in judging the validity of an improvement. It includes the questions:

Is it timely?

What is its probable cost?

Is it feasible?

Does it improve methods?

Does it reduce cost?

III. SELECTING AN EVALUATIVE TECHNIQUE. It is presumed that the particular methods used in judging the worthiness of innovative ideas are infinite in number. Some of the better ones that are available range from a simple ranking method to an elaborate one devised by Derek Castle which even evaluates the potential ease of implementation.

Following are descriptions of a few of these evaluative techniques:

*a*) *Ranking.* In this method, the evaluation criteria are applied consecutively to each of the ideas to be judged. Using a scale with the highest value at the top, the ideas are arranged in declining order of their desirability. For example, where a single criterion, such as the practicability of an idea, is used, each idea would be rated on this basis. The ranking of ideas may be done by one individual or by a group consensus. In any case it will clearly indicate which ideas offer the best potential for improvement.

*b*) *The weighted choice.* This procedure is an evaluation technique that is useful when group judgment is available. It involves the determination of the high-quality ideas by having each member of the group vote on whether the idea satisfies a wide range of criteria. Each person may vote for or abstain from voting for each of the ideas being judged. The votes are tallied and those ideas with the highest number of "aye" votes are considered most likely to be successful innovations. A feature of this technique is that the criteria selected can vary in vote value based upon their importance as selection criteria. Thus the final score can be weighted more heavily in favor of those criteria that are likely to have a greater impact upon the success of an innovation.

*c*) *The Castle evaluation.* This method was developed by Derek Castle and is, by far, the most intensive judicial technique available. This evaluation procedure employs a wide range of criteria, including an assessment of the influence of persons in the company in terms of the ultimate acceptance of the innovation. This approach assesses the particular idea; but, in addition, it goes beyond this point to assess alternate plans of action to implement the idea. The first step employed is the examination of objects, functional areas in the company, and company personnel that may be affected in some way by the proposed innovation. If the effects are judged to be negative, the idea may be rejected at this point. However, if this test is passed, the idea is further analyzed in terms of its various stages of applicability, such as its usability now, whether it should be modified, or whether the idea should be set aside for the time being.

The third stage of the Castle evaluation process involves the use of judgment in setting up the plan of action. At this time the innovation is reviewed in terms of the following considerations:

Who might do this?

When might it be done?

Where might it be done?

How might it be done?

It is of particular interest to note that though we are in the process of evaluating an idea, further ideas must be created that take the form of critical questions to test the practicability of the innovation. The above group of questions is just one example of ideas that become criteria in evaluating other ideas.

In the fourth stage of this judicial procedure, the advantages offered by each of the alternate ideas are emphasized. In addition, these ideas are expressed in terms of a plan of action to implement an innovation. The innovation may be judged in terms of such additional criteria as:

The best idea for action.

The best person to accomplish this.

The best time to do it.

The best place to do it.

The best means of action.

Finally, the fifth and last stage of the Castle evaluation anticipates the challenge the innovator faces in gaining acceptance of his ideas. To overcome this challenge, an inventory should be prepared that would identify the possible objections that are likely to be raised by others. To prepare this inventory is, incidentally, a creative process in itself, even though it occurs during the mental activity of passing judgment. Inevitably, creative thinking is required to generate ideas that offer possibilities of overcoming the objections to a particular innovation.

The ideas that have passed the "acid test" of the Castle evaluation are potential candidates for innovation.

*d) Regenerate ideas.* Evaluation of all the proposed ideas and selection of the best ones provide the basis for generating additional ideas. It is often said that some of the best ideas are combinations, rearrangements, or adaptations of other ideas. It is therefore essential to repeat the process of a search for ideas, except that this time the "culled" list of ideas will form the springboard for further creative thinking. The basis for this step is that good ideas can spark *additional* ideas. No less an authority on creativity than Thomas A. Edison has stated:

Make it a habit to keep on the lookout for novel and interesting ideas that others have used successfully. Your idea needs to be original only in its adaptation to the problem you are working on.

The technique of building upon ideas to develop further ideas can be improved even more by designing a group of questions that may extend the boundaries of the imagination into multiple directions. Some of these questions might include:

*What adaptations can be made in . . . ?* The problem at hand may concern a search for new or improved product ideas, or it may be the need for a slogan or a change in service. Indeed, anything that may be varied slightly can form the basis for additional ideas.

*In what ways can a modification or substitution be devised?* In a "copy" of the idea that would be cheaper, better, or in some way preferable to an improvement of the idea originally proposed?

*In what ways can we reduce, increase, divide, subtract, etc.?* This question centers about the characteristic of size as being one of the most productive keys to generating ideas. In addition to considering each variation as a potential source of additional ideas, the extremes of maximizing or minimizing may be productive also. For example, in packaging, the effect of a "jumbo" or of a miniature size may have a dramatic impact upon sales.

*How else can this be arranged or continued?* Answers to such a question may lead to alternate means of laying out facilities or to ideas for changing the sequence of any series of tasks. The questions may also provoke ideas for a tool or machine that is designed for several purposes rather than a single use.

*e) Final selection of ideas.* This stage would once more include the application of evaluative or judicial thinking and techniques that would select the most worthy ideas. One outcome of this final evaluation is that a proposed innovation is subject to a "pilot" test of the feasibility of an idea in advance of implementing it on a larger scale. The testing process is most appropriate in such areas as the design of a new product, where consumer acceptance would be studied. The type and extent of the pilot test is in itself an important area for applying creative thinking.

**6. Gaining acceptance of ideas as a basic creative decision.** The energy devoted to generating ideas has too often been completely wasted because the process of creative decision making is stopped one notch too soon. Quite simply, generating an idea, evaluating it, and preparing it in the form of a decision to innovate are *not enough* to assure its implementation. What *is* necessary is to concentrate additional energy in gaining acceptance of the innovation as the last and vital step in the cycle of creative decision making.

An imaginative (creative) approach in proposing the innovation for acceptance by others should include some of the following ingredients:

The problem of gaining acceptance should be so clarified as to highlight the substance of the innovation, the persons who should become convinced of its value, and the actions these persons would be expected to take on behalf of the idea.

In addition, a list should then be prepared that would crystallize the advantages—and to what departments, persons, company, etc. Another list should be prepared revealing the ways in which these advantages can be made to appear "obvious" to the persons concerned. For example, the devices used might include visual displays of tables, charts, pictures, three-dimensional models, or samples. It might include as well an array of arguments on the advantages and possibly the results of some tests on a pilot level, or the successes of similar kinds of innovation. Before making a presentation, it is essential to prepare a written proposal as well as an outline to be used in guiding an oral proposal.

In any case, a determined effort at this stage of the creative process should lead either to a total acceptance of the idea or some kind of a trial period for the innovation. What is to be avoided is an outright rejection of the idea.

## Critique of Creative Thinking

The techniques described have proven themselves tremendously successful in generating ideas that were converted into profitable innovations. However, these principles, if applied in a faulty manner, can prove useless, even harmful. In addition, the achievements of creative thinking may blind some enthusiasts to the realization that there are limitations to its use.

One of the strongest critics of creative thinking is Levitt, who cries out that:

Creativity is not the miraculous road to business growth and affluence that is so abundantly claimed these days. . . . The trouble with much of the advice business is getting today about the need to be more vigorously creative is, essentially, that its advocates have generally failed to distinguish between the relatively easy process of being creative in the abstract and the infinitely more difficult process of being innovationist in the concrete. **(6)**

Levitt goes on to explain that in too many organizations, "idea men" undertake the task of generating ideas, but these people are unwilling, or unable, to translate these ideas into workable and profitable innovations. Indeed, it is true that the skills of creativity are quite distinct from the judicial mental process or evaluation. Moreover, it is also true that many people find it immensely difficult to guide the implementation of an innovation.

It is not that one ingredient is more necessary to succeed in innovation than others. What *is* important is that *all* of these skills be applied. The four ingredients a manager must have to be innovative are: creative ability; skill in evaluating ideas generated by creative thinking; the ability to concretize the proposal for innovation (enumerating the pros and cons); and, most critical, the ability to prepare a program for implementing the innovation that overcomes the obstacles to the change.

Levitt's appeal to managers on how to handle creativity is capped by the advice:

For those critics of and advisors to U.S. industry who repeatedly call for more creativity in business, it is well first to try to understand the profound distinction between creativity and innovation, and then perhaps to spend a little more time calling on creative individuals to take added responsibility for implementation.

To the extent that Levitt has shown that the ideas generated must be translated into purposeful profitable change—or innovation—he has certainly done a service to the business community.

### Sources of Innovative Ideas

I strongly believe in an ongoing program for stimulating creativity as the prime vehicle for developing a continuous flow of innovative ideas. Indeed, it is the largest single factor in developing an exciting "spirit of innovation" in an organization. Let us now move somewhat afield from examining the *process* of creativity and review some of the potential sources from which the innovative ideas may spring.

*Internal sources of ideas.*   One general category that may prove a valuable source of ideas is from within the company itself. In the search for internal sources, it is desirable to recognize that no single source is to be stressed to the exclusion of others. Certainly a prime source for innovative ideas remains the formally constituted research department, even though generally in it is to be found an ebb and tide of cycles of ideas. Formal research is most productive when it includes not only work on technological innovations but on administrative ones as well, and when the research is oriented towards company goals.

*Managers,* on all levels, are a prime source of ideas for innovation, since they are particularly sensitive to company needs and goals. Indeed, the McKinsey study has shown that managers are the most important single source of innovative ideas, principally for the above reason.

The *sales force* can be a valuable source of ideas, since they are in a position to become acutely aware of customers' needs and desires.

The *service* personnel who are involved in correcting difficulties with the company's product or service are in a particularly favorable position to develop ways of increasing customer satisfaction via innovative ideas.

In addition to the above groups, any person who has achieved, in some fashion, an identity with the company's interest and an awareness of the customers' needs is a potential source for ideas.

The *systems or industrial* engineering persons are completely involved in the search for ways of improving management methods. They are a prime source of administrative innovations.

In summation, it should be understood that the machine operator or clerk—yes, even the janitor—represent the source of potential ideas for innovation. The way to tap this potential is to provide them with the tools that will make it easy for them to express these ideas.

**External sources of ideas.**   In general it is considered that external sources provide less opportunity for ideas than internal sources. Nonetheless, there is no way of telling when a most valuable idea may be drawn from an outside source or, just as important, when a "spark" drawn from the outside may provoke some fruitful ideas from internal sources.

*Customers* are the major source of innovative ideas. For that reason it is important to develop warm relationships with customers whenever possible. The value lies in the fact that they provide a critique of company products or service. It is important, therefore, to encourage their free flow of suggestions to be used as innovative ideas.

*Trade associations* and their publications are very important sources of ideas. Being aware of industry trends in general and specific innovations by competitors can often provide the basis for developing a company's own innovations.

*Unsolicited ideas* by persons who have known of the company's activities can prove a helpful source of ideas. These may be actual or potential customers or they may be inventors seeking commercial application of their work. These ideas will usually flow to the companies that have created the strongest innovative "image" with the public, either through advertising or other means. General Electric's "progress is our most important product"; Du Pont's "better things for better living, through chemistry"; and U.S. Steel's and Sylvania's use of the word "innovation" in their promotions have helped to implant this image with the public at large.

*Financial institutions,* such as banks and insurance companies, often provide helpful ideas for profit opportunities because of their continual search for places to invest their resources.

*Vendors* can be another helpful source of ideas, particularly if the company has encouraged long-term associations under such approaches as reciprocal purchasing. Moreover, many vendors provide a counseling service that is designed to lead to profitable innovations.

*Government* sources provide a wide and voluminous source of ideas, both in terms of published materials such as the *Official Gazette* of the patent office, the patent office itself, and the *Products List Circular* of the Small Business Administration, as well as advice from various government agencies.

### Some Problems in Generating Ideas

Just as we have examined some limitations in the use of creative thinking for innovating, there are other problems that may arise in the midst of encouraging a greater flow of ideas.

**Creative destruction.**    One of the dangers that should be recognized stems largely from the very process of proliferating ideas. This is the danger of "creative destruction," which has the net effect of rendering a previously profitable innovation (product, service, process, and so forth) completely obsolete. This destructive cycle may be, at times, completely unavoidable. At other times it may even prove desirable, as a recognition that competitive forces may bring about the demise anyway, so why not "beat them to the punch?" Levitt's example of the threat facing the utility industry from sources that would replace electric power with the energy cell makes it clear that: "To survive, they themselves will have to plot the obsolescence of what now produces their livelihood." **(7)**

**The overemphasis on R&D.**    Another danger that may arise when encouraging creativity is to go "overboard" in using the R&D department as the source of innovative ideas. The evil it may create is success itself—success which may induce stagnation and complacency. As one authority has seen this danger:

Some individuals possess deep-seated motivation to be able to cope with good fortune, but all too often this is not the case. I have seen few "fat cats" who were truly creative. **(8)**

This is pointed out by Levitt as one of the dangers that is beginning to build up in the electronics industry. It is their growing emphasis upon technical development that tends to draw them away from a customer orientation in research and results in a sharp drop in innovative ideas that, by serving the customer, have good potential profit. Since their expansion has been totally devoid of marketing effort, they are building the seeds of ultimate decline through their indifference to consumer wants. **(9)**

CHAPTER 7

# EVALUATING THE PROFIT
# POTENTIAL OF AN INNOVATION

Leaning heavily upon creative thinking may well have produced a crop of innovative ideas. But whatever may have been the technique employed or the origin of the idea, it must immediately be exposed to a preliminary test of its potential profitability. Indeed, the first test of "profit-ability" of an idea often proves the most difficult task confronting the would-be innovator, because he finds it difficult to remove the bias of creation and to replace it with the objectivity of judgment.

It should be remembered that the task, at this point, is not merely to determine whether the idea has any potential profit merit; it also must be judged in terms of its relative profitability in comparison to other proposed innovative ideas that are available for consideration. Since it is profit value (relative worth) to the *firm* that is the governing factor, it is essential that any evaluation be tied together with company planning projections, first.

### Evaluation Based on Company Planning Objectives

The most significant relationship between planning and innovating is that the criterion for evaluating the profit potential of an idea should be drawn directly from the objectives of the company planning program. Indeed, even before this takes place, one has to be

106

certain that the philosophy or company approach stressing "management by objectives" is the guide for top management as well as the lowest management level. Actually, the heart of planning is the setting of sound objectives and then plotting steps to achieve them. But managers who are dedicated to planning as a way of life prefer the added intensity expressed by "management by objectives."

Stew Thompson points out that "This phase seems to emphasize management's determination to strike to create markets and to control the future of the business rather than to react on a piecemeal basis to oncoming events." As a matter of fact, this same apparent restlessness with the status quo is exactly the kind of attitude managers must have to be successful innovators, as well as successful planners. Thompson also clearly focuses on the use of objectives as providing the standard for evaluating innovations; or, as he puts it, "objectives enable the manager to evaluate the merits of unforeseen opportunities when they occur and to weigh alternative courses of action." **(1)**

As Merrill has summarized in his review of current best planning practice, the criteria against which innovation will be judged are the objectives that are crystallized by two key steps in the planning process that answer the questions, Where do we want to go? and, What may *get* us there? From the reply to these questions evolve the general strategic plans of the company, which are then translated into objectives and plans in terms of organization units: divisions, products, and/or functions. **(2)**

**Assessing company circumstances.**   In relating profit evaluation of innovations to basic company planning, one important criterion will result from an analysis of company circumstances and capabilities. The final stage of the operating plan (to become the *actual* guide for installing the innovation) starts with the question, How much will be required of company resources? At this point the fiscal aspects of carrying out the plan are probed: how much financing would be required for the necessary people and facilities, and how much should be assigned to the various segments; what kind of financing should be adopted; and where the money is to come from.

It is essential to recognize that an innovation has profit potential to a company only if *that* company has the resources and capacity to *implement* it. From a talk given by Dean Emeritus O'Brien of

UCLA, Bright discloses that an assessment of company circumstances should include: "cash position, competition, and know-how." (3) It's interesting to note that, just as innovations must be judged in terms of the company resources and capabilities, the very process of setting objectives must also be developed within the limitations of company capabilities.

In the matter of studying a firm's capabilities, the analysis should place a greater emphasis on nonphysical assets, such as the managerial and technical capabilities of its personnel. Moreover, this examination should extend beyond the boundaries of the company. Thompson has said,

> In appraising the capabilities of a firm, the focus is less and less likely to be solely on the industry in which the firm has traditionally operated. Broad industrial classifications will become less and less meaningful to managers as they seek unique opportunities to exploit the capabilities of their business. (4)

*Resources necessary.*    Present company resources should be assessed with great care. The implementation program should be tailored, in size and rate, to be consistent with the available company resources. This should reflect a realistic assessment in terms of management's objectives and in terms of the urgency for the innovation in question. This issue is presented strongly by Craig in his study of a conversion to electronic accounting: What are the objectives of top management? Are these objectives realistic in terms of resources available and time required to accomplish the task?

He further asks, What additional strain in terms of cost, work load, manpower, and executive manpower will this rate of conversion represent over and above the performance of normal functions of the organization?

*Cost analysis of the changeover.*    Even before the change actually occurs, it is essential to make some cost projections of the innovation in operation. These analyses should cover two things: first, the actual cost of making the changeover; and second, the operating costs of the innovation during the early period after implementation. It is essential to make projections of the changeover costs so that enough funds are available to support the implementation of the innovation. It is also necessary to make projections of the early operating phase to have some yardstick to measure against the *actual* operating costs.

*Determination of work load.*  It is essential to make accurate estimates of the work load that will be necessary during the change-over and in the period immediately thereafter. This will be necessary so as to provide an adequate number of people with the appropriate skills during the tension-filled period of transition. It is also wise to provide additional personnel or standby people available upon immediate request from other departments. And it is desirable to explore the possible need for multiple shift operations during the transition period and beyond.

*Planning for growth.*  Another significant objective that may evolve through planning is that involved with identifying an emphasis upon growth as a means of perpetuating the company. A caution that is appropriate here is that by "perpetuating" I do not mean merely continuing the status quo. Indeed, exploiting opportunities for growth (through innovation) may very well mean a vast change in the characteristics of the business, to wit:

Setting business objectives often involves *creating* new business opportunities as well as discovering them. It is the managers task to determine whether the capability of his business can and should be restructured to take advantage of new products, new markets, and new methods of operating.

To properly guide the direction in which innovations will proceed and to properly place company growth as a criterion to be used in evaluation innovative ideas, limits must be established for company growth. Some managers believe that setting *any* limits tends to restrict innovation altogether. Not so! For companies to seek growth with no restraints is to risk foundering by going off in too many directions searching for innovations, and thus to drain company resources.

The very process of setting objectives is, in itself, "a means by which the limits to company growth are narrowed so that order can be brought about. Within those limits may be a large number of potentially profitable opportunities for growth."

A final comment on the relationship of planning objectives to the process of innovating, and particularly to the evaluation of the profit potential of a proposed innovation. The objectives established and the innovation programs designed to carry them out are not to be approached as possibilities merely for consideration, but rather for the making of decisions that bring about *action*. Merrill brilliantly pinpoints this characteristic of the *intensity* of modern corporate planning as requiring a commitment from all managers and that it be *action*-oriented. He concludes that planning

. . . must deserve and attain the total involvement of the entire organization. The process of company planning is not the place for ivory-tower thinking. The plan that comes out of the process must be designed for action. Otherwise, it is bound to fail. **(5)**

## The Evaluation Process

We have acknowledged that to proceed with an evaluation of innovative ideas without having established planning objectives is senseless. Having explored planning objectives, let us now analyze some of the approaches used in judging the value of innovative ideas. It should be understood that the atmosphere surrounding the evaluation process should be one of a search for truth, no matter how harsh it might appear to be. That is, we must be alert to the two dangers of biased evaluation. This bias (as mentioned in the preceding chapter) may discard a potentially valuable idea, *or* it may lead a company to "stick with" an idea that is hopelessly unprofitable.

*Barriers to proper evaluation of innovations.* Let us examine the signs of potential barriers to honest evaluation that may lead to bias. One such barrier is created by the administrative-financial structure of many companies whose commitment to a budgetary expenditure is often considered a license to squander. In this fashion, a proposal for *developing* an innovation is often considered synonymous with approval to *implement* the innovation. The result is the continued pouring of funds down the drain, even though it is clear to all that the innovation is a failure.

Bright provides insight into another barrier to proper evaluation that grows out of being tied too closely with the status quo and therefore is unduly harsh in evaluating *any* new proposal. He notes the contributing factors to this condition as:

A successful commercial enterprise has little stimulus to change present practice. Its energies pour into filling its current needs.

Training, education and experience of a firm's personnel generally are rooted in present practice. It is unlikely that a firm will have technical skills or technical knowledge (or for that matter, managerial skills and knowledge) in other fields.

There is an emotional and social attachment around present practice which inhibits the unbiased exploration of new possibilities. **(6)**

***Evaluation techniques for judging profitability.*** There are almost as many approaches as there are companies trying to judge the potential profit of an innovation. In general, whatever is used, rarely is the process critical and disciplined enough to provide sound projections of potential profitability.

One of the most thorough appraisal techniques is that used by Monsanto Chemical Company, which projects potential profitability of product innovations on a device called a new product profile chart. **(7)** This analysis examines such factors as the financial research, marketing, and production aspects. Under each of these areas, criteria are established and weights assigned to the criterion governing each area that bears on the success of the innovation. The resulting profile provides a judgment of the value of the innovation, ranging from completely negative to completely positive. In this fashion, profit projections of an array of criteria can reveal whether an innovation leans heavily towards profit or towards loss.

This profile chart was validated as a useful tool by applying it to past innovations, some of which succeeded and some of which failed. Those innovations that succeeded consistently had positive scores and those that failed consistently had negative scores.

Another valuable tool, devised by Modern Packaging Machinery Corporation, is used to rate the potential of innovation in what is called the chance of commercial success analysis. This company uses nine factors in its evaluation, including: relation to present distribution channels; savings to customer (labor and material); effect on quality; availability to customer; cost of changes by customer; price; exclusiveness of the innovation; and place in market. Each of these factors is scored on the basis of very good (100) down through five levels to a bottom of very poor (0%), with the final score representing the degree of potential success for the innovation.

In general, some sort of rating scale or profile is used with the technique of determining potential profitability of an innovation. The analysis device should include all the factors that have a bearing on profitability as criteria for profit evaluation. It should make provision for weighting those factors in terms of which ones may have a greater impact upon profitability. The evaluation procedure should include a range or scale of values for each factor and criterion to be examined. A qualitative value is helpful for each level. Provision should be made for commenting on each criterion so that the evaluator clearly understands the basis on which an innovation is to be judged. The particular and unique characteristics and circumstances of the innovation should be clearly stated.

### Preparing the Proposal Resulting from Evaluation

After employing any one of a number of evaluative techniques to determine the potential profitability of an innovation, a decision is required in terms of whether the proposed idea is to be discarded, or whether it proceeds to the next step on the road to implementation. Having been discarded at this point doesn't mean that the idea is eliminated for all time, but that it will receive no further consideration for implementation at present. For those innovations that pass this test of potential profitability, the findings of the evaluation should be incorporated into a written proposal that presents the overview for implementing the innovation. This proposal should include: the proposed recommendation for change, clearly pinpointed; supporting data showing the summary justification for the innovation; a preliminary programming of the steps required for implementing the idea and some of the critical points in this process; and finally, an economic projection of the consequences of the implementation, including the costs to be incurred in the changeover stage. At Quaker Oats this last stage even includes a detailed estimate of the effect on company personnel, including costs of training, transferring, or other personnel impact resulting from the change.

*Planning the implementation.* The proposal should include a presentation of the schedule to be followed (estimate); the resources to be used; the personnel to be involved, and their tentative duties and responsibilities; and a step-by-step procedure for implementing the innovation. It should also include an identification of the problems that are likely to arise in the changeover, both technical and human. Moreover, the critical points in the program for innovation should be highlighted so as to receive particular manager attention.

***Economic projection of the innovation.***     This analysis starts with an estimate of the possible economic returns from the innovation, coupled with the estimate of expenditures necessary to put it into functioning form. It should also include a cost analysis of the actual operations, once the changeover has been achieved. Also identified should be projections of the payback period for investing in the change and an estimated rate of return on investment, as well as identification of the break-even point for the innovation in operation.

# CHAPTER 8

# IMPLEMENTING THE INNOVATION

Before examining some of the issues that arise in preparing to implement an innovation, let us consider the seven stages of innovation that might be best applicable to a business enterprise.

## The Phases of Innovation

Scientists have been hard at work to devise and distinguish the steps that must be traversed to develop and implement an innovation. One reservation is that the stages are necessarily distinct (there may be overlapping), but they do not necessarily follow in an exact sequence. Many of the original advances in the theory of innovation and the formulation of an orderly sequence for the process of innovation were achieved by Kurt Lewin. His findings suggested three stages of planned change or innovation. His description of this is as follows:

A change toward a higher level of performance is frequently short-lived; after a "shot in the arm," group life soon returns to the previous level. This indicates that it does not suffice to define the objectives of planned change in group performance as the reaching of a different level. Permanency for a desired time should be included in the objective. A successful change includes, therefore, three aspects: unfreezing (if necessary) the present level, moving to the new level, and freezing group life on the new level. **(1)**

This statement presents us with insight into the practical problem of successfully implementing innovation, in that it must result in lasting achievements. Here are the seven stages of innovation:

1. Identifying a need for innovation.
2. Creating the idea for innovation.
3. Developing a relationship for innovation.
4. Designing an innovation program that serves the needs of the company.
5. Implementing the planned change.
6. Concretizing or stabilizing the innovation.
7. Termination of the agent-client relationship.

**Phase 1. Identifying the need for innovation.** The motivation for exploring a planned change may grow out of a specific challenge or problem that arises. This does not mean that where a problem *does* exist that management in a company actually recognizes it here. The essential part of this first phase is to clarify the problem or problems that may exist. Quite apart from crystallization of the problem is the even further understanding that its solution lies in implementing planned change. There must be management as well as companywide acceptance of the proposition that it is desirable to proceed with an innovation. The double step in this phase involves the identification of a need for change, plus a willingness *to* change. This may be achieved either through a slow process of evolution or from a sudden event that takes place outside the company.

**Phase 2. Creating the idea for an innovation.** The generating of an idea from which a worthwhile innovation can develop requires a number of ingredients. The first requirement is to have a well-established company emphasis upon the value of creativity as the springboard for encouraging the flow of ideas. To facilitate this flow it is healthy to identify an avenue through which ideas may be presented. It should be openly declared that *any* employee is the potential source of an innovation. The final step in preparing the idea for innovation is for it to go through the process of intense evaluation as to its possibilities for becoming a successful innovation.

**Phase 3. Developing a relationship for innovation.** In the relationship between the client system (company) and the change agent lies one of the keys to the success of the innovation. Incidentally, it should be remembered that the change agent is not necessarily or literally an "outisder." He may be an adviser or consultant drawn from one of the staff groups in the company. Very often he might be the head of the systems department or of an industrial engineering department. Nonetheless, he still may be regarded as an outsider, since he is not a member of the social, status, and working group which will be involved in the change.

If there is mistrust or lack of confidence either for personal or professional reasons, this produces stresses. Lippitt and his associates brilliantly express some of the misgivings that arise in the mind of the client, as well as what they view as essential in the change agent in the following passage:

Often the client system seems to be seeking assurance that the potential change agent is different enough from the client system to be a real expert, and yet enough like it to be thoroughly understanding and approachable. What the client system really wants is two change agents in one. It wants an agent who identifies himself with the client system's needs and values, but who will at the same time be neutral enough to take a genuinely objective and different view of the system's predicament.

The joint development of goals, the exchange of ideas on how to implement the innovation, and mutual respect are vital parts of a healthy relationship between client and agent.

**Phase 4. Designing an innovation program that serves the needs of the company.**   A program should be developed (again, jointly) that delineates the steps to be followed in producing an innovation. This should include an identification of the best method to proceed, the resources necessary, the dislocating effect of the change, and the means of motivating others to accept the innovation. This program—what to do, who's to do it, how much to do, what to do it with, and when to do it—for planned change should result from an accommodation between agent and client.

**Phase 5. Implementing the planned change.**   The relationship between the client and change agent should not end before this phase begins, or even immediately after it. There are many unfortunate cases where the installation of the change is handled alone by the client without having the advice of the change agent available.

It is at this stage that the innovation is put to the test in terms of achieving the goals projected for it. To determine the success of the change it is desirable to have established standards for measuring the effectiveness of the innovation. This is particularly true at the early part of the implementation, for misunderstandings and errors may arise that require corrections. Another reason for keeping a close check on the progress of the change is that the pace of the installation may have to be changed, due to the amount of resources available at the time.

**Phase 6. Concretizing or stabilizing the innovation.** As Lewin has warned, success with a change may only be fleeting until a "sliding back" occurs. Since a vast expenditure in energy, time, and funds has usually been committed, it seems ironic that so little effort is used in "nailing down" a change that has been successfully installed. It is here that Lewin's deep understanding of the process of change is important. Lippitt and his associates also reveal the critical nature of this phase in the following comment:

One of the important questions about any process of change is whether or not the change which has been accomplished will remain a stable and permanent characteristic of the system. Too often change which has been produced by painstaking and costly efforts tends to disappear after the change effort ceases, and the system, which wanted to change, slips back instead into its old ways. **(2)**

**Phase 7. Termination of the agent-client relationship.** As indicated earlier, it is certainly desirable to maintain this relationship until after the actual installation stage has been completed. It is still better to continue this relationship beyond the concretizing stage. Even better, some form of the relationship should be established even for a considerable period beyond. This would assure that the agent offers assistance during the critical stabilizing phase and he may even be available (on call) should some problems arise long after the installation has been completed.

Now let us review the sequence of the implementation process and analyze some of the problems in changing over. A primary consideration, even before proceeding to the implementation stage, is the need to relate this changeover to the company's operating plans. Where there are no detailed plans, then it is still necessary to *tie in* the implementation of a *particular* innovation with whatever activities are contemplated by the company. This is true even for localized administrative innovations that may affect but a few people in a single area.

### Relating the Innovation to Company Operation Plans

The innovative manager must be conscious of the need to use companywide operating plans as the framework for innovating. As a result, developing a commitment to innovating induces great pressure for improving company planning.

Preparing the implementation of an innovation is therefore now examined in the context of Merrill's guide (mentioned in Chapter 7) for developing a company plan. **(3)**

It has been pointed out that company planning, including the key stage of pinpointing objectives, should be the basis for developing innovations. Referring to Merrill's outline of the planning steps, the operational planning phase of this sequence answers the questions, How are we going to get there? and, Who is going to do what? This becomes the guide for implementing an innovation because it accomplishes the following: physical planning is activated, for the people and facilities needed to carry out the strategic plan. Assignments are made to develop operating plans in the various units of the company.

These operating plans are made concrete by delegating responsibility for each segment of the total operating plan to a specific person. The data to spell out the exact nature of putting the plan into effect result from the next two phases of Merrill's planning guide that answer the question, When will results be achieved? The answer becomes a timetable or schedule.

### Programming the Implementation of an Innovation

The two basic ingredients for the implentation of an innovation are now set: the sharpened objectives and the clear operating plan for the company, covering each unit of organization. Following are some of the considerations that will arise in developing the steps that will be necessary to carry out the change to the innovation.

**Composition of the change group.**  An important factor in the successful implementation will be the nature of the group actually administering the change. Ideally, this change group should be made up of people with different and complementary backgrounds, each related to some aspect of the innovation. For example, the group should include the person who developed the innovative idea; it should have a representative of the department that will be affected by the change; and it should include a staff representative who is technically familiar with the type of change (this might be a product or process engineer, a systems analyst, or industrial engineer). In this way, persons with varying interests at stake in the outcome and effect of the innovation may be able to bring their talents as well as point of view to bear on its implementation.

**Events to take place and their sequence.**  A clear description, in concise and logical form, should be prepared for each step in the program of change. It is helpful to supplement a detailed summary of the sequence of the implementation with flow charts and other devices which sharpen the relationship of events. Another device that may be used is the route sheet, which has been a useful tool for decades in planning production programs. This provides the added information of a time estimate, the organization unit involved, and the volume of activity at each step in the sequence or route.

**Scheduling the changeover.**  Based upon a flow analysis of the sequence of steps to be performed in making the changeover, it is essential to identify specific starting times by day, date, hour, and minute of each activity in the program.

## The Timing Factor in Innovation

An extremely critical factor in determining the success of an innovation is the attention given to the selection of the appropriate time at which the innovation will be introduced. The strategy of selecting the opportune, psychological, optimum or what may be the "best" time can never be prescribed with certainty. But the expressions "the time is ripe" and "when the iron is hot" typify the preoccupation with timing. Certain criteria can be weighed before selecting the right time for implementing an innovation. One of these considerations was raised earlier, in the concern for timing in relation to the business cycle. Best results are achieved, with the greatest return, when the innovation is introduced early in the business cycle.

Another consideration of timing is to select that seasonal period which provides the greatest resources available to support the innovation. Another timing consideration is to avoid introducing an innovation on the heels of a previous one and before it has been fully "digested." A variety of other timing considerations exist that may be most appropriate to the particular company, its personnel, and its unique operating conditions.

*A new approach to programming innovation.*   Recent developments of an administrative innovation called Critical Path Method, or PERT, described earlier, have now been put to use in programming the implementation of other innovations. An example of the amazing value of CPM in guiding innovations is its use by the Diamond Alkali Company in planning the introduction of product innovations. It is interesting to note the tremendous impact this technique has had in helping Diamond Alkali to introduce new products. Some of CPM's achievements are as follows:

While still in the early stages of planning, it forces us and everyone involved to really think through the entire program in advance—in detail. Thus we were able to pinpoint difficulties before they arose, and solve them in advance.

Enabled us to meet what at first seemed an impossible deadline.

Provided good control over progress of the program.

Helped us level out manpower requirements.

Served as a remarkable means of communication within a large complex organization.

Helped top management fully understand what a new product entails and what it takes to market a new product. (4)

In effect, by using the Critical Path Method of network analysis, Diamond Alkali was forced to think through the entire program of implementing an innovation well in advance. It was also forced "to consider every related activity that might affect the scheduling of jobs that had to be done," to successfully implement the innovation. It certainly is *not* to be assumed that this technique completely eliminated the possibility of errors. What it *did* do was to minimize them so that the resulting changeover turned out to be the most successful implementation of an innovation in Diamond Alkali's history.

## Making the Change

The change that takes place may have been a conversion from some previous means of operation, or it may be a wholly new innovation. In making the change there are often two distinct stages. The first stage may be a trial run or pilot stage used to test a "model" of the innovation. In turn, the second stage may involve the complete implementation of the innovation to full-scale operation.

It is important to consider whether the changeover will take place in two stages or whether the innovation will be installed without a trial run.

*Verifying sequence and schedule.*    Before proceeding with either degree of change (trial run or full-scale), it is essential that a final check be made of the sequence and the schedule of implementation. Any adjustments should be made at this time, to eliminate any stumbling blocks that can possibly be anticipated.

*Weigh parallel operation.*    Another issue which should be explored before proceeding with the change is whether two activities be installed in parallel with the old operation. This, in effect, is the practice of maintaining old activity in operation for a while after the innovation has been installed, in order to maintain the old practice until the innovation has proved to be completely satisfactory. Another reason for parallel operation is so that a comparison can be made with the old method and minor malfunctions of the newly installed change can readily be corrected.

An important thing to bear in mind is that parallel operation is a very costly process. The cost incurred must be balanced against its possible advantage. In any case, it should be eliminated as soon as practicable.

*Trial run stage.*    Assuming that the implementation will proceed in two stages (trial and then full-scale), let us examine some of the factors to consider in the first stage, or trial run. The principle of using the trial run approach is to test the innovation under, as nearly as possible, true operating conditions, to discover any difficulties which were not readily anticipated during the programming of the change. In this way it is many times possible to make simple adjustments of problems that may prove very burdensome, or even endanger the innovation, once the innovation proceeds to full-scale operation.

There are, of course, some limitations to the use of the pilot or trial run. One limitation is that even a trial run often does not produce a *full* test of the efficacy of the innovation. Also, in making the trial run, the conditions that are created may not faithfully duplicate the conditions to be faced in actual full-scale operation. Canning reveals this issue as he explores the test run used in converting to electronic data processing: "The limitation of the test problem approach, of course, is the human's ability to select problems which adequately test the operation." **(5)**

***Full-scale implementation.***   The *rate* of introducing the change should be fully evaluated, whether the change proceeds in a trial run first or not. In the case of a technological innovation, it may involve introducing the change all at once or only at a gradual rate. One way to make the changeover all at once is to completely shut down operations while the change is made. The classic example is the late-summer shutdown in the auto industry during the change-over to a new model. In implementing the change on a *gradual* basis, operations are converted bit by bit, until the operation is completely under the innovated method.

The above conditions apply whether the innovation is technological or administrative. Each approach has problems of its own. The company must choose what, for it, is most advantageous. The gradual approach offers the advantage of gradual assimilation of the innovation so that any learning necessary by the people involved does not take place under pressure. However, this piecemeal approach may prove costly because of the slow rate of change. It also has the disadvantage of perpetuating a state of flux, with continually shifting activities and resources as the changeover proceeds further.

The approach of the complete changeover presents contrasting advantages and disadvantages. Each has its application to specific conditions, but requires a great deal of deliberation before selection.

***Analysis of problem areas.***   Presuming that the innovation has been placed into operation, it is appropriate to provide for a high degree of vigilance during the early period of the changeover. It is reasonable to expect that if the programming of the change has been carefully developed, the persons supervising the implementation can readily eliminate any dislocations at the start. And yet, problems do occur with facilities, materials, equipment, procedures, personnel, and finances, and warrant extra standby observers to be alert to *any* difficulty. For example, equipment is liable to break down through faulty use and unanticipated overloading. It should be a policy that—insofar as possible—productivity and customer satisfaction should be maintained at normal levels so as not to damage the company's profit.

One of the most delicate types of problem that may arise is in the area of personnel. It is essential to probe whether difficulties may be anticipated. This issue will be explored more deeply in Part III. Meanwhile it is appropriate to ask, What effect will these changes have upon the reasonable expectation of individuals in the organization?

***Making adjustments during implementation.***     As a result of keeping in touch with events of the changeover, corrections can be made of problems that arise before they become serious ones. Equipment difficulties can be attended to, personal shifts may be arranged, and other resources may be applied wherever support is needed.

***Establishing procedures to monitor the innovation.***     As part of the programming stage of innovating, steps should be taken to establish a procedure to review the operation of the newly installed innovation. The substance of this procedure should include methods of collecting all performance data that will be appraised in the light of steps to be explored in the next chapter (the actual performance will be evaluated to determine whether the innovation is to continue in operation). The ingredients of the monitoring procedure should include the following:

1. COLLECT OPERATING DATA.   Procedures and forms should be prepared to collect all information on performance from production statistics, employee performance data, cost data, sales data, consumer reactions, and any other pertinent information that gives a picture of the performance of the innovation.

2. PREPARE PERFORMANCE STANDARDS.   At the time the procedures are being prepared it is desirable to establish a whole range of

operating performance standards. These should include physical standards, cost standards, and personnel performance standards. The personnel performance standards should cover professional, supervisory, and manager standards as well as those for employees.

3. SET UP REPORTING ROUTINE. Part of the procedure should be to establish routines for the format of preparing and submitting reports on the innovation's performance. This should include summaries of the operating data as well as conclusions growing out of the comparisons with expected results. It should cover the organization unit involved, the person responsible, and the source and destination of the operating report.

# CHAPTER 9

# EVALUATING THE PROFIT PERFORMANCE OF AN INNOVATION

Successful implementation of an innovation does *not* end when it apparently "gets off the ground." This event can either mark the beginning of a successful change, or merely signal the last burst before collapsing in failure. The essential and demanding period that follows right after implementing the innovation should be a time when a determined and speedy check is made of the profit performance of the innovation. The results of this review will be used to make the harsh decision of ceasing its operation or of continuing on with the innovation. These are the extremes of the decision required, but the alternatives the manager faces with regard to the future of the recently installed innovation include: continue the innovation at its present pace; completely cease operation; postpone a decision until a further evaluation has been made for a given time period; or reduce the pace of operation of the innovation.

It is the objective of the postimplementation review to determine whether the innovation has achieved, or appears likely to achieve, its primary objective—increased profit for the company. Another key purpose of the review is to rate the performance of each of the managers who had a role in programming or implementing the innovation. This is necessary for two reasons. First, the performance of managers involved in the change may have been a large factor contributing to the success—or failure—of the innovation. In effect, by rating the innovative capacity of managers, we are dealing with a significant *determinant* of company profits and growth. The analysis may reveal that in the case of a failure of innovation, it may have been due to the way the implementation was managed rather than to an inherent lack of profitability of the innovation.

A second reason for the evaluation of managers' performance in innovation is to discover the strengths and weaknesses of each manager. Thus, efforts can be made to raise the innovating capability of managers who have shown deficiencies. Those managers who reveal high skill in innovating can, forthwith, be assigned greater responsibilities for further innovations. The result of evaluation and then action is to raise the *total* innovative capability of the company's managers.

A more harsh approach in using the results of the evaluation is proposed by Hertz of McKinsey and Company, who suggests the following:

The worst men are either developed and make their contribution, or they are eliminated. The better men are reassigned to places where they can make better and better contributions. **(1)**

The essential question that is raised, and hopefully affirmatively answered, is, as Merrill presents it, Can we really do it? **(2)** More appropriately, have we accomplished what we said we could do? If standards for accomplishment have been established, if our procedures for monitoring performance have been developed and installed, and if responsibility for each step in the innovation implementation has been pinpointed, then we certainly should be able to get the answers and to *act* on what we find out. However, before going in to a review of some techniques that can be helpful in assessing profit performance, let us first examine the meaning of profit. Let's further see how profit is related to innovating, and this may lead to alternate ways of measuring profit performance.

### Profit: Its Nature and Measurement

The major underlying premise I have made is that a fundamental motivation for innovating—by definition—is that the change brings about a profit to the innovator and/or his company. In other words, the innovation must provide an economic rationale. Otherwise, it is not an innovation; it is, rather, a planned change.

The two other widely held justifications for profits are, as a *reward for risk taking,* justified as a compensation for the fact that the higher the risk, the higher the rewards should be; and *profits as a result of frictions* and imperfections in the economy, resulting from temporary adjustment of the economy to some dislocation. This theory views profits as a result of imperfections in competition which result in temporary advantage (profits). It gives no consideration at all to the risks assumed by the entrepreneur.

The third widely held theory of profits, and the one I advocate, was most brilliantly conceived by Schumpeter as the theory of innovation profits. (3) This theory holds that the individual "who sees the value of a new idea and is able to organize and carry out the job of turning it into cash" deserves the profit. He is, in other words, the one who *implements* the innovation rather than the one who merely comes up with the idea for change in the first place.

As Joel Dean states regarding this position, "By this theory, then, profit is the reward for disrupting the status quo." (4)

**Profit measurement concepts.** Another issue that arises in using profit as an evaluation criterion for innovations is the problem of which of two basic measuring approaches should be used: the economic or the accounting. The contrast between the economic measurement of profit and the accounting approach centers on a conflict over the futurity of profit. The economic measure of profit, conceptually, is a measure of future profits that are likely to accrue. On the other hand, the accounting measurement is a historical approach which deals solely with profits in a *past* period.

The most important differences that are evident between the economic and accounting approaches are emphasized in the following points:

(1) the inclusiveness of cost, i.e., what should be subtracted from revenue to get profit; (2) the meaning of depreciation; (3) the treatment of capital gains and losses; and perhaps most important, (4) the price-level basis for valuation of assets, i.e., current vs. historical costs. (5)

For the purpose of determining the innate profitability of an innovation, based upon a short period of operation after installation, it would seem that the economic approach towards measuring profit has immense possibility for evaluating the *future* profitability of an innovation.

***Use of profit for evaluating manager performance.*** It is growingly recognized that a factor which has helped to improve manager performance is the use of profit results of a department as a measure of executive performance. This has come about from the practice of pinpointing manager responsibility in terms of organization units. This has required two significant changes in company operations.

The first is the realignment of the managerial organization to shift the basic breakdown from a functional basis—to break the company into several integrated operating units, divisions, and give the executive authority over all functions in his division, and make him responsible for profits.

The second common trait is reorientation of accounting reports to conform to the areas of executive responsibility.

The advantages of profit as an evaluation criterion should not obscure, however, an issue that may complicate its use. This is the question of whether the measure of profit should be in terms of total dollars or whether profit should be considered relative to the sum of invested capital or return on investment.

Dean argues that the measurement of profit should be in terms of aggregate dollars because the investments made by previous managers are beyond the control of current managers. However, we must not fail to distinguish between return on *total* investment of the division or department, and return on the investment in a *single project*. This last condition is essentially what prevails when evaluating a newly implemented innovation.

I advocate return on investment (or relative profits) because aggregate (total) dollar profit does not serve as an effective measure of success for a *particular* innovation. On the other hand, return on investment (for an innovation project) is one tool that very definitely can achieve this evaluation. In this way the effectiveness of a control tool can be employed without contaminating the measurement of a newly installed innovation with investments in previous changes directed by previous managers.

***Earnings improvement budgeting.*** There are a number of ingredients vital to budgeting for innovation that are not necessarily found in regular budgeting practice. Some of them are:

1. There should be a particular emphasis on developing manager and supervisor participation in—and enthusiasm for—budgeting. To that end, each manager should initiate the budget for his own department. Moreover, no changes should be made either by his superior or an accounting office without the full consent and understanding of the particular manager.

2. Forms and reports should be prepared in such a manner that data covers only those expenses over which a manager has a direct influence. This may require additional effort by the accounting department, but only in that way can the department manager fully exploit the possibilities of reducing losses. Another feature of these reports is that they should be kept concise but clear.

3. Performance measures should be developed to help guide the department manager in determining the effectiveness of his innovating efforts. Performance standards could be established to appraise each individual activity. In turn, performance during any period could be so analyzed as to reveal the particular department's contribution to total company earnings.

4. Speeding up report preparation is very desirable for budgeting that is designed to encourage innovation. Admittedly, fast reporting is always desirable. However, it is particularly frustrating for managers to attempt a vigorous vigilance for ways to improve operations through innovation while being hamstrung with *outdated* information that is to be used to evaluate the innovation's performance.

**Break-even analysis.**    Apart from those control measures of evaluating profit performance of an innovation that are peculiar to an earnings improvement program, a whole "arsenal" of control tools is available. One such control technique is break-even analysis, both mathematical and graphic varieties. This analysis projects the comparison between expenses and income to determine at what point, in terms of dollar revenue, a break-even condition is achieved. The effect, also, of changes in the characteristics and amount of expenses or of income is projected with unusual clarity to reveal how the break-even point may shift as a result. In turn, the analysis highlights—especially through graphic presentation—the impact of these changes on future profits, or losses, of an innovation. This tool has been particularly useful in evaluating product innovations. In this situation the rate at which profits of the innovation are rising (or losses are declining) can be compared to the rate at which expenses are rising, particularly at different levels of output.

Gardner makes use of this tool to evaluate profit performance in terms of what he calls "profit efficiency." Following his guide, the influences of such factors as volume of output, mix-of-product variations, cost performance at a given volume, and selling price varieties are interpreted and measured over a period of time.

It is within this context that the break-even point becomes fundamental in defining Gardner's profit efficiency. In another way, it helps determine to what degree there is a *variation* from a projected profit picture (in the case of an innovation, it compares proposed profits before installation to the actual profit results of the period immediately after implementation.)

The break-even analysis is an extremely useful tool in forecasting the *future* profit potential. Moreover, it is done in a dramatic fashion by using just a short period of operation of the innovation as a basis for projecting its future profit performance. It will also clearly indicate the *rate* at which the profits of the newly installed innovation should rise. It is thus very useful when the manager faces the critical decision point of whether to continue operation of the innovation (and for how long) or to cease operations.

***Return on investment.***    Return on investment, as a control tool, has proved to be a magnificent boon to guiding business operations for decades. It has been used (as already stated) with enthusiastic acclaim at companies like Du Pont, Heinz, and Monsanto. It is an absolutely key measure in evaluating an innovation, because it is capable of clearly measuring the particular contribution to company profits achieved as a result of the innovation.

Return on investment is, simply, the result (in percentage) of comparing profits with the investment necessary to generate those profits. As used by Du Pont, return on investment is derived from two key factors that have a direct bearing upon profits. They are: first, earnings as a percentage of sales (which is an indication of how efficiently the company produces and sells its wares); and second, turnover (which reveals the intensity with which a given amount of investment is put to use in generating sales). In this fashion, the return-on-investment concept is then traced to the contributing source, that is, the individual department and individual project or product that has contributed to the profit, or failed to contribute, in the rate of return established for it before operations began for a particular time period. In this way the profitability of a department or of a project is evaluated together with the capability of the manager of that department or project. This indicates the usefulness of this control technique for evaluating innovations. (6)

One offshoot of the return-on-investment concept has been used by Olin Industries in what they call an "index of return." This has been used to evaluate the profitability of an innovation. This technique is used, not only as an evaluation after the innovation has been installed, but as a screening device used during the preliminary evaluation of an innovative idea.

The sequence of Olin's use of their index of return is as follows: When the innovation is first proposed, an estimate is made of the additional earnings the change may provide when installed. After the change is made, data is collected every three months for a whole year's time on the results of operation. In terms of the different kinds of technological innovation that this technique may be applied to, Olin computes this operating data on improved processes for one year, on improved products for one year, and on new products for three years. Thus, the estimated index of return (for each innovation) is compared to its corresponding *actual* index of return (performance) at three-month intervals. The effectiveness of this control tool (a variation of the return-on-investment concept) in achieving successful innovation is summarized as "one measure of the success of the corporation as a whole in replacing current products with better ones." (7)

*Network analysis—PERT and CPM.* A growingly important tool for both planning and controlling (evaluating the profit performance) of innovations is the concept of network analysis. These include both the Program Evaluation and Review Technique (PERT) and the Critical Path Method (CPM). More recently, cost considerations have been added to the time factors in PERT, resulting in the technique of PERT/cost. The sequence of steps in using PERT/cost, for example, are as follows:

1. Identify all the jobs that make up the project.
2. Relate them to each other in a logical network.
3. Estimate how much time each step will take.

4. Estimate how much each step will cost.
5. From the above determine a realistic budget and target date.
6. From time to time compare results with the original plan—and revise it if necessary.

PERT/cost has admittedly achieved its greatest triumphs in producing innovations in defense industries. However, its use is extending into every conceivable area of technological and administrative innovation. It has been proved both in planning the program for installing the innovation and in evaluating performance after it is in operation. In a particularly exotic application of the CPM technique of network analysts, a Colorado hospital has used it for planning and performing open-heart surgery.

**Cost analysis.** Underlying the other control techniques, but no less a significant technique in itself, is the area of cost analysis. To get a reliable picture of present profits and a sound evaluation of future profits of an innovation, a sound method of accumulating costs is essential. However, the form of the cost analysis is as important as having one at all. This is because the traditional cost systems (such as process, job order, and so forth, with or without standards) *fail* to clearly distinguish the innate profitability of a particular product or project.

*Direct costing* overcomes this difficulty by more *truly* applying costs to specific projects. There is a growing recognition of the value of direct costing for executive control. In some companies it is replacing tradition cost techniques, while in others it is used as in parallel with the regular cost system in effect. Direct costing has proved to be a uniquely helpful tool in determining the true earnings improvement achieved by the production and sale of a particular product line. This results from the contrast with regular cost systems. With the traditional system, typical overhead allocation penalizes a product line, department, or project (by raising its cost) when production vaolume in other areas declines. This "false" fluctuation in unit cost is eliminated or minimized by direct costing.

A leading authority on the use of direct costing indicates clearly the virtue of this tool in helping managers to project the future profitability of an innovation. It is of particular value in allowing a *decision* on whether an innovation should continue in operation or not. Ray Longenecker of Armstrong shows this:

The direct costing approach provides a completely understandable insight into cost elements and their behavior characteristics, thereby permitting soundly conceived decisions. . . . The very nature of direct costing sets up the statistical records as well as the data related to *future* expectations, in a manner which facilitates sound analysis. This is so because direct costing recognizes the basic distinction between those costs relating directly to units produced and those costs relating to a period of time.

Cost analysis—specifically the direct costing technique—is particularly useful in profit evaluations of product innovations whether they are new products or improvements in old ones. The cost data compiled (as a basis for profit evaluation) should cover development costs as well as operating costs of the product. These will be necessary not only for assessing innate profitability, but also for establishing a price structure for the innovated product. In spite of the techniques available for determining costs of new products, it should be recognized that conditions exist which make costing of new products extremely difficult. Virdon Scranton of Motorola summarized the essential ingredients necessary for proper costing and analysis of new products as including:

1. Good communication channels between management, the operating groups and the accountant.
2. A good budgeting system for control purposes.
3. A well-defined costs system for proper cost identification. We prefer to handle the engineering functions all the way through pilot production on an engineering project system, with all charges and time reported by project number. Labor and other expenses are broken down by a sub-account numbering system.
4. A clear reporting system showing actual accumulated costs at each checkpoint, with a re-evaluation of projected costs. **(8)**

Another particularly significant area of cost analysis of an innovation concerns the installation period itself. It is not unusual for the greatest impact on immediate profitability of the innovation to be felt during the implementation period. In discussing the installation of a certain computer, Canning points out that "the total costs are 10 percent higher than was budgeted." **(9)**

## Making the Decision to Cut or Continue the Innovation

The importance—and urgency—of evaluating the profit performance of a newly installed innovation grows out of the pressure facing managers as to whether the innovation should continue or not. In the vernacular, managers are faced with the need to "fish or cut bait" as soon as possible after implementation. This may actually involve one of three alternate possibilities.

First, it may be clear that the innovation falls far short of profit expectations and, therefore, the operation should be stopped. A second possible decision is to continue operation—under close observation—and reevaluate performance after another period. Finally, the decision may be to proceed fully ahead because the innovation gives every evidence of complete success, profitwise.

The delicacy, urgency, and sheer discomfort during this period soon after an innovation has been launched with the highest expectations is crystallized by Milton E. Mangel, vice president of product planning at Burroughs:

Unfortunately, not all products come up to estimates in the market place for any number of reasons. Therefore, our product program reviews the results obtained against projections. If these reviews disclose a lack of profitability or a trend toward that condition, we plan as good a retreat as we can, even though we have no replacement. **(10)**

# CHAPTER 10

# AN EARNINGS IMPROVEMENT AND LOSS REDUCTION PROGRAM

A vital ingredient in the process of managing innovation is the development of a sound program for earnings improvement and loss reduction. The gains that may result—quite apart from its place in conjunction with innovations—are widespread. As one significant indication of the general acceptance of earnings improvement and loss reduction as a continuing way of life, companies bidding for defense contracts are openly advised that one criterion for consideration in granting an award is whether a company has a functioning earnings improvement program.

However, the value of such a program is magnified by having it used, in addition, as a tool of the innovation process. The importance of EI and LR is as a means of determining the feasibility of a proposed idea for innovation, by evaluating the ability of the project to bring economic benefits to the company. Since the basic challenge to any innovation is its profitability, it is essential that the proposal undergo a thorough test of its potential in that direction. The EI and LR procedures also are important in the innovation process for evaluating the innovation *after* it has been installed. In that way, evidence is accumulated that will reveal whether the innovation has achieved the earnings goals established for it, or not.

The insight revealed by the comparison of achievement and goal may have far-reaching effects in planning future innovations.

Before examining the use of EI and LR as a yardstick for judging a proposed innovation, it is in order to explore the meaning I will place on the two terms, loss reduction and innovation. The concept of *loss* reduction is far more compelling than the more usual phrase, cost reduction. Under the idea of reducing losses, the emphasis is placed on separating that part of expenditure that is wasteful from that part which is absolutely necessary to maintain operations. The portion that is identified as wasteful I would consider an outright *loss*, just as though these resources were consumed by fire. With the evil thus made more glaring there is also less danger that—as often happens in cost reduction efforts—arbitrary cuts will be made in vital activities. On the contrary, it is recognized that loss reduction involves the elimination of practices that tend to drain the energies of the company.

One area of loss reduction that has been found particularly amenable to correction is the area of bad debts. Ironically, many companies follow the practice of accepting a given quantity of bad debt expense as reasonable in terms of its relationship to sales volume. This handling of bad debts is particularly shocking because any reduction in this *loss* becomes a direct addition to company earnings. The writer and his associates have developed policies and procedures which managers sheepishly acknowledged achieved dramatic results in loss reduction.

Another point worthy of brief exploration is to clearly identify the two types of innovation once more: innovation involving technological, and innovation involving administrative, changes. The more familiar one is technological innovation. However, administrative innovation is the area that has far greater untapped potential. This last type represents all the vast possibilities for changes in company operating methods.

It is this last type of change, administrative, that Eels and Walton categorize as social inventions. They strongly suggest that the innovations of greatest number and impact will be social rather than technical. When applied to business operations, this would include such areas as: the arrangement and nature of work, marketing, and customer service, and dramatic changes in the nature of the manager's job on all levels of the company.

Such a view of innovation makes it quite difficult to confine the process to one compartment of the company, whether that group be called research, systems, planning, or engineering. As expressed earlier, there is need to recognize innovation as one of the basic functions of *every* manager's job and in many cases it is becoming his most *important* function. The process of innovating is thus tied with planning, organizing, and controlling to give a *dynamic* intent to the manager's activities. The addition of innovating as a basic function gives the manager conscious recognition of the fact that he is committed to a continuous improvement of operations by challenging the status quo.

Applying the critical test—profitability—to an innovation demands a deliberate and well-thought-out program that is made an intimate part of the substance and spirit of innovation. The major elements in such a program are:

*First,* develop sound policies and procedures incorporating all aspects of earnings improvement and loss reduction and involving a total company commitment—from the "top brass" to the lowest worker. Such a program should be so constituted that it can be maintained with or without a direct tie to a program designed to encourage innovation.

*Second,* apply principles and techniques that are designed specifically to assess the additional earnings that may be contributed by an innovation.

*Third,* prepare executive control tools that will permit an appraisal of the results accomplished by a particular innovation after it has been in operation for a given period of time.

## Developing an Earnings Improvement and Loss Reduction Program

The interest in and pressures for a stable and effective earnings improvement program are growing each day. Not the least of these pressures has come from government agencies which have clearly stated that their selection of vendors will be guided to a significant degree by the existence in the vendor's company of an earnings improvement plan. This government pressure is designed to encourage innovations in products, services, and administration, as well as reduced prices to government agencies. However, the development of an earnings improvement effort requires more than just mechanical techniques. It demands thorough reflection which results in a philosophy and attitudes which provide a *positive* basis for applying the techniques of earnings improvement and loss reduction. The broad outlines of such a plan that would operate in conjunction with an innovation program include:

1. Defining the purposes and goals of earnings improvement and loss reduction.
2. Developing the right attitudes and atmosphere.
3. Involving *all* company personnel to the greatest degree possible.
4. Establishing key performance measures.
5. Organizing for earnings improvement and loss reduction.
6. Providing tools, techniques, and training in their use.
7. Highlighting areas of greatest improvement potential (where innovations are needed most).
8. Defining procedures for developing and implementing EI and LR projects.
9. Documenting project results.
10. Providing recognition of achievements.
11. Establishing periodic evaluation of the earnings improvement and loss reduction program to determine whether its goals are being achieved and/or if they need revision.

*1. Defining purposes and goals.* The purposes of a specific company's earnings improvement program should be clearly spelled out. This provides guidance for specific projects that ensue, and also presents a rationale for undertaking such a program in the first place. It should be made clear that the EI and LR program is not an activity that is set apart from all other functions of the company. Rather, it should be conceived as a convenient vehicle for improving *all* company operations.

*2. Developing the right attitudes and atmosphere.* The risk of failure in attaining the broad as well as the specific objectives is greater from faulty attitudes than from inadequate techniques. An essential ingredient for success is a grass-roots enthusiasm for the aims of earnings improvement.

To capture this spirit among managers and employees alike, a couple of issues are helpful. One point to stress is that the program will be on a continuous basis rather than just for a short period, to attain a few successes. Also it is appropriate to stress that the goals set for earnings improvement are essential to all concerned and they *are* attainable. This last point is important, because people will get a great deal of satisfaction when they experience the feeling of having attained realistic objectives.

Furthermore, remove all hint of contamination by an air of crisis to cut costs, because this inevitably leads to the feeling that changes will be arbitrary and obnoxious. Instead, stress should be laid on the fact that earnings improvement and loss reduction are as applicable in good times as in bad. Moreover, they should be viewed as part of one's everyday responsibility, rather than as some extraordinary activity set apart from regular operating duties.

It should also be emphasized that the organization of EI and LR projects does *not* imply that improvements could not occur without such projects. What it does mean is that energies already committed to that end could be more effectively combined and channeled than left on a piecemeal basis. In addition, some ongoing activities would continue, quite apart from the relatively formal EI and LR program. These activities would thus complement one another.

This implied appeal to the self-interest of each employee—developing a common interest of personnel and company—can best be established by the *example* and dedication of each manager. In his daily concern for earnings improvement, he can search for increased revenue opportunities as well as instances for eliminating wasteful practices. The manager's attitude can be infectious in leading to an atmosphere that is the *substance* underlying the form of an earnings improvement and loss reduction program.

**3. Involving all company personnel.**   If the support of and enthusiasm for earnings improvement is to be maintained, each person should find a definite role in achieving the established goals (the key role must be assumed by top management). Primarily, all are to pledge their support in both word and deed to a companywide (without exception) emphasis upon earnings improvement.

Full involvement of people is the best avenue for gaining acceptance for the EI and LR program. However, the price of *continued* acceptance is a constant emphasis upon the importance of the goals established and the dependence of the company on each person to achieve those objectives.

**4. Establishing key performance measures.**   Another essential
ingredient of the EI and LR program is the development of performance measures. There is an unmistakable trend towards adding
measures of all kinds of effort, including managerial and professional tasks. Indeed, there is hardly anything new about being
measured or appraised. What is new is our growing ability to extend
performance measures to those areas where it has been thought
difficult or "sensitive." This has been accomplished by developing
objective standards where only subjective ones existed before.

The idea of placing performance measures in all company activities provides the basis for sound supervisory and executive control.
For this reason, it results in a more effective management quite
apart from the direct results of the EI and LR program.

It is necessary that the measures developed be comparable between departments, so that friendly competition can be encouraged.
For example, if departments vary greatly in size, a dollar comparison of earnings improvement may not be as meaningful as a percentage gain in earnings. Moreover, since results may be achieved
more easily in some units than others, recognition should be given
in terms of the degree of *difficulty* of achieving improvement in
various departments.

**5. Organizing for earnings improvement.**   Some companies
structure an EI and LR program as a function of a specific department charged with initiating and implementing all projects. For
example, it may become part of the regular activities of an industrial engineering department, or it may be assigned to a new unit
whose sole concern is earnings improvement. However, there is
compelling reason for giving a significant role—or even the dominant one—to the line manager, making him responsible for selecting and implementing particular earnings improvement projects.
The philosophy involved is the deemphasis of the expert approach.
Coupled with this is the recognition that since the line manager is
held accountable for his department's operations, it should be *he*
who directs the efforts towards improving those operations.

**6. Providing tools, techniques, and training in their use.**   The
initial phase of preparing employees for a cooperative effort in
earnings improvement should involve orientation. This may be
achieved through conferences led by the management, as well as by
written descriptions of the program distributed to all personnel.

This is designed to set forth the role of the group in the program. It will also serve to indicate the kinds of skills and training that will need to be applied in achieving the ends of earnings improvement.

Training in skills and techniques should be provided for managers, supervisors and key employees. Among the areas to be covered are the following:

*a*) Change as the basis for improvement.
*b*) Skills in eliminating wasteful practices.
*c*) Preparation in developing performance standards.
*d*) Training in selecting and proposing projects.
*e*) Hints on establishing targets and reporting results.

**7. Highlighting areas of greatest improvement potential.** The cornerstone of any EI and LR program consists of actual projects to improve specific areas of operations or to develop entirely new areas. It follows that the skill used in selecting these projects is vital to the success of the entire program.

To satisfy the definition of an earnings improvement project, the Le Tourneau-Westinghouse Company prescribed the following five criteria:

*a*) It has a specific goal.
*b*) It involves some specific action.
*c*) Its progress can be scheduled and its earnings improvements are of a continuous nature.
*d*) Its results can be measured and attributed to the action taken.
*e*) It produces a tangible improvement in earning level over current operations for the company as a whole.

**8. Designing procedures for developing and implementing projects.** Having prepared the philosophy, organization, and techniques for the program, it is essential to provide a companywide vehicle for implementing earnings improvement, namely, specific procedures. To make the procedures readily understandable, it is desirable to accompany them with a flow chart and an organization chart. The flow chart will serve to summarize the sequence of the major steps to be followed from the time an idea for improvement arises to its implementation, and finally, the recording of the results.

**9. Documenting project results.** It should be made a part of the process that regular reports be accumulated that reveal the results of all earnings improvement projects. Summaries of these results should be prepared in table form, showing the actual achievements in one column and the degree to which the goals of each department have been attained in another. Participants (line managers) should be encouraged to establish realistic and yet demanding goals. The degree to which these targets are achieved will represent a significant barometer of the enthusiasm for the program.

**10. Providing recognition of achievements.**    A program of earnings improvement will persist just so long as company personnel believe in and support it. Certainly there is no single means of obtaining continued support. However, one highly effective motivating force is to provide some recognition for individuals who have made a contribution towards increasing company earnings. An excellent way to do this is to formally appraise candidates for promotional salary increases on the *specific* efforts towards the earnings improvement program. In this way all come to recognize that their future progress is tied to their own efforts in increasing their value to the company.

**11. Establishing periodic evaluation of the program.**    In some regular and deliberate fashion there should be a review of the EI and LR program to determine whether the goals set for it are being achieved. As a result of this analysis, questions may be raised as to whether it should undergo substantial changes. A significant criterion of the program's success might be the determination of whether earnings improvement has kept pace with or advanced beyond unavoidable increases in expenditures, such as for salaries.

### Return on Investment Projection of Profit Potential

A valuable device for projecting the future profit potential of a proposed innovation is the return on investment technique. The most effective use of RI to assess future profit potential (as well as to appraise actual performance) of an innovation has been made by the Du Pont company. The RI technique is used as an overall control tool for Du Pont operations, but what is of particular interest is how the individual manager can use RI in his own area of responsibility. In the case of a department manager, his estimate of the future profit potential of an innovation centers on the projection of the future profit on the amount of investment required to implement the innovation. What is unique about Du Pont's approach is their breakdown of return on investment into its two contributing ingredients, earnings as a percent of sales (profit margin), and turnover (amount of sales generated by a given investment).

In appraising the profit potential of an innovation through RI, Du Pont encourages the department manager involved with a particular innovation to determine the underlying ingredients that may contribute to (or fail to contribute to) the future profitability of an innovation. This drives home the manager-oriented emphasis in using RI as a tool for appraising the inherent profit potential of a proposed innovation. In this way the manager can determine if investment in the project is justified.

### Profit Testing of Proposed Innovations

Having once established a sound EI and LR program, the framework has been prepared for determining the profitability of the proposed innovations. These innovations should be judged on their potential for either increasing revenue or reducing losses. In both cases they may contribute to increased company earnings. It is necessary to develop procedures for giving a fair appraisal on each innovation in such a way that they can be integrated with the earnings improvement program. Such an evaluation procedure should include techniques for analyzing the earnings potential, projection of the consequences of the analysis, and a follow-up to trace the actual earnings contribution of the innovation after it has been implemented.

*Earnings evaluation technique.* The steps defined for judging the earnings potential of a planned change should be flexible enough to evaluate loss reduction as well as revenue-increasing innovations. In addition, they should be equally valid in examining technological and administrative innovations.

It is required that the first step in the evaluation process be the preparation of a proposal describing the nature of the innovation and *estimating* its effects, either in increasing revenue or in reducing losses.

The typical kinds of expenditures from which losses can be eliminated include: direct labor expenditures, material costs, indirect hourly labor expenses, salaried personnel expenditures, and many others. These areas may be summarized as being concentrated in the use of human, material, mechanical, and data resources. A few examples of areas that may prove fruitful for increasing company revenue include: product design, marketing distribution, customer services, and sales promotion.

Before examining a sample format of the evaluation, let us agree on the purpose of an evaluation form. In addition to providing projection of future earnings, it helps to organize the data to facilitate the comparison of the estimated with the actual earnings. Following are some of the data that should be generated for use in evaluating the potential earnings improvement of a proposed innovation:

1. The source (specific department of the proposal and the activity to which it will be applied).
2. A description of the present practice, if one exists.
3. Description of the proposed innovation and what it will accomplish.
4. The estimated reduction in loss per unit of product.
5. An estimate of annual number of units of product multiplied by the unit savings, resulting in annual loss reduction.
6. The estimated increase in revenue on an annual basis.
7. The impact upon the total company earnings from loss reduction and/or revenue increase.
8. The capital investment necessary to develop the innovation.
9. The expense required to implement the innovation.
10. Where funds are required, to determine the breakeven point (in dollars and date) and the return on investment rate.

The above samples of the kind of data that might be developed for projecting the profitability of an innovation can be gathered for most business activities. However, these can be supplemented or replaced by additional information that is peculiar to the needs of a particular company.

The specific proposal should be prepared and submitted by either line or staff management in an appropriate, uniform type of format. It is desirable to have some coordinating agency or individual receive the proposals and arrange for some preliminary review before they are subjected to intense examination.

*Deciding on the feasibility of the innovation.*   The selection of an appropriate technique for making the evaluation has included the determination of the data required, arranging the format of its presentation, and organization of the persons involved in the evaluation process. The critical phase involves the actual determination of the feasibility of the innovation. To do this involves the following three steps:

1. Verification of the proposed data.
2. Selecting the criteria to be used and applying them to the issue at hand.
3. Clarifying the alternate decisions that may be possible in each case.

Verification of the data appearing in the proposal is essential at this early stage of innovation evaluation. To begin with, it is important to check carefully the mechanical accuracy of the information (proper selection of data, accurate calculations, etc.). In addition, the projections of the anticipated achievements of the innovations (potential profits, etc.) should be examined to determine whether they are too extravagant or too modest.

Among the factors to consider as criteria in evaluating the potential profitability are the actual amount of estimated earnings improvement, how quickly these earnings will be achieved, how long the earnings will persist, and what positive or negative effects the proposed innovation may have upon other sources of company earnings. The criteria that may have a bearing upon the feasibility of the innovation include: the degree of difficulty in implementing the change, the number of persons affected by it, and the nature and extent of the consequences to these people. These criteria should be arrayed in some scale of values and an acceptability point should be established for each one. For example, earnings improvement should be rated in terms of its importance as a criterion. Moreover, a minimum level or standard of earnings improvement should be established for this criterion.

Before making a determination on the disposition of a proposed innovation the specific alternate possibilities should be explored. For example, the evaluation should lead to any one of four alternate decisions. These are:

1. Complete acceptance of the proposal, accompanied by a recommendation for implementation immediately.
2. Setting the proposal aside, due to lack of feasibility at that time. This is *not* rejection; the proposal may be reconsidered.
3. Adoption of the proposal, but implementation to be delayed for a specific period of time.
4. Qualified approval of the proposal, with implementation to proceed on a small-scale or pilot basis, with a review of results to take place before *full* implementation of the proposal.

**Recording the status of innovations.**    After a decision has been made on a proposal, it is essential to record its progress and status, as in a ship's log. Among the items of information to include in these progress records are: the date and nature of the evaluation decision, a report on the events that take place with regard to the project, and data on the achievements of the innovation.

# CHAPTER 11

# ORGANIZING FOR INNOVATION

It is unquestionably the *duty* of each manager, regardless of his level or the area of his work, to engage in advancing innovation. Nonetheless, since this is an issue of great significance to the whole company, it is not enough to have it remain a matter of an individual manager's discretion. It is necessary to provide guidance, resources, and coordination in the planning and implementing of change. To accomplish this, it has proved effective to organize a group that devotes its full energy to the activity of innovation. Traditionally, it has been the practice to develop innovations on a strictly functional basis. For example, the marketing division would make provision for studies to improve marketing techniques, market penetration, product acceptability, and a whole range of matters. The manufacturing function would, in turn, develop innovations in equipment as well as product and administrative techniques. The engineering activity might involve changed products and invent new lines of products. The accounting department could explore changes in accounting procedures. In turn, other departments typically pursue innovations—when they are so inclined—on this separate basis.

The means of directing effort on change via the key area route has two main shortcomings. To begin with, in a great many cases, considerations arise which require that an innovation overlap the boundaries of functional areas. Quite simply, some projects require the combined efforts of many groups. Secondly, the efforts in innovation are too confined to the narrow interest and viewpoint of the head of the functional area. To overcome these restraints, many companies are centralizing the activity of innovation. The names of such departments vary, but nowhere at this time does the description I would offer exist. The title that seems most appropriate is the "Innovation Management" department.

## Innovation Management Department

To foster innovation and to coordinate the energies of managers in that direction, it is essential to establish a vehicle for orderly companywide innovation. Since innovating is a process that is purposeful, continuous, and companywide planned change, this agency should be called the innovation management department or section.

The approach of this unit should emphasize assuming of the role of catalytic agents for innovation devised by others. From this position, it becomes evident that there is to be a deemphasis of the "expert" as the sole possessor of innovative talents. The personnel of this agency should have the combined talents that will enable them to stimulate the efforts of others for innovative ideas, to evaluate proposed improvements, and to help develop programs for the actual implementation of innovations. With such broad scope, it would be desirable to have this staff group report directly to the highest operating officer in the company. This would be a further indicator of the companywide emphasis on innovation.

## Organization for Innovation

The organization unit to be designated as innovation management should perform duties that run the gamut of innovation. In many situations the tasks required from development to implementation of an innovation may actually be performed by other groups, but they should be supervised and/or coordinated by this organization unit. The range of activities should include: preparing materials and methods of communicating the nature of the approach to innovation in the particular company; engaging in the training of personnel to develop the requisite skills and attitudes; developing the means for generating ideas that form the starting point for innovation; evaluating the feasibility of proposed innovations; preparing the programming to implement potentially profitable innovations; and determining control practices that will monitor and appraise the achievements of those innovations that have been implemented.

In effect, this department should provide the inspiration, the broad framework, and an unlimited amount of guidance to assure that managers throughout the company devote a significant portion of their energies to the process of innovation.

The organization of an ongoing innovation program in the above manner is still quite rare today. It is far more common to find that planned change (where it receives any degree of recognition) is the responsibility of a great many areas in the company—which results in multiple approaches to innovation. Generally, these activities are found under the sections identified as research and development, product planning, systems analysis, and industrial engineering. The first two departments (R&D and product planning) generally confine their activities to technological innovations, while the latter two are usually more involved with administrative innovation. In either case, this more typical approach has a number of shortcomings. Perhaps the greatest limiting factor is that the persons in these departments are solely responsible for the design and implementation of the particular innovation. In other words, these are the experts on planned change. The average manager is, therefore, typically ignored as a major source of innovative ideas. Improvements in the company are conceived of as the sole responsibility of these highly trained experts.

Another shortcoming of the "spread-eagle" attack on innovation is that where innovations are developed by a few key departments that are all-time "change agents," this compartmented approach (developed in isolation from other groups) tends to ignore the companywide impact of a potential innovation. Each of these departments tends to deal with planned change in terms of the viewpoint of its own area of influence.

Let us review some examples of companies that have established the responsibility of planned change as separated into different departmental areas, rather than under a single group that corordinates all innovation activity in the company.

**Company approaches to innovation.** It may be worth noting that to this date there is no evidence that any company has established anything that in substance is like my innovation management department. At the same time, there are indications that many of our most successful companies have developed the philosophy and tools to harness the innovative talents of their employees. In a recent study of our country's most persistent growth companies, *Dun's Review* reveals what might be considered the keys to their success. Charles Thornton of Litton Industries stated that the fundamental reason for his company's success is: "Our company has made a business out of change." **(1)**

The study reveals that the primary reason for the sustained growth in company profits and size was that these firms have provided the means for capturing those innovative ideas that every company has lying dormant until aroused. William Norris declares that: "You must have an organization that encourages and makes it possible for people to exercise their individual creativity and initiative."

An example that comes closest to the development of a single companywide agency for planned change is found in the Westinghouse Air Brake Company. In this particular case, the department is called simply "the planning department." However, it is a highly developed instance of a company that has organized the development of planned change on a companywide basis. Let us examine WABCO's approach and note in what ways it may be improved to facilitate even further the objectives of innovation management that I recommended earlier.

First, there is companywide acceptance of the attitude expressed by Edward J. Greene, vice president of planning and marketing, that: "If something is worth doing and if it is important or urgent that it be done, it is worthwhile to designate someone to see to it that it is done properly." **(2)**

Implicitly, WABCO is convinced that an informal or "hit-or-miss" attitude towards the company's future is unacceptable. A second aspect of WABCO's program is that planning (for innovation) is done within the marketing department, and therefore places greatest emphasis upon product innovations. A third and most significant aspect of this company's innovation planning is that the personnel in this agency are not designated as experts. Thus they do not regard themselves as responsible for doing the innovating; rather, they are committed to see that this is done by managers throughout the company.

The most important features of the WABCO program are as follows: the development of sound procedures to be used throughout the company; the use of full-time personnel; and achieving the enthusiastic participation of key people to foster the planning of innovation.

The two ways in which this highly successful program may be improved are by broadening its base to include all functional areas of the enterprise under the department's wing, and by adding to the planning department efforts to include more facets of innovating; that is, to make the program more extensive (innovation covering more company activities) and more intensive (a rigorous application of the innovative process). WABCO's success is attributable to the centralized approach towards innovation.

Though I have recommended that they go even further in that direction, it must be pointed out that a great many companies reject *any* degree of centralization of planned change.

One of these companies is General Electric, where the stress is upon encouraging operating executives to plan changes as part of their regular work and without the assistance of a central guiding and coordinating agency (such as WABCO has). As GE's George L. Chamberlin states: "We don't want a planning group off to one side. We have had experience that planning by live people is most efficient where the subject of the plan is within the line department."

However, it should be pointed out that though WABCO's approach to planning of innovation is more organized, there is absolutely complete agreement with General Electric that the actual planning should be done by the line manager.

Somewhere in between WABCO's emphasis that a full-time department coordinate and "see to it" that the line manager plans and the GE emphasis upon complete self-direction by the line manager is the committee setup of the Cleveland Electric Illuminating Company. The committee consists of operating officers who exchange top-level information and stimulate planning on a variety of problems confronting top management. Clearly, this is *not* a full-time agency and yet there is more centralized effort to innovate than was described by Chamberlin of General Electric.

As evidence of the success of a centrally coordinated innovation program, the president of the E. P. Hauserman Company makes this claim for the superiority of his company's relatively recent program over a looser program in effect previously: "We have brought out more innovations in the current year than we had in the previous five years."

Such revelations are clear proof of the value of placing a greater emphasis upon a well-coordinated companywide innovation program. Nonetheless, in many companies with no sign whatsoever of management encouragement of innovation, ridiculous claims are made that "innovation goes on all the time." These preposterous statements are made in spite of the fact that the company has no organization unit involved in innovation, no procedure for it, no staff, no means of appraising the success of innovation, and absolutely no records of innovations that have been implemented.

It is interesting to note that the traditional corporate planning staff has some of the earmarks of my innovation management department. However, there are a number of important distinctions that are to be found in the innovation management department I am advocating which are not found in the corporate planning activity. These include the following:

1. The innovation department would be committed to motivating *all* company personnel to participate in fostering innovation, either as innovators or in supporting the innovative ideas of others.
2. The innovation department would have persons skilled in evaluating innovation proposals and in helping to coordinate innovation programs, either on a companywide basis or in single areas of the company.

Since the corporate planning staff is concerned with guiding the future growth and prosperity of the firm, it is a "natural" to assume the additional responsibilities of an innovation management department. It can thus expand its activities to include fostering innovations that may tend to "guarantee" the company's future.

**The philosophy and goals of the innovation department.**    An essential part of the innovation management department's work—indeed, basic to its very existence—would be the clarification of its philosophy and goals. As implied throughout the previous discussion, this agency should have as its primary goals (1) inspiring persons throughout the company to innovate and (2) guiding and coordinating the development and implementation of the innovation proposals. This department would *not* be constituted to be the source of innovation, and therefore would not be staffed by experts on change. The purpose of this group would be to effectively exploit the improvement ideas created by others. Its aim is to improve the *process* of innovation, so that more and better administrative and technological innovations are forthcoming.

The underlying philosophy of the innovation management group should be to encourage in others a challenge of the status quo. This attitude should be pervasive and continuous, whether the company is faced with "belt tightening" or is in a period of economic good fortune. As a matter of fact, the danger sign, complacency—the seed of eventual decline—is quite likely to arise during a period of profitable operation. It is desirable to examine and criticize company activities during a period of prosperity to determine the reasons for success, as well as to find ways of improving company practices, products, and services. Only in this way will success *follow* upon success. It is too late for innovation to start when the decline in company fortunes has begun.

## The Duties of the Innovation Management Department

It is essential to clearly define the tasks of the department that will direct company innovation. These duties are *not* designed to generate innovation from the department itself, but rather, to see to it that innovating takes place in the company. This is analogous to what Shaffir has defined as a catalytic agent. In his case, his frame of reference is the planning function which, as he says, "establishes the system and discipline to make planning function successfully." **(3)**

Indeed, it is Shaffir's outline for the duties of the corporate planning staff that has formed the basis for the activities that might be performed by the central innovation department:

1. Developing corporate innovation goals as an outgrowth of company goals.
2. Educating, stimulating, and counseling managers on every level to undertake innovations in their departments.
3. Reviewing divisional and department proposals for innovation.
4. Combining and integrating innovation programs from various sources, where appropriate.

5. Providing study of the innovation for feasibility, profit potential, and other advice.
6. Coordinating the efforts of multiple departments when an innovation affects them both, or all.
7. Providing specialized assistance in the department itself to help them in clarifying innovations.
8. Undertaking innovations that are outside the scope of every department.
9. Acting as a consultant to top management in evaluating innovation proposals.
10. Measuring the innovation performance of departments and their managers.

***Relationship of innovation department to other activities.*** It is vital to identify the place of the innovation department with regard to other company activities. Once more Shaffir's guidelines for corporate planning are helpful in assigning a role to the innovation department. To begin with, the department should report to top management because it *must* concern itself with the total corporate innovating effort. Moreover, it cannot be an effective force in stimulating effort by other departments unless it is identified with the top level.

As a staff group reporting to the president or executive vice president, the innovation department should bear an operating relationship to all divisions and departments. The selection of the place of the department should also give full weight to the executive to whom it reports, for, "Location can be determined by looking at the organization chart; status can be found only from the reaction of key people."

The relations with other divisions and departments should be carefully thought out so as to define the role and duties of the innovation department. Suspicions and even distrust must be allayed in terms of the duties pursued and in the *way* they are fulfilled.

## Organization Approaches that Facilitate Innovation

To facilitate effective operation of the innovation department, it is appropriate to examine approaches in organizing the effort of *other* groups in the company. There are some new approaches to organization that can more effectively use the efforts of people to enhance innovation. In this regard there are two issues: first, organizing the entire company structure to facilitate innovation; and second, organizing the efforts of those people directly engaged in innovating.

**Company organization for innovating.**   There have been studies recently of major revisions in organization structures that would array activities to achieve greater results from innovating. One such proposal has been developed by Gerald Fisch. **(4)**

His *functional team concept* is designed to replace the traditional line and staff, which he considers an arbitrary division of functions. Instead, he advocates the division of activities into three major areas: resources (human, material, and financial); operations (making, marketing, and distributing); and relations (all groups dealing with the company). In this way, innovative ideas can more readily be assessed and, after evaluation, implemented. Moreover, the implementation of an innovation (for example, a product) deals with the entire process from conception to operation under the functional team: "The logical flow begins with a product idea and ends with a finished, workable product that has been market-tested and that can be made at a reasonable cost and sold at a profit." In other words, this whole sequence will take place under a single major organization unit, the operations division.

***Organizing for specific innovation—the innovation team.***   The basic unit of organizing to implement a specific innovation that is here advocated may be called the innovation team. The approach of program management was developed in the defense industry to achieve stability of personnel, and yet to attain flexibility in moving from completion of one project to work on another. It is designed to overcome the shortcomings of traditional organizational approaches to innovating. Even decentralization and creating separate divisions to meet changing conditions must cope with the demands of managing innovations. These approaches only further strain the demands in coordinating many skills. On the other hand, program management involves building a *team* drawn from various disciplines and relating these interests and skills to achieve the most economical and speedy results of innovation.

The simplest form of project organization, by all odds, is to pull the people concerned away from all other duties to create a team or task force dedicated solely to the particular program. Hertz of

McKinsey & Company believes the trend is growing in the direction of the team concept that he calls "the matrix approach," which permits a close exchange of information, benefits specialists, and develops generalists. Furthermore, specialists can work on several projects at one time, and despite the fact that a man winds up having several bosses, the flexibility apparently pays off handsomely. **(5)**

One use of the team approach uses profit goals to single out innovation projects. Such an approach has proved extremely effective at Proctor and Gamble, General Electric, and other top companies. In essence, it is a group headed by a top-flight man within a corporation, which works closely with top management.

The major distinction between the "profit team" and the "innovation team" is that the profit team concentrates on a crash program, usually confined to a given operation area. As applied at one division of General Electric, the team looked for ways to "utilize material more effectively, to develop new and lower cost materials, to reduce the manhours needed to build and test motors and generators and to develop better methods, equipment, processes and sheer organization in the entire department." In short—a concentrated application of technological and administrative innovation.

The master in the profit team approach is Proctor and Gamble. They have developed excellent guidelines for operation of the profit team. Underlying their use, however, should be the determination *first* of, What is the organization's ability to tolerate change?

The Proctor and Gamble profit team guidelines are:

1. Make sure that groups have surveyed all potential for profit in their area.
2. Plan to use your entire management group.
3. Be sure goals are established.
4. Be sure some person is assigned to give the program continuing follow-up and coordination.
5. Keep the responsibility for success where it belongs—on the line organization.
6. Take positive stage to provide recognition. **(6)**

More and more we are realizing that the most vital force of organization is not its structure but its spirit. This has been reenforced by research on organizational behavior.

To achieve effective organization of a company innovation it is also necessary to develop an attitude or spirit among company employees that leads to a company designation of "innovative organization."

There is some dispute as to whether there is a simple way to categorize organizations as innovative types. Some companies that employ great effort at innovation often show only meager results. Nonetheless, there seem to be certain conditions which *do* make for an innovative organization and assure that this kind of company *will* enjoy greater success in innovating.

Becker crystallizes what an innovative organization is like. He indicates that an organization which seeks to stimulate innovation should be structured to:

(1) Encourage the diffusion of ideas by diversifying an individual's tasks and his contacts with others; (2) use its slack to reward innovation, or behavior that leads to innovation; (3) centralize to be better able to install the innovation and at the same time decentralize to produce the innovation; (4) provide for individual and job security; (5) while doing all this, make certain the organization's goals are being attained. **(7)**

## Elements of Strategy for Innovating Change

A vital element in successful innovating is an understanding and proper use of strategy in organizing and implementing the innovation. The issue of strategy is usually discussed behind closed doors, for its connotation is that it is devious. Properly approached and morally supported, strategic considerations form a perfectly valid practice of a manager's function. Many times, the use of strategy comes closest to the *essence* of managing.

The attempt by the manager to determine his own posture is fundamental to developing sound strategy for managing innovation. Positive responses to these questions will help him achieve this:

Are we personally receptive to new ideas? Have we devised some type of program whereby we are systematically made aware of new ideas or new approaches initiated outside the company? Do we encourage innovation? Are we truly effective in implementing ideas? And finally, are we taking measures to ensure personal knowledge of the valid applications of the various specialized techniques now prevalent in the management field?

Part of the problem over strategy is the vagueness of its meaning. It is often, for example, confused with tactics. The difference is a matter of scope: "strategy expressed the more general and larger concept; whereas tactics conveyed the idea of the more specific and smaller." Another view is that strategy is: "the general outline of the ways of achieving certain goals." Game theory has given us a fuller understanding of strategy, especially in such treatments as Williams' *Compleat Strategyst*.

Using the concept of game theory to emphasize strategy, Hardwick views the word strategy as signifying: "the general concept and salient aspects of gamemanship as an administrative course designed to bring success." **(8)**

**Strategy for implementing change.**    It is essential to decide which strategy is appropriate for a particular situation and then use it. A number of strategies are revealed by Hardwick and Landuyt that are appropriate for varying conditions of change. They provide three categories of strategies, including those for: overcoming precedent, overcoming opposition, and selecting the appropriate opportunity.

In *overcoming precedent* the strategies are:

1. Show drastic changes to exist in circumstances.
2. Demonstrate to administration that there is a better way of doing the thing in question.
3. Make the new plan appear as similar as truth will permit to the existing plan or other accepted norms of operation.
4. Give as much as honorably possible, if not all, of the credit for the new idea to those who support precedent.
5. Show, when appropriate, that competitors, particularly the effective ones, are planning for change or actually taking new steps.
6. Plan for gradual change.
7. Announce the new plan as a completely revolutionary idea when grounds exist for so describing it.

Some strategy to forestall or *overcome opposition* may include, "trust more to subordinates." All the ingenuity in the world is of little use compared to the power of morality reflected in past dealings with associates.

A further strategy consideration is in selecting the *appropriate opportunity* for making the change. The components of opportunity selection are: the critical moment, possession of adequate power, the availability of means of exploitation; absence of effective resistance, and the possibility of gain.

A particularly noteworthy consideration is that occasionally the use of the *fait accompli* strategy of change may prove effective. It is "sometimes more effective to introduce the changed operation first, before attempting to bring about the desired attitude change." However, Watson and Glaser suggest that, for the most part, it would be well to consider the following steps in making a change:

1. Make clear the needs for change or provide a climate in which others feel free to identify such needs.
2. Permit, encourage, and secure relevant group participation in clarifying and expanding the concept of these needs.
3. State the objectives to be achieved.
4. Establish broad guidelines for achieving the objectives.
5. Leave the details of change planning to the parts of the organization that will be affected by the change and must implement the plan.
6. Indicate the benefits or renewals to individuals and to the group expected as a result of successful change.
7. Materialize the benefits or rewards: i.e., keep promises.

The two ingredients that are necessary to support the innovation strategies conceived and applied are: high management and supervisor capability in handling the change; and clear and open communication between all persons and all levels in the organizing of innovation.

# PART III

# Human Problems
# of Innovating

# CHAPTER 12

# RESISTANCE TO INNOVATION

A key aspect of the process of innovating is the recognition that successful implementation of an innovation is dependent upon overcoming many obstacles to its installation. The most significant obstacle facing the manager is in the form of resistance to the change by people in the organization. The nature and intensity of this resistance may vary from company to company. We shall examine how and why this develops to get some insight into how resistance can obstruct change, as a prelude to removing the obstruction.

In the opinion of a leading authority on the problems of change, Paul R. Lawrence, "One of the most baffling and recalcitrant of the problems which business executives face is employee resistance to change." (1) The statement labels resistance—though perhaps unintentionally—as a "disease" restricted to employees only. *All* company personnel, as a matter of fact, express resistance to a change occasionally, regardless of their roles. Failure to appreciate this is one reason for difficulties over resistance.

Instead, by trying to understand this issue a manager can develop positive steps towards change that may prevent the appearance of resistance, or at least minimize its influence.

## Background of Resistance to Change

The background of resistance to change is sprinkled with all kinds of incidents, some amusing and many replete with tragic events. The sabotage at the textile mills of England is but one form of worker resistance to massive and widespread change. Far less noted by historians has been the kind of conflict which persisted for decades during the industrial expansion of the late 19th century in this country. The conflicts were usually over the amount of work to be performed, and pitted individuals and groups of workers against works managers. This was during a period when production quotas became a common device for supervising workers' efforts. This piece-rate system was, in effect, a carry-over from the period when work was performed in the home, before factory days.

It was upon this scene, sprinkled with conflict and resistance against production standards, that Frederick Taylor appeared. The heart of his attempts to alleviate these conflicts and eliminate re-striction on work was not time study or scientific management. Rather, it was his advocacy of a "mental revolution" which required that managers recognize their common interest in improving pro-duction output. He felt that where this was achieved, the worker benefited through higher wages while, at the same time, the com-pany benefited through lower labor costs and higher profits. In spite of Taylor's efforts, no significant progress was made in eliminating restriction of production and outright resistance to changes.

There were continued examples of the difficulties in overcoming resistance. What is interesting to note is that resistance to change was as prevalent, if not more so, in the upper levels of organization as in the lower levels. One of the most dramatic examples of this condition is found in Morrison's delightful account of how difficult it was for a junior officer in the American Navy to persuade his superiors to adopt improved gun firing techniques. **(2)**

It is of particular interest to note that in this case it was someone from the low echelon who was trying to persuade the "top brass" to adopt an amazingly successful technique for all the ships in the Navy. Indeed, it was only by going outside the organization—to President Theodore Roosevelt—that the change was actually made. Subsequently, we shall examine this and other examples of resist-ance to change, at high as well as low levels of the organization, to determine their causes.

This brief review of some of the highlights and trends in resist-ance to change reveals that through the centuries whole societies, as well as individuals and small groups, resisted the adoption of change in a variety of ways and with varying intensity. Today, in our society, the manager should be particularly sensitive to the possibility of the appearance of resistance to innovation. The issue is unusually critical because the accelerating rate of change will bring increasing demands for the swifter adoption of innovations, with economic survival in the balance.

Understanding the existence of resistance as a *possible* accompaniment of change should not lead to the conclusion that it will appear. Rather, by at least remaining alert to it the manager can more fully consider its implications. Indeed, he can make it one of the factors worthy of study as he prepares the program for implementing an innovation.

## Kinds of Change

Before examining some aspects of how and why people resist change, it is appropriate to take note of the gamut of changes that may occur to alter the status quo in a company. In its broadest sense, any kind of change tends to have an unbalancing effect upon the equilibrium of the organization.

**Work methods changes.** The most common kind of change that confronts a manager is that involved in any adjustment or revision of the method of performing a job. It generally is found to be the change that evokes the most immediate reaction by the persons involved and is the largest cause of resistance, since it goes deepest in affecting a person's daily routine.

**Changes in work standards.** At one time it was commonplace for a change in work standards to spark open hostility. Occasionally this happens today. Very often it is centered in a dispute over whether the new standard requires greater effort from the worker. Some of the extreme forms of reaction to this type of change have included violence.

**Economic changes.** Often ignored in studying changes that induce resistance are those brought about by economic changes that have been brought on by fluctuations in the economic fortunes of a particular company or industry. These economic turns, either down or up, may lead to expanding or contracting operations. Whether they materialize or not, there may be a threat of layoffs. Other adjustments the company may make may induce resistance by employees.

**Technological change.**    The form of change that has had the greatest historical significance, and also generated a great deal of resistance, is change in technology—of product or process. Changes that have occurred in various regions of our country have had significant impact on communities and areas, particularly in shifts from an agrarian to an industrial economy and in the industry shifts from the north to the south.

**Changes in policies and procedures.**    A type of change that, on the surface, seems to be a rather tepid one is a change in policy and/or procedure. And yet, these changes can prove rather unsettling and may generate a good deal of resistance. It may be a change in pension policy, which affects employee interest, or some budgeting procedure, which may produce an adverse reaction.

**Personnel shifts.**    Replacements, transfers, reassignments, layoffs, or dismissals are the kinds of changes that have a lasting effect upon people. Another kind of personnel shift, such as a shakeup in top management, can have a reverberating effect, even though most people have not been directly affected. It may grow out of a merger, purchase, or internal battle for control, and the scars of these massive changes may filter down to many people and cause doubts about future operating conditions. Another type of personnel shift that can have a marked effect upon a group is the transfer of a single employee to that group. The adjustments that may be made necessary in this situation can be as upsetting as for more widespread shifts in personnel. Another kind of personnel change that can lead to intense repercussions is the introduction of a new supervisor into a work group. A lot will depend upon the relationship with the previous supervisor: if it was negative, the group may welcome the change; if not, they may resent it.

**Organizational changes.**    Changes in organization structure require varying adjustments by people in the organization. In addition, these changes almost always are accompanied by personnel changes, changes in functions, creation or elimination of activities, and an increase or decrease of a department's status. It is this kind of change that may directly involve only a single department and yet affect all others. Moreover, the dislocations can persist for some time, particularly if the former structure was a long-standing one.

**Status and social change.**   Some changes may appear totally innocuous in size and scope, and yet the change may actually induce a social change or one involving shifts in status. Managers may be completely unaware of the rigidity of the "informal organization" and the social relations within a work group. Indeed, there may be no deliberate attempt at disrupting them. However, these kinds of change have a dramatic impact upon people. As Roethlisberger has said:

Any person who has achieved a certain rank in the prestige scale regards anything, real or imaginary, which tends to alter his status adversely as something unfair and unjust. It can be seen that any move on the part of the company may alter the existing social equilibrium to which the employee has grown accustomed, and by means of which his status is defined. (3)

**Change in company or department location.**   A most unsettling experience for most company personnel occurs when there is a physical change in the location of department or company. In some cases it may mean a transfer to another locale; but even where this doesn't occur, a move can be very upsetting. Even shifts of company or department facilities to the same floor in a building can cause amazing reactions. In addition, very often a new location represents a loss in status or convenience for employees and this may induce adverse reactions.

**Physical environment changes.**   There are also the kind of changes that alter the physical surroundings of the work setting. The change in a fixture, furniture, lighting, air conditioning, or redecorating the area may set off negative reactions. This is often deeply resented by managers when the changes are decided improvements that represent a considerable investment. Nonetheless, it is wise to remain sensitive to *any* unsettling influence, even though it is disconcerting to notice adverse reactions to improved work environment.

## The Groups Involved in Change

An important condition for examining resistance to change is to note the different groups that are a party to the change. From this we can learn what each group typically considers its role in the change and how they may shift these roles depending upon how the change affects them. What is important to recognize is that *any* or *all* of these groups may, at any time, become the seat of resistance to change. Typically there are four groups involved in a change, including: employees, staff specialists, managers, and supervisors (first line).

As I have found in an earlier study of resistance problems:

. . . it is not only the "production" employees whose attitude may affect the success of the installation, but any of the three other groups as well—managers, methods analysts, and supervisors. **(4)**

Let us examine the characteristics and the role of each of these groups more closely.

*Empoyees.*    The category called "employees" is distinguished from other company personnel by their position as the lowest level of workers. Further, their job description includes no supervisory duties and thus they are responsible only for performing their own tasks.

*Staff specialists.*    The staff specialist usually fills the role, with regard to innovating, of the full-time change administrator, whether he is a company employee or a consultant. He has absolutely no line authority and his title may include any of the following: methods analyst, project engineer, systems engineer, or industrial engineer. Though he may not have originated the innovation, he will usually have some role in programming its implementation. He may thus acquire a "proprietary" interest in the change.

*Managers.*    This group includes middle as well as upper level managers. It will include managers whose departments are to be changed as the result of their own initiative, and managers whose departments are changed because of an innovation developed "outside" the department. Among this group will also be managers who are authorized to approve the implementation of the change.

*Supervisors.*    Supervisors should clearly be distinguished from the manager group. Certainly they may be considered members of management, but this group has the unique management task of directing the work of lowest level employees. The supervisors often are the key group in the change, for they may be responsible for the actual implementation of the details of the innovation. They are also in a key position because they are first to learn of any adverse reaction to the change on the part of the employees. Moreover, their own attitudes toward the change may be directly transmitted to the work group around them.

**Nature of resistance to change.**    Before examining some expressions of resistance, let's pinpoint what resistance is. According to Zander, resistance is an expression of "behavior which is intended to protect an individual from the effects of real or imagined change." **(5)** A further point that Zander stresses is that mere opposition to change does not mean what we have characterized as resistance to change. For example, some opposition to change or criticism of it may represent sound and justifiable reasons. It may reflect opposition to the substance of the change or to the means of implementing it. Indeed, this opposition may be combined with specific suggestions that would tend to overcome the shortcomings that were opposed. For the tendency to be labeled as resistance to change, "The behavior must be attempting to protect the person against the consequences of the change." **(6)** In other words, does it represent a reaction in terms of, How does it affect me?

For further understanding of the nature of resistance to change it is well to reflect on the general conditions which seem to underlie the development of resistance. Such underlying general conditions may include the state of the nation's economy (whether it is expanding, contracting, or stable)—a significant condition which may affect a person's attitude towards a specific change. Also, whether the period is one of national or local crisis will have a bearing on whether resistance tends to develop against change. The social and political climate may also have a distinct bearing upon the reaction towards change. As Bright has pointed out,

A striking example was the change in public attitudes towards education, scientific research, development, and government support of such work after Sputnik I was launched in October, 1957. **(7)**

## Forms of Resistance

With resistance identified as attempts at self-protection against the effects of change, it is fascinating to note the different ways people express resistance. Zander feels that the general form resistance takes is an expression of hostility. This may be revealed as aggression against "the change itself or against the administrator.

What is done depends on how the person can safely resist without further endangering himself in the situation." **(8)**

**1. Forms of resistance found in all groups.**  There are some expressions of resistance that may appear as readily in any of the four groups (managers, employees, staff specialists, and supervisors). They simply reflect reactions of any individual who is required to make an adjustment to a change that confronts him. In the sense that most changes are generally directed towards a first-line employee, these forms of resistance are, perhaps, more likely to appear among the employee group.

Zander identifies these forms of resistance or "symptoms of resistance" as

. . . sloppy effort; fawning submissiveness which is a hybrid of apple polishing and apathy. It can occur by lowering the level of aspiration to an inefficient degree, discouragement, or the development of unhappy cliques and outspoken factions. **(9)**

In their classic study of resistance to change, Coch and French describe expressions of resistance as they found it:

This resistance expressed itself in several ways, such as grievances about the piece rates that went with the new methods, high turnover, very low efficiency, restriction of output and marked aggression against management. **(10)**

Of particular note were the expressions of resistance to changes in personnel shifts to which Coch and French commented:

In addition to resentment against management for transferring them, the employees typically show feelings of frustration, loss of hope of ever regaining their former level of production and status in the factory, feelings of failure and a very low level of aspiration. **(11)**

Davis has developed a particularly notable view of the way people express their resistance to change by noting that many times individual expressions of resistance are channeled into social action which provokes some group reaction (i.e., a strike) to individual forms of resistance. Some forms of individual expressions of resistance to change he has observed include, "Absenteeism, strike, demands, sullenness, and harder work." **(12)**

Lawrence reveals his finds on the forms that resistance to change takes as including:

Persistent reduction in output, increase in the number of "quits" and requests for transfer, chronic quarrels, sullen hostility, wildcat or slowdown strikes and, of course, the expression of a lot of pseudo-logical reasons why the change will not work. **(13)**

**2. *Forms of resistance by managers.*** It is vital to recognize that a significant human barrier to successful innovation sometimes arises in the form of resistance by managers. In identifying this source of resistance I have grouped all persons with managerial responsibilities, including top-level managers and first-line supervisors. It should be recognized that resistance by managers can have a far greater impact than on the employee level. One interesting example of the form resistance may take when expressed at managerial levels is revealed in the resistance by Navy "top brass" to gunnery innovations. The resistance to the innovation was described as occurring in three stages: "First stage: no response; second stage: rebuttal; and the final stage: name calling." **(14)**

In my own experience I have discovered managerial resistance to change expressed in a variety of ways. Following are some profiles I have observed of the "types" of managers and the form of resistance they express. **(15)**

THE NEGATIVE VIEW. One of the most common forms of resistance is found in managers who inevitably take a negative view of any change that is proposed. As soon as a change is suggested, this type of manager is ready to express his resentment and apprehensions, pointing out all the reasons why it won't work and the shortcomings of the plan. If the plan is adopted in spite of his protests, he can easily destroy its prospective advantages by taking a "Look what we've been saddled with now" attitude—and transmitting it to his subordinates.

There are times, of course, when an essentially negative and fault-finding attitude can be useful in forcing proponents of a change to question their assumptions, check their facts, and strengthen the weak points in their proposal. This was the case in an independent telephone company which transferred its customer billing to tabulator equipment and then to a computer, over the protests of one of the company's line managers. "The main problem," the manager felt, was that, "the methods people had ideas on how the system should go, and we were always explaining how *we* thought it should go." The net result of this running battle, however, was that the manager's ideas were considered and, when appropriate, utilized, so that the final installation was an excellent one.

In many cases, however, the hypercritical executive often has no solid basis to his objections, and his cynicism and fault-finding can be seriously disruptive to the organization. In any event, a little bit of this goes a long way.

UNCONSCIOUS DISSENSION.    Perhaps the opposite of this kind of resistance to change is an attitude that seems on the surface quite cooperative, but can destroy the company's chances of successfully installing a change. This is the "organization man" kind of unquestioning acceptance of everything that comes from on high. Managers with this view of change feel compelled to bury any doubts or misgivings about the workability or value of the proposed plan, even to the extent that they may not even be aware of their own opposition to it.

In a southern commercial bank whose records were being changed from a completely manual system to a punched-card system, the head of one department submerged his displeasure, even though he lacked confidence in tab record keeping as compared with visual means and was unsatisfied with the fact that the old system was to be maintained for an indefinite period while the new one was being installed, thus adding to the department's work load. When questioned, he grudgingly admitted that he was "not sold completely on the usefulness of machine accounting," but he went along with the plan with obvious lack of enthusiasm until its almost inevitable failure.

Does this kind of hidden resistance spring from an unconscious desire to let an unwanted change come to grief? No one can be sure, but certainly it does no one—including the company—any good. Indeed, in this case, it was a significant factor in the collapse of the installation.

APATHY AND INDIFFERENCE.    Another essentially hidden kind of resistance is exemplified in the kind of manager who sees his role as merely implementing whatever changes are presented to him by top management or a staff group. Despite the fact that he has no strong feelings either for or against the change, his indifferent attitude can be as fatal to the change as outright defiance, since it is easily transmitted to his subordinates, thus all but dooming the plan before it even gets off the ground. Moreover, an executive with this attitude, who takes the position that "he just works here" and has no responsibility for the success of any methods or procedures, is extremely unlikely to take steps to anticipate any possible difficulties that may arise during the installation of a change. Obviously, then, the indifferent manager who refuses to commit his energies to the successful implementation of changes frequently causes them to fail by default.

FREE TRANSLATION.    Another attitude that may cause difficulty is the kind of manager who does not resist change so much as he bends it to his own purposes and ideas. Since he is the one most familiar with his department and its personnel, he feels justified in making changes in his own way, without regard for the overall plans of top management. There are cases, of course, when this freewheeling approach to change can work well—usually when the manager is intelligent and capable, and the original plan is flexible enough to withstand the variations of content and application to which it is subjected. Even then, however, it would be far better to discuss the "variations" with higher management; then, if they prove desirable, they can be incorporated into the plan and coordinated with other aspects of the operation.

In many cases, a manager's improvisations lead to serious difficulties, especially when the change cuts across departmental lines. This was clearly demonstrated in one company where a manager, told that his department would be eliminated in gradual stages, took it upon himself to arrange his employees' transfers in his own way. From time to time, employees who became in excess were to be transferred to the tab department, the fastest growing in the organization. The department head, however, "adjusted" the transfers to suit himself, selecting the poorest employees for transfer and retaining the most efficient until the bitter end. Unfortunately, this "variation" made the better workers subordinate to their less capable colleagues when they were finally transferred to the tab department. Obviously, the net result when the change was completed was dissatisfaction on the part of the workers and a less efficient organization.

THE PET PROJECT ATTITUDE.    But not all the obstacles to change come from those who resist change, whether overtly, covertly or unconsciously. On the other side of the coin there are habits of thought and action on the part of *proponents* of change that can also hinder its effective introduction.

One of the most frequently encountered of these roadblocks is the attitude of the manager who has formulated the plans for a change—or at least has been in on the planning of the change from the beginning—of what might be called the "pet project" attitude. Under some circumstances it can be a big help in introducing a change, since the manager involved not only believes deeply in the wisdom of the change, but usually identifies himself so strongly with its success that he expends unusual amounts of energy to gain acceptance to his plan. Ironically, though, his zeal may create difficulties that would not otherwise arise. He may be so determined to have his pet ideas accepted that he becomes unduly sensitive to criticism of his plan and thus overlooks helpful suggestions. Moreover, his "push" tactics may engender resentment on the part of the people who will be taking part in the change, and thereby create resistance to the entire plan.

THE AUTHORITARIAN APPROACH.    Another attitude found among the proponents of change might be called the authoritarian approach. This attitude is not uncommon among the upper echelons of management; everyone has probably known at least one executive who believed in change by fiat and, by his apparently (or really) arbitrary pronouncements, created unnecessary difficulties for what might have been a useful and easily accomplished change.

Sometimes an officer or senior executive will learn of a new piece of equipment, a new technique, or a new method of doing a job and will summarily demand its introduction into the organization. At times, the change so demanded is entirely inappropriate to the company's needs; at other times, the change is desirable in itself, but it can be misunderstood, resented, or resisted if the executive hasn't taken time to prepare his subordinates and win their acceptance.

An example of this attitude appeared in a New England firm that was preparing to install a computer. One highly placed officer saw a computer demonstration and came away so impressed that he ordered the changeover date to be advanced two months. Although a considerable amount of preparation had already been made, this unreasonable pressure created such havoc that for a time the entire installation was in serious danger of collapse. In this case, the executive abused the authority of his position by imposing his will; despite his lack of capacity in the area, he failed to distinguish between authority of position and authority of knowledge.

**3. Forms of staff specialist resistance.**   It may seem incongruous for the change agent (staff specialist) to become "contaminated" by resistance to change. However, as a human being who has become involved in an emotionally charged situation, the staff specialist may also give vent to his feelings towards the change in a negative manner. It is more likely, however, that in the case of the staff specialist the form of resistance will be expressed by erecting barriers to the ideas of *others* regarding the change. Nonetheless, this attitude seriously endangers the installation of change. As Lawrence has noted:

> All too frequently we see staff specialists who bring to their work certain blind spots that get them into trouble when they initiate change with operating people. When he goes to some group of operating people to introduce change, his very identification with his ideas tends to make him unreceptive to any suggestions for modification. **(16)**

## Why People Resist Change

After exploring the nature of resistance as well as its forms and the groups that express it, let us examine, simply—Why? Most of us, from experience or observation, certainly have some opinions as to why people resist change. Let us look deeper, however, to learn how varied these reasons may be and how readily resistance may flare up. This is a necessary step before trying to develop methods of preventing resistance (to be explored in the next two chapters).

To begin with, let's examine two commentaries on range of causes for resistance. One of them is drawn from my own study and reveals that some of the causes for resistance were:

1. Inept approach of methods analysts.
2. Personnel shortage during implementation.
3. Failure to justify reasons for the change.
4. Top management pressure for fast installation of the change.
5. Lack of participation by supervisors and key employees.
6. Poor planning for transfers of personnel.

7. Insufficient guidance of people affected by the change.
8. Lack of enthusiasm for the change by managers and supervisors which affected employees.
9. Lack of advance information on the change. **(17)**

The composite that Davis has prepared on the causes of resistance is interesting because of his classification of resistance to change under the three broad headings of economic reasons, personal reasons, and social reasons. His summary of why people resist change is:

1. *Economic reasons*
   Fears technological unemployment.
   Fears reduced hours.
   Fears demotion and reduced wages.
   Fears speedup and reduced incentive wages.
2. *Personal reasons*
   Resents implied criticism that present method is inadequate.
   Fears that his skill, and personal pride in it, will be reduced.
   Expects greater specialization, resulting in boredom, monotony, and decreased sense of worthwhileness.
   Dislikes effort required to relearn.
   Fears harder work will be required.
   Resists change because he doesn't understand it.
3. *Social reasons*
   Dislikes making new social adjustments.
   Dislikes breaking present social ties.
   Fears the new social situation will bring reduced satisfaction.
   Dislikes outside interference and/or some of the persons making the change.
   Resents lack of participation in setting up the change.
   Visualizes the change as mostly benefitting the company, rather than him, his fellow workers, or the general public. **(18)**

Saltonstall adds, to the above categories of reasons, technical causes of resistance. He gives an example of the technical barrier that may induce resistance by showing that changes

   . . . are likely to be explained in technical language and supported by facts and statistics that management is familiar with. However, when the engineer tries to explain his proposals to a union committee or to the work group affected, his problem is fundamentally different. **(19)**

Some highlights of the causes of resistance that Boyd has found include, economic loss, emotional shock, and implied criticism. He also points out that the history of past changes in the company is extremely important as "unfortunate experiences with past changes of a similar nature have made people distrustful, suspicious, or even angry." **(20)**

Morrison's analysis of Navy resistance to change revealed three reasons, namely:

. . . honest disbelief in the dramatic but substantial claims of the new process; protection of the existing devices and instruments with which they identified themselves; and maintenance of the existing society with which they were identified." **(21)**

According to Lawrence, one of the most important reasons that people resist change is caused by the attitude of the person making the change, usually a staff specialist. Indeed, Lawrence feels that resistance is not to the *change* itself, but to the way it is presented and the social effects it will have. He considers the staff specialist as the key to the whole question of resistance. As an example of how the employee resists the social change and *not* the technical fact of change, he shows the approach of one staff specialist:

The new engineer was introducing not only a technical change, but also a change in the operator's customary way of relating herself to others in the organization. By his brusque manner and by his lack of any explanation, he led the operator to fear that her usual work relationships were being changed. And she just did not like the new way she was being treated. **(22)**

Finally, in our review of the reasons why people resist change, Zander has identified conditions that are conducive to resistance to change:

1. Resistance can be expected if the nature of the change is not made clear.
2. Different people will see different meanings in the proposed change.
3. Resistance can be expected when those influenced are caught in a job

between strong forces pushing them to make the change and strong forces deterring them against making the change.

4. Resistance may be expected if the change is made on personal grounds rather than impersonal requirements or sanctions.
5. Resistance may be expected to the degree that the persons influenced by the change have pressure put upon them to make it.
6. Resistance may be expected if the change ignores the already established institutions in the group. **(23)**

# CHAPTER 13

# THE INDIVIDUAL EMPLOYEE AND HIS ADJUSTMENT TO CHANGE

This chapter will deal with the steps *managers* may take to facilitate the individual employee's adjustment to change. It will explore plans of eliminating and preventing resistance to change or minimizing its influence should it appear. The net objective is to develop an understanding of how to remove one of the most trying and costly obstacles to successful innovation.

It should be understood that facilitating the *individual's* adjustment to change is but one of two approaches in overcoming resistance. The other approach is to grasp the issues involved in organized group resistance to change. On this level, overcoming resistance requires joint labor-management exploration of the problems leading to resistance and of solutions to it. The results of this effort are usually incorporated in a labor-management contract. This *joint* action approach will be explored in the next chapter.

In the present chapter we will examine the steps that management may take unilaterally to achieve individual adjustment to change. Managers should recognize, however, that the techniques underlying *both* approaches—unilateral and joint labor-management—should be employed in a *total* program of achieving adjustment to, and cooperation with, the implementation of innovations.

179

In this chapter, the following issues will be explored: an examination of two contrasting philosophies toward change (the positive versus the negative); an analysis of some of the conditions that should be developed to eliminate resistance; presentation of concepts as well as successful techniques for achieving individual adjustment to change; and finally, a review of the unique role played by communications as a catalytic agent for achieving adjustment.

## Philosophy and Attitudes towards Change

Factors that affect the appearance of resistance to change are the philosophy and attitudes toward change that pervade the company.

Two contrasting philosophies are worthy of note. On the one hand, change may be regarded by company personnel as a circumstance that automatically induces resistance among people to its installation. It is considered a phenomenon of "human nature" that people resist change and this philosophy produces an atmosphere of "fear." It is a decidedly negative view of change, or, more appropriately, of people's *reactions* to change. Expecting resistance, in itself, inevitably contributes to its appearance.

In the contrasting view of change, the phenomenon may be viewed with a touch of lightheartedness, as something the human being *naturally* accepts (after "getting used to it") and adjusts to. By presuming that people are capable of adjusting to change—the positive philosophy—we might likewise call upon "human nature" as the basis for *accepting* change. This is particularly true when we recognize that human beings have been created as self-regulating beings endowed with the capacity to adjust readily to a change in environment, be it temperature, physical pressure, or emotional stress.

Given this positive view of change the atmosphere in the company abounds in the recognition that change, in itself, is not to be feared. Moreover, if the *manner* in which the change is made is sound, there should be no difficulty in adjusting to it. By pursuing a positive attitude towards change—with top management taking the lead—it is possible to build a healthy attitude towards change throughout the company. This is the first essential step in achieving individual adjustment to change.

This point of view was emphasized at a Harvard conference on fostering technological innovation as follows:

To cope with technological change management must orient the entire organization towards acceptance of change. This requires a top management attitude of welcoming change as an opportunity and not a burden. **(1)**

## Conditions for Reducing Resistance to Change

Let us review some basic conditions that are desirable for reducing resistance to change. The rationale is that by "neutralizing" resistance a significant obstacle may be removed to facilitating adjustment to the change.

*Creating readiness for change.* In the above reference to the conference on technology there was a stress on creating or "orienting" the organization towards change.

Certainly an essential step is management's affirmation of change. However, it is naive to expect that this step alone will be enough to achieve the "readiness." In addition to this step it should be made clear that employees have, in the past, been given consideration as to their interests and needs in situations that arise. Long-standing employee sentiments of company loyalty and belief in the common goals of company and its employees are indications of the atmosphere needed. Another is the knowledge of how company personnel has fared in past changes. All this may lead to a total attitude of good will that may characterize employee reaction to innovations.

What should be developed is personnel motivation for change. It is absolutely possible to achieve the kind of readiness where people not only accept but *welcome* change.

Mann and Hoffman point out some ingredients for creating the readiness for change in their study of technological innovation in a power plant. In effect, before people can be motivated on *behalf* of change, it is necessary to create conditions which, at least, make them *ready* for its introduction. To wit:

The readiness of an organization for change—the management-union relations, the level of employees' overall satisfaction with the company, the extent to which there is mutual trust and goodwill—is an important factor in the acceptance of innovations by its personnel.

Moreover, it is suggested that managers should be aware of certain cautions if this readiness has *not* been achieved.

If the organization is not ready for change, it may be less expensive in the long run to forego the apparent advantage of an immediate conversion to automation until some attention has been paid to creating a more favorable climate.

Of significance in determining readiness for change is whether change has been present enough to become a familiar condition. When employees have been used to a stable organization, change can produce considerable apprehension when it suddenly becomes the order of the day. When, on the other hand a company has continually had to adjust to varying external demands and the workers have come to expect change, or when the workers' personalities make them eager for change, technological innovations can probably be made much more easily. **(2)**

Another aspect of achieving readiness concerns the role employees have felt in the process of change. Management may do everything to foster a climate for change, but may fail to identify any significant role for the employee as making some contribution to the change.

If members of an organization are encouraged to think about what they are doing, and how to do it better, if they feel free to take occasional time out from their immediate tasks to discuss half-formed notions of innovations with their associates, if they know that those at the next upward level of authority are eager for their creative help, suggestions for improvements are likely to flow more abundantly, and more ready cooperation in the changes is likely. **(3)**

Certainly having implanted the feeling of contribution in the employee the atmosphere for innovating will be enhanced. Some specific techniques for extending this idea will be explored later in this chapter.

***Reducing the causes of resistance.***    In the previous chapter some of the widely accepted causes for resistance to change were explored. It is these *causes* for resistance that we should try to neutralize. It is urgent to remove these irritants as a basis for achieving individual adjustment to change. Bennis *et al.* recommend that fortifications be provided against these stresses:

Considering the stressful aspects of change with its attendant uncertainties about the future and fearful fantasies about loss, successful change can only be realized, it would seem, by providing the actors in this situation with enough emotional nutriments for them to cope with the anxiety-producing situation. **(4)**

One of the desirable ways to neutralize resistance is the manner in which the innovation is presented, with emphasis on the prestige of the person proposing the idea for change.

Acceptance is governed by definable controls, and their existence may be ascertained in advance of a given introduction (of change). One set of such controls relates to the auspices of the presentation of a new idea, specifically to the personal and social characteristics of its advocate. **(5)**

A most significant contribution has been made by Zander in suggesting means of neutralizing resistance. His principle states that:

Resistance will be prevented to the degree that the changer helps the changees to develop their own understanding of the need for change and an explicit awareness of how they feel about it and what can be done about those feelings. **(6)**

Zander amplifies this principle by noting four implications it generates.

First, the administrator can use resistance as an important symptom in localizing the cause of resistance. The second implication is that there is value in allowing "blowing off steam" or catharsis. The third implication is that resistance may be less likely to occur if the group participates in making the decisions about how the change should be implemented, what the change should be like, how people might perform in the changed situation, or any other problems that are within their area of freedom to decide. The last implication Zander draws from his principle is that resistance will be less likely to develop if facts which point to the need for the change are gathered by the person who must make the change.

Some interesting conclusions have been reached by Cartwright for neutralizing causes of resistance to change. He views the groups involved in change in three ways: as a medium of change, as a target of change, and as agents of change. His recommendations grow directly out of the distinct roles and give significant insight into removing causes for resistance. **(7)**

Other means of neutralizing the *causes* of resistance include: offering guarantees of economic security against reduced earnings or dismissal; pledges of retraining and guarantees of employee rights such as promotion, tenure and pension. To strengthen these pledges machinery should be set up to solve any difficulties that arise. "Grievance systems give the employee a feeling of security that his benefits will be protected and differences about them fairly resolved." **(8)**

Another caution in change is to be careful of the techniques used to convince people to change. Avoid the use of what Feinberg calls "sure-fire" techniques that may work the first time they are used, but, because they are essentially manipulative and undemocratic, will breed resentment against the person using them. **(9)** This will make convincing people to accept change very bitter the next time.

### Achieving Individual Adjustment to Change

Let us examine some approaches which may help to achieve individual adjustment to a change that has been introduced.

***Developing overall strategy for adjustment.*** One approach in achieving adjustment is to prepare a step-by-step program for the individuals affected by the change. One such approach, by Becker and Murphy, includes the following steps recommended for changes to office automation:

1. Notify operating people in advance that a study of the possibility of automation will be made.
2. Assure those who are affected that they will be suitably placed elsewhere.
3. Inform first-level supervision as to the responsibility that results when routine clerical operations become mechanized.
4. Show understanding to those who must live with the difficult day-to-day problems.
5. Give ample credit to those whose intimate and thorough knowledge of the details of procedures permits an analysis to be completed successfully.

6. Make certain, when approaching operation people for their opinions, they understand that what they say is of valuable help to the company. **(10)**

Another example of the package approach to gaining individual adjustment is given by Boyd:

1. Get ready to sell.
2. Identify sources of help.
3. Anticipate objections.
4. Sell benefits.
5. Listen in depth.
6. Follow up. **(11)**

The danger in the canned approach is that it may become mechanical in spite of the worthy thoughts expressed.

**Participation.**    One of the widely acclaimed techniques for achieving individual adjustment to change is participation in the process of change by the persons affected by the change. The classic study of the use of participation was that of Coch and French at the Harwood Manufacturing Corporation. **(12)** The study was designed to discover why people resist change and what could be done to overcome it. They used three different work groups in conducting experiments on the introduction of change. They found that, overwhelmingly, the greatest success in introducing change was achieved through the active participation of the people whose work was changed. This success was confirmed by the fact that this group had the highest production and no resignations after the change. Since this study, further support has been provided for the value of participation.

In contrasting the traditional approach to change with the participative approach, Saltonstall indicates that

. . . the participative approach suggests that the technical specialist sincerely wants and needs the opinions and ideas of both the foreman and the group to be affected by the change.

He goes on to show *why* participation works by stating,

If people in the shop sense this as a genuine need on the part of the technician and can see that their ideas and reactions are being carefully weighed in the final formulation of the plan, the plan itself may become "our plan" and they have a vested interest in seeing it work. **(13)**

In spite of the wide acclaim participation has received, there are some who feel we have overrated this approach. Lawrence is one of these critics who indicates the difficulty of having managers actually apply the technique largely because of misunderstanding of the word "participation." He indicates that the real problem is

. . . how to *get* this thing called participation. And as a matter of fact, the question remains whether participation was the determining factor in the Coch and French experiment or whether there was something of deeper significance underlying it. **(14)**

It is interesting to note that Lawrence's skepticism about the place of participation may be well founded, as studies by Argyris and McGregor probe deeper into the problems of motivation.

**Team management.**   The significance of the team management, or the visible management, approach is that it goes far deeper than participation in involving the employee in change. It does so by attempting to achieve an accommodation of the employees' goals with the company's goals. Moreover, this technique is not merely a laboratory approach but is used regularly in implementing change by a number of leading companies.

The results of team management have been achieved by the "collaboration" of research efforts with practical steps to apply the current research findings to business operations. The two works most responsible for the impetus of this technique are Argyris' widely acclaimed *Personality and Organization,* and the late McGregor's brilliant *The Human Side of Enterprise.*

In his work, Argyris sharpens the potential conflict between the individual and organization and suggests a possible remedy by indicating that job enlargement may be the key to minimizing this "incongruency" between the individual and the organization. Implicitly, it is this incongruency which is a vital factor in delaying individual adjustment to change. Argyris further noted that employee-centered leadership (team management) is of possible value, but points out that "How management controls may be modified is a crucial area that requires such exploration." **(15)**

It is precisely this *crucial* point—the type of control over employee effort—that was McGregor's starting point. He examined the two contrasting attitudes towards employee motivation for work. In the essentially negative attitude, which he labels as "theory

X," the traditional managers view people as essentially avoiding work and as a consequence having to be "pushed" into it. In the positive assumption of employee motivation, which he calls "theory Y," McGregor proposes that work is natural to people; they seek to achieve objectives and, moreover, they tend to accept and even seek responsibility. The recommendation that is proposed, in the light of research findings and McGregor's synthesis, is that the directing of human effort no longer follow the exercise of authority via the scaler principle but that instead it should stress the integration of authority and self-control. By integration McGregor means, "the creation of conditions such that the members of the organization can achieve their own goals *best* by directing their efforts toward the success of the enterprise." It is this approach which he suggests will lead to greater realization of both individual and organizational goals. **(16)**

It is in the last few years that the practical effects of the McGregor and Argyris proposition—higher employee material and psychic rewards as well as higher company profits—have actually been achieved. The translation of what they have advocated is called, popularly, "team management." The achievements of IBM and Non-Linear Systems are particularly worth of note.

In the case of IBM, it was found that in one plant, called Plant A, the performance record was excellent in terms of costs, productivity, and quality. In this plant, methods and output standards were *not* established by the engineer as in other plants. Instead, they were set jointly by the employees and managers in the plant. It is interesting to note that the underlying assumption for this approach was that,

The plant's management felt strongly that the man on the job could outsmart any engineer coming in to set methods and standards. **(17)**

It has been shown that under these conditions of operating, not only is there ready adjustment to change, but many innovations are suggested and even implemented by the employees themselves.

In the case of Non-Linear Systems, since 1960 its top management has developed companywide production on the basis of individual work teams of six or seven each. **(18)** Moreover, each team of workers is free to organize and work as they wish. After some months of adjustment, the production has consistently been 30 percent higher than the old way, and costs and customer complaints (over quality) have been sharply reduced. What is of particular interest is that there has been a dramatic improvement in the individual adjustments to change. Since model change and work assignment change were a recurrent problem, it is amazing to note that, "where it used to take eight to ten weeks to crank up a new model, now it takes two to three."

Indeed, these results are being intensely studied by such companies as General Electric and others, to extend the benefits of team managing.

*Result sharing.*   Either in combination with other approaches such as participation and team management or alone, sharing the results of change has been successfully used in facilitating adjustment to change. It offers an opportunity for appealing to self-interest. Essentially, however, it is a motivating influence because it reflects concern for the individual who has been exposed to change. It offers other tangible benefits also. Methods men are learning to use every opportunity to make the job easier and less exerting. Along with their process changes they attempt to install floormats, hoists, chairs, ventilators, and other conveniences, thereby showing that they are interested in the whole job process, including the worker.

The basic approach of sharing will be explored more fully as a joint labor-management technique for achieving adjustment to change.

### Communications: The Catalyst in Achieving Adjustment

Underlying any approach to facilitating adjustment to change is the impact made by the process of communicating between management and employees. As Pigors has so clearly focused the issue, it is a question of "keeping in touch with workers when making a change." Indeed, it is particularly during a process of change that conflicts may be magnified by the barriers in communications, perhaps endangering efforts at facilitating adjustment to change. As Pigors sharpens the challenge:

The misunderstandings that hinder cooperation are the worst kind of waste because they are avoidable. Understanding can be achieved by getting agreement on such questions as: What are the facts, feelings and purposes of everyone involved in the change? How can this whole meaning be shared by all concerned? **(19)**

Another point to note is that the disruptions of change may seriously damage normally effective communications that may have existed before the change. In other words, certain stabilizing social processes are weakest at the time they are needed most; therefore management needs to make special effort to maintain them in times of change.

CHAPTER **14**

# LABOR-MANAGEMENT
# ADJUSTMENT TO CHANGE

The basic approach underlying efforts at achieving labor-management adjustment to change is the development of a company-wide, goal-directed program. This will assure both continuous, profitable growth and peaceful relations between employee groups and management. In this way the company is spared the disrupting effects of economic conflicts between labor and management. Instead, it can apply its resources towards achieving benefits for the company as well as its employees.

It was essentially this philosophy that was suggested by Taylor about three quarters of a century ago and was largely rejected by both management and labor. Let us examine some attempts by management and labor, jointly, to achieve adjustments to change by the use of cooperation, and thus provide a companion to the previous chapter on individual adjustment to change.

In this way we may develop some approaches that will help to solve human problems of change by working towards group as well as individual adjustment to the implementation of innovations.

Finding the perfect solution to all the labor-management conflicts is next to impossible. Yet there have been some significant steps taken in the labor relations field that are worth noting.

A former prizefighter, open-hearth worker, steel company cost

accountant, union local president, and a lecturer in industrial relations at Massachusetts Institute of Technology was the author of the
Scanlon Plan. Joseph Scanlon was concerned with the mutual interests of labor and management. His plan was created to cut the
worker in on the project, the decisions, and the profits of increased
productivity, and to help management utilize the ingenuity of employees as a way of improving production.

Scanlon had long felt that the workers could help improve production if they had an incentive to do so. In 1938 an incentive was
created. He was, at that time, president of his Steelworkers local.
Management informed him that if the plant could not do better, it
would have to be shut down. Scanlon and the company's top management went to the CIO steel headquarters in Pittsburgh and there
worked out a union-management productivity plan. Besides rescu-
ing the plant, it put it on a profitable basis.

According to this plan, the union and management in the plant
fix a productivity norm, and the labor force is promised a bonus
from the savings the workers can bring about by producing at a
lower cost per unit. This plan is noncompetitive, and unites the
work force in a common goal rather than putting them opposite
each other. The Scanlon Plan also calls for a system of production
councils in which union and management attack production
costs. **(1)**

In 1945 Scanlon finally took the various solutions he had tried
out in many companies and put them together at the Adamson
Company, located in East Palestine, Ohio. This firm was a small
manufacturer of steel tanks. The owner, Cecil Adamson, commented: "I give the union everything it asks for. But still the shop
isn't working well. Let's get together and work out something so
that you'll get something and I'll get something." Joseph Scanlon
went into the plant, checked the records, and derived a normal
labor cost per unit. Then he set up a system for a 50–50 split of the
savings the workers made by producing at less than normal cost. **(2)**

It did not take long for the new joint union-management to be
swamped with workers' suggestions. Welders who had wasted time
waiting for materials started helping to unload. Workers who were
previously indifferent to substandard work turned out by slackers
began raising a fuss because it lowered their bonus. The employees

and executives formed a team working to attain a mutual goal. After a year, the Adamson Company was five times as profitable as in former days. Even after sharing the productivity savings 50–50, management still received twice as much income.

In 1947 Scanlon came into the Lapointe Machine Tool Company at Hudson, Massachusetts, where there was constant conflict over the piecework system. For some workers the rates were so easy that they earned big bonuses and held back production out of fear that the rates would be cut. For others, rates were so difficult that only the most skillful could earn any bonus at all. Workers not involved in piecework had no incentive rates and resented those of the others. There were innumerable production delays, spoilage was too high and deliveries were bad.

Under the Scanlon Plan, Lapointe's working force receives, as a bonus every month, all of the savings it can effect on its own cost for that month. Concurrently, management profits from greater production with no corresponding increase in total overhead.

This improved productivity evolved mainly because of suggestions as to how time and effort could be saved. With the Scanlon Plan the reward for valid suggestions goes to the entire shop. The suggestions are handled by a screening committee made up of representatives of management and labor from the various departments. The screening committee at Lapointe received 513 suggestions in 24 months. A total of 380 were accepted.

Management and labor have been cooperating so effectively at Lapointe Machine Tool Company that it is difficult to tell where the contribution of one ends and that of the other takes over. Another plus factor is the reduction in complaints based on imperfect workmanship. The policy at this company is to take back any unsatisfactory product and fix it without extra cost. With the Scanlon Plan, this means a loss to labor as well as management. Consequently, great care is taken all along the line.

The Scanlon Plan was tested in companies where labor-management relations were relatively successful.

The Parker Pen Company at Janesville, Wisconsin, was a progressive firm that had an intelligent management and union, a standard incentive system, an up-to-date retirement plan, a very modern, air-conditioned factory with production aids such as piped-in music for their workers. Even so, the company found that a good incentive plan created trouble. There were some men in low-paying jobs who took home more pay than the men in highly skilled divisions.

Joseph Scanlon was asked to come in and help. He eliminated the existing incentive system, which promoted individual effort at the expense of the group. He spent several days with the finance and accounting people, whose role he deemed very important, and arrived at a productivity norm. It was the fiscal year March, 1953 through February, 1954. Scanlon arranged that the savings on output made at less than the costs of the base year figure, as measured by sales value, should go into a bonus pool. One quarter of the pool money was automatically set aside as a reserve fund to be paid out in the break-even or deficit months when no bonus was earned. The rest of the pie, made up of increased value through productivity savings, was split. Labor got 75 percent, management 25 percent. The bonus for the first month, paid in September, 1954, totaled $43,199, a 13.8 percent wage increase. In January, the pen and pencil industry's seasonal low, the workers failed to earn a bonus, but it was the only month they missed. Payments from the reserve pool were made only at the end of the year. Labor earned a peak 27.1 percent over their wages in September.

The companies who have tested the Scanlon Plan have laudatory things to say about it. President Leo Beckwith of the Market Forge Company at Everett, Massachusetts, said, "Maybe it isn't the Utopia that some people try to make it, but it has been a fine thing. If for any reason we ever had to drop it, the boys in the plant would be very unhappy and so would I." The vice president of an Illinois concern had this to say: "As far as I'm concerned, Joe has the answer to the future for American free enterprise capitalism."

The Scanlon Plan is now operating in approximately 60 firms, from furniture to steel, where profits were excellent and where they were nonexistent, where labor relations were good and where they were substandard. But this plan has two prerequisites: the union leadership must be intelligent, and there must be men in top management who are not only 100 percent sold on the plan but are willing to accept in an impartial way any criticism thrown at their own management.

A labor relations plan of more recent origin is the Kaiser–Steel Union Long-Range Sharing Plan. Only time will tell if it will have as wide an application as the Scanlon Plan. At present, it is operating effectively at Kaiser Steel, Fontana, California.

On January 11, 1963, the Kaiser Steel Corporation workers agreed to give a four-year trial to an experimental labor contract, subject to annual review and revision. They felt that they had nothing to lose and much to gain.

This plan affords greater protection than ever before against the loss of jobs or income because of technological change. It insures labor a share, 32.5 percent, of any cost reductions brought about through increased efficiency. It guarantees wage and benefit increases equal to or better than what might be offered by the rest of the industry. Incentive workers' earnings are assured to be at least as high and possibly higher than they have been receiving in the recent past if they choose to get off incentives. **(3)**

For Kaiser Steel the plan means an escape from the annual or biennial debates over wages, and from possible strikes. It gives the company a chance to get rid of an incentive pay system. Most important of all, it gives them an opportunity to introduce changes in technology and work systems without the usual employee resistance.

To Kaiser Steel there are two main goals in this plan. One objective is to find a better way of solving mutual problems. The second goal is to stimulate in Kaiser's employees the same interest and desire for the success of the business as that of management. The gains-sharing section of the plan is considered as an initial step to generate this interest. "If we can get 7,000 people interested in two-thirds of the cost that they have never been interested in before, we'll really have something," remarked one company official.

Mr. Walter Reuther called the Kaiser Plan "one of the most important developments in a long time." The UAW, he said, would investigate "progress sharing." The Rubber Workers Union also announced that it would introduce a plan to share productivity increases at its next bargaining session.

Here is the plan. Every month Kaiser Steel will divide up among its workers 32.5 percent of whatever savings the company achieves through increased productivity or by cutting the cost of its supplies. The 32.5 percent figure was chosen because labor accounts for about a third of Kaiser's costs. If the savings to be divided grow big enough, the union will allow Kaiser to save up some of them to be used to pay future increases in basic steel wages.

The Kaiser local of the United Steelworkers will not have to do any wage haggling at all. They will automatically get the same increases that the union receives in its negotiations with the eastern steel companies.

No Kaiser Steel employee will be laid off from the effective date of this plan because of technological change, new or improved work methods and systems, or any other innovation in operations not resulting from a decrease in man-hour requirements caused by a decrease in finished steel production, or a change in product or production requirements. This protection shall be provided by the creation of a plantwide employment reserve. No employee shall, however, be entitled to employment in the plantwide employment reserve, or to share in the protection provided by the above-mentioned, until he has worked for the company in 26 weekly pay periods. If the employee is forced to move to a lower paying position, he will go on being paid at his old rate for one year.

After Kaiser Steel Corporation signed this unique plan with the Steelworkers union the workers had one major concern: Just how big a melon would Kaiser share? Their answer came when Kaiser announced that its costs in March, 1963, were $962,000 less than the 1961 base. The eligible workers' 32.5 percent share averaged out to $79 each for the month. "The payoff was considerably more than we anticipated," said George Sirolli, local union president. "We were pleasantly surprised."

Admittedly, the payoff to individual workers has many times dipped well below the early share given by Kaiser. It is interesting to note, however, that it has bounced back to an attractive figure. Moreover, the occasional sharp dip in the employee share has *not* caused disenchantment with the program itself by the union leaders or the rank and file.

A contrary approach to the same industry was David J. McDonald's approach in arriving at a new tack towards dealing with the problems of innovation. This entailed the creation of a Human Relations Committee made up of four top representatives of the United Steelworkers and of the steel industry. This committee developed an approach consisting of year-round discussions of innovation as well as other problems so as to relieve both sides of the pressure arising from deadline negotiations on specific issues. These discussions were held in secrecy to protect the parties from friendly and unfriendly pressures and to enable a frank exchange of ideas.

The Human Relations Committee worked exceptionally well in facilitating the application of numbers of innovations in the steel industry while at the same time affording protection to the employees. Many imaginative approaches were developed to prevent dislocations to the worker, such as a unique extended vacation plan and early retirement arrangements. Unfortunately, the secrecy surrounding the work of the Human Relations Committee coupled with seemingly modest wage settlements generated the opposition to McDonald that led to his defeat as president by I. W. Abel, who ran on a platform of returning the union to the rank and file.

The significant point to remember about the Kaiser plan is that it is the most ardent effort yet made by a major American industry to do something of substance about the problems incurred with technological innovation. The Kaiser plan is a reaffirmation of the belief that technological advances can be utilized to benefit all parties concerned. The agreement gives evidence, in the words of Labor Secretary W. Willard Wirtz, that "by serving mutual interest, individual interests can be served."

Now we turn our attention to an industry that is amphibious. On October 18, 1960, the Longshoremen's and Warehousemen's Union and the Pacific Maritime Association signed a mechanization and modernization agreement extending to July 1, 1966. The pact was the result, achieved after five months of concentrated negotiations, of discussions and planning by both groups which had started in 1957.

Harry Bridges, president of the International Longshoremen's and Warehousemen's Union, and J. Paul St. Sure, president of the Pacific Maritime Association, appeared before a congressional committee on October 8, 1963 in order to describe the mechanization agreement between their organizations. The union members gain a high degree of protection against layoff and declining earnings, to the extent that these threats are the result of increasing productivity; while the employers gain greater freedom to mechanize and modernize. The negotiations were relatively friendly, without the threat of a strike, and were conducted without the assistance of any third party. The pact has quickened the introduction of laborsaving equipment on the West Coast waterfront and has tempered the effects of technological innovations. (4)

The West Coast shipping industry dispute is an example of a militant union and an equally militant employer group that formulated a unique solution for the irksome problem of restrictive working rules which may have far reaching influence. Harry Bridges had urged the union members, in October, 1957, to give up their policy of guerrilla resistance and adopt a more flexible policy so that they could buy specific benefits in return. As it turned out, the union gained sizable payments as its "share of the machine" and the assurance of security for its members. Meantime, the employer, the Pacific Maritime Association, achieved a high degree of freedom to manage its operations effectively and established its right to introduce laborsaving innovations.

Other industries may find it possible to develop modifications of this approach in solving their own work rules problems. The primary significance of the West Coast development is in the fact that it illustrates that management can solve this difficulty by giving labor a share in the gains brought about by increased technological innovation, while simultaneously protecting worker security.

There is a similarity of policies between the International Longshoremen's Union and the Pacific Maritime Association, and those followed by John L. Lewis and the miners.

The United Mine Workers adopted a policy of promoting the modernization of the coal mines in exchange for improved wages, hours, and working conditions. In the last decade, the mining of bituminous coal experienced an unusual transformation as the result of an astonishing rate of technological innovation in that industry. In 1950 a miner was producing 6.77 tons of coal each day; in 1958 the national average was just under 12 tons. Meanwhile, over the years the miners have established one of the highest hourly wages of any industrial workers in the world. Along with increased wages came a detailed pension and medical care program, improved working conditions, and reduced hours. The estimated 400,000 miners in the bituminous coal industry in 1942 have today been decreased to 200,000, and production is not much below what it was 10 years ago. John L. Lewis has accepted shrinking employment and a decreasing union membership as the price of technological progress.

Unfortunately, the long period of peace in the mining industry has been broken in recent years. The shrinking of jobs has had drastic *direct* impact on the union members. In addition, the *indirect* impact of reduced employer contributions to the union welfare fund has been particularly difficult to accept. In effect, at a time when the fund could be an aid in mitigating the problems of innovation, employers are deliberately reducing their contributions to it.

In both the coal mines and West Coast longshore industry, the rise in labor productivity comes about from mechanization. New machines are taking over operations previously performed by hand, but a man is still needed to control and operate the machine.

A recent study was published in which top managers were interviewed about their views on how to cushion the impact of technological innovation on labor.

There was a general consensus that the first step is to create a receptive atmosphere. And all who were interviewed felt that advanced planning reduced the human fatalities lying in the path of technological innovations.

We can, for sure, anticipate more automated plants, computerized offices and laborsaving devices of all kinds. Of course, this means displaced workers and more difficult problems for management.

The greater success managers have in increasing productivity and decreasing labor cost, the more attention they must give to human relations and related social problems. Sociological problems arise as the technological innovations are instituted. It is important, therefore, to create the right climate. A people-oriented program should be established. With it comes the absorbing of as many displaced workers as possible. In order to set this receptive atmosphere, management should call in representatives from the working group for an open and straightforward discussion. By thorough planning and proper timing, management should be able to alleviate most of its problems.

Any company which has its workers' interests at heart will be more successful, while instituting technological innovations, in securing worker cooperation than the firm that treats labor as a commodity. As a company becomes more machine-oriented, its managers must become more people-oriented.

Let us now examine the steps that Armour and Company took to lessen the impact of technological innovation on its displaced workers.

In March, 1962, Armour and Company announced the forthcoming shutdown of its main meatpacking plant in Fort Worth, Texas. The greater number of the layoffs took place in July and August, and the plant was not completely closed until December. Approximately 1,000 production and maintenance workers were displaced.

After the public announcement of the shutdown, the Automation Fund Committee initiated a special program to assist the employees in the bargaining unit who would be affected by the closing. This committee was established by contract between Armour and Company and the United Packinghouse Food and Allied Workers AFL–CIO and the Amalgamated Meat Cutters and Butcher Workmen of North America AFL–CIO. This was the second such project handled by the Automation Fund Committee. The Fort Worth project was aided by a betterment in the employment market in the Fort Worth area. However, an earlier experience of this committee was not as successful. In Oklahoma City (1960–61) unemployment increased sharply while the committee's retraining and relocation efforts were taking place. This illustrates the importance of understanding that what can be accomplished by retraining is closely related to the general availability of jobs.

The Fort Worth project was handled throughout as a joint effort by the company, the union, and the public members of the committee. In the early stages of the project, especially when the work was being planned and organized, the cooperative approach was very beneficial, producing results that would have been hard to obtain if this had been a project primarily handled under committee control by an individual expert or subcontractor. The objective of the Fort Worth project was to aid the displaced employees to find other job opportunities. In particular, the project involved efforts to facilitate the direct placement of former Armour employees in new jobs, and to retrain the displaced workers in different occupational skills for which there seemed to be some demand in the local labor market and surrounding areas.

The placement program encountered limited success, but did result in finding jobs for several workers, especially for those who had physical, social, or educational disabilities. The program also served to orientate job seekers to the labor market.

Although the project is not yet completed, the results so far allow a preparatory evaluation of the experience that may provide guides to future activities in similar situations.

The situation at Armour and Company in Fort Worth demonstrated an instance where job retraining helps. It was a crash program of retraining, and therefore had its limitations. On the whole, however, modest success has been reported in helping to relocate workers displaced as a result of the shutdown.

### Conclusions Based on Labor-Management Cooperation

The basic guidelines for labor-management adjustment to innovation were clearly set forth in the contributions of Scanlon. He provided the philosophy and goals as well as many specific techniques that are fundamental to encouraging innovation. Essentially, they involve enlisting workers' cooperation and involvement in planning and implementing innovation to some degree, and thereby preventing resistance to its introduction.

As recounted in this chapter, many companies, with the aid of union leaders, have developed programs that were designed to prevent crippling strikes or other less dramatic obstructions to the introduction of innovation. These strides in labor-management adjustments to innovation are not particularly impressive, however.

In the first place, the efforts to date have been largely confined to production industries. Indications are that in the coming years the most significant impact of innovations will be among vast numbers of white-collar, civil service, and technical employees.

Another disappointing aspect of recent attempts at labor-management adjustment to innovation is the varied picture of success. In some cases the results have been heartening, while in other situations they have ranged from mediocre to poor. In still other attempts initial success was followed by collapse of the program.

What is important to observe from these experiences are those ingredients which seem necessary for achieving successful adjustment to innovation through the joint efforts of management and labor. As a result of analyzing these experiences, following are some suggestions to managers for developing an approach that should go a long way towards an adjustment in both white-collar and production industries.

Managers should seek to encourage some deliberate program in dealing with the labor groups in their company and to adopt the following thoughts to guide them in their own departmental activities.

1. The first stage of a successful program for achieving labor-management adjustment to innovation is the adoption of a philosophy by managers—and then urging that labor leaders join them in it—in which cooperation between labor and management is viewed as beneficial to each side. It is to their mutual benefit to foster innovation.

2. Managers should offer a guarantee that either of two things will result from job displacement: either there will be a guarantee of job security or there will be a commitment to help find a job in another company if a jobholder is displaced.

3. Develop relationships (whatever the mechanism may be called) on a year-round basis to discuss and resolve major issues that might retard the introduction of innovations. This machinery should be created in addition to that for a basic grievance process. It may well be patterned after the Human Relations Committee of the steel industry, or the Kaiser committee which includes outside representatives. In their operation, these year-round discussions should draw in wide representation from employees. In addition, results of these labor-management deliberations should be freely communicated to all employees.

4. Managers should encourage their subordinates, whether union members or not, to concern themselves with company and union affairs. Indeed, union affairs are very much the concern of the manager, and the more informed union members are encouraged to become, the greater likelihood they will become key ingredients towards facilitating innovation.

5. Managers should advocate, for their own departments as well as the company as a whole, a basic change in the labor-manage-

ment contract so as to place less emphasis upon *bargaining* aspects of the agreement and concentrate more on *facts* as a basis for a just contract. Contract conditions such as rates of pay and fringe benefits should draw upon data such as the economics of the firm, productivity of employees, industry conditions, employee real wages, and the like. These are a far better device than the use of bargaining "muscle" on each side. This is particularly true in areas where the public interest may be affected. Should the "fact" approach to negotiations fail, managers should recognize the potential desirability of compulsory arbitration as a necessary alternative to crippling strikes which may result from either side's assumption of "impossible" bargaining positions.

# Conclusion

# CONCLUSION

Someone has said that the meaning of "news" can be defined in a single word: *change.*

*Change*—the only thing in our existence of which we can be certain. In all walks, in all phases of life, change is our greatest challenge.

The purpose of this book has been to bring out, through a deeper understanding of one small segment of change, *innovation,* how this "controlled, directed and purposeful activity" can be harnessed for man's benefit, particularly in the area of business. It is addressed specifically to the business manager in his focal position in innovation management.

Here are compiled the extensive findings of today's successful innovators, with a liberal sprinkling of yesterday's pioneers.

Here we take up the manager's basic functions in innovating, and the implications of a *new* dimension in his job of managing and the necessity for him to keep pace with his "own expanded capacity to innovate." In other words, how he has to plan, organize, control, and *innovate* company resources in order to achieve greater profits —to apply new technologies "that revolutionize existing industrial structures."

In sum, as quoted in our Introduction, "Innovation is risk-taking change introduced for the purpose of satisfying economic wants and resulting in increased profitability."

And may I also respectfully quote from Machiavelli's *The Prince:*

There is nothing more difficult to take in hand, more perilous to conduct or more uncertain in its success than to take the lead in the introduction of a new order of things, because the innovator has for enemies all those who have done well under the old conditions and lukewarm defenders in those who may do well under the new.

# Appendixes

# NATIONAL FOOD COMPANY

The experience of the National Food Company (name and industry disguised) in managing innovation at one of its plants is notable for two reasons. First, it represents a particular approach in a company program designed to manage—plan, organize, control —innovation. It assigns the *primary* role in achieving innovation to operating management, with staff providing guidance and assistance where needed. In addition, a group of operating managers whose departments participate in implementing innovations directs and coordinates the individual innovation projects. The net effect is that the managers develop the conviction that innovating is an inherent and ongoing part of their job. Moreover, they learn to cooper..te—give and take—with other managers on their own level in getting an innovation planned, installed, and assessed, even when a particular innovation seems against a particular manager's own interest. It is, "pull together, or we don't improve the performance of our plant."

This case has a second feature in that a condition of urgency prevails in spite of a rather tense atmosphere over past failures to bring about any significant innovations at the plant.

The company has had some difficult times in recent years competing with others in the food industry. Low margins on its products, vigorous competitive promotions, and widespread innovations in the industry place high demands on both the marketing and manufacturing division of the company.

As far as the manufacturing division is concerned, its top management is constantly struggling to keep the operating costs of its plants in line. With this in mind, the Danville plant stands out strikingly. Home office management is particularly anxious to bring about some innovations that would result in greater operating efficiency. In turn, the Danville plant manager and his staff are thoroughly convinced that the home office manufacturing people are "down" on them and are unwilling to extend themselves to "bail out" from the poor operating position.

It is in such an atmosphere that the vice president of manufacturing is sending a team of industrial engineers and consultants to Danville. It will be their goal to work with the plant management to develop an innovation program that will achieve a "turn around" in the operating picture at Danville. The visiting team has the blessing of the home office, but aren't exactly welcomed at the plant.

Before exploring the events that took place in this effort to manage innovations, let's get a better picture of the company.

The National Food Company, with its executive offices in Chicago, is engaged in the processing and distribution of a wide line of food and snack products to the retail trade and to institutional users. The products distributed to retail outlets include coffee, shortenings, desserts, frozen fruits and vegetables, and assorted snack foods. The institutional customers, such as restaurants, bakers, hospitals, and schools are sold such products as coffee, desserts, shortening, and frozen eggs, fruits, and vegetables.

National has processing plants in four locations around the country, with its largest and oldest one at Danville, Illinois, about 110 miles south of the home office at Chicago. Each of the four plants handles the complete line of company products. The products are sold through six regional sales offices, one of which is at the home office, serving the midwestern region. Due to the competitive nature of the industry, deal packs, wide product lines, continuous research on new products, and testing of special markets resulted in a condition where short runs proved to be the way of life at the plants. This is particularly true of the Danville plant, which was near enough to the home office to provide convenient testing of ideas for new packaging, products, or special promotions. This is a carry-over of a tradition born when Danville was the only plant and was regularly called upon to produce "special orders."

In the opinion of one Danville manager:

I'd like to see the production superintendents get together. We operate on an almost day-to-day basis for production scheduling. We can't get a minimum firm schedule from the home office.

Some of the other internal operating problems at Danville that were mentioned include:

Out-moded equipment, bumping system among personnel when lay-offs occur, shortage of key people resulting from budget reductions, lack of understanding by the home office and top management, and self-defeating overtime arrangements and customs.

Whatever the real or imagined problems at Danville, National Food's top management feels that time is running out and the plant must begin to move faster to raise performance. What's more, if there's going to be more help or support from the home office, initiatives by the plant will have to be made *first*.

Over the past few years home office men have tried to bring about operating innovations at Danville with little success to show for it.

The plant's managers did not see the company's technical staff people as allies, but more as additional sources of pressure and consumers of precious time. They recognized the competence of these men, but kept putting them off with such rationalizations as: "We are too busy"; "We don't have time to do that"; "I'd need another supervisor full time just to conduct that project"; "Why perfect that process? I hear we're going out of that business;" and dozens of others. Thus the plant management, which was sorely in need of help, kept at arm's length the very technical staff people who could help them get on top of the situation.

Now another major attempt was to be made.

## A Fresh Approach

Right from the start it was agreed that little would be gained by arguing with the plant's managers, who insisted that any improvement efforts by the plant were doomed to failure unless accompanied by massive injections of new equipment, better people, and improved manufacturing schedules with fewer line shifts. (The corporate staff engineers already had a collection of facts which *proved* that Danville's managers weren't running the plant as well as they might. But these "facts" never produced much change.)

This time they decided to seek out, wherever and however they could, areas where the plant's people themselves, with a minimum of help, could make some measurable improvements in the plant's operations. Instead of pointing out what was wrong with Danville (and pointing "sound" solutions), the engineers' approach was based on locating strengths and capabilities in the plant and helping them to put them to better use. This meant the experts would have to roll up their sleeves and get to work with Danville's people on jobs they were ready to tackle.

A series of interviews was held with all department managers and supervisors, who were asked a very simple question: "What can you and your associates do to make your department run better?" The answers came back at first in the stereotyped fashion. The result was a long list of reasons why everything was out of the hands of the supervisors and why it was up to "them" to provide the tools, the improved equipment, the materials, the scheduling, the trained employees, the time, and everything else needed for innovating.

The engineers found that there was some justice in the plant's feeling of being a stepchild. Company policy had indeed restricted the flow of capital investment into the plant, which resulted in a most discouraging and discouraged atmosphere. Control tools were inadequate—there were no profit and loss measures by product groups. There was a feeling that general management used yardsticks for performance which were inadequate, with too many variables to be valid.

Danville's managers hoped that the engineering team, seeing the odds against which the plant was fighting, would carry the word to top management. But the engineers did not feel it would serve any purpose to become message carriers from the plant. They stuck doggedly to their original question: "What can *you* do here to improve operations through innovations?"

This was not an easy question for the plant managers. To answer by saying "Nothing" was to admit complete defeat. Down deep they *really* knew they weren't going to get relief from corporate headquarters until they did better. But to say there were things that could be done might be construed to mean that they hadn't been doing their best job. And that possibility wasn't something they wanted to face.

Nevertheless, as the engineers moved around the plant talking with managers and supervisors informally and in meetings, the ideas began to come forth—ideas on where improvements could be made in the plant's performance.

The trouble with the suggestions was that most were prefaced with words like, "If they would . . .," or "If only we could. . . ." The theme that some mysterious "they" should be responsible was common to both foremen's suggestions and manager's complaints.

Gradually, by bits and pieces, ideas on how to make the plant *really* run better came into view. A bag-filling machine could run faster with no ill effects. A valve could be opened to permit greater flow of raw material. A "rush" maintenance order could wait a day or two. Signs could be put up to help direct outside truckers to the right unloading docks, thereby eliminating a lot of confusion as to where incoming supplies were to be located. The personnel department could help put together an instruction manual for certain operating jobs. These were modest innovations, but they were clearly profit-oriented.

## An Unexpected Report

After several weeks of listening, the engineering team collated its notes. They were surprised by the great number of specific suggestions they had received in every department. Many of the ideas didn't impress them as being exactly on the mark, but plenty of them did. They began to discuss how to separate the good ideas from the poor ones, and how to summarize the findings in a report, along with their recommendations on steps that might be taken to follow up on each idea. They were actually dividing this task among themselves when one of the team pointed out: "If we take the responsibility of judging their ideas, saying which should be done and which ignored, telling them how to do it, won't we be back on the very same merry-go-round? They'll end up shrugging their shoulders and telling us they'll get to it when they have time." His colleagues readily accepted the wisdom in this observation, and after more exploration they decided on another tack.

All of the data gathered in the initial reconaissance were simply assembled and organized by department in a set of notes. Then a meeting was held with Danville's top management group. At this meeting the engineers reviewed their conversations and outlined the scope and nature of the suggestions they had received. The plant management listened with interest; and when the engineers were finished, one of the managers said, "Well, you sure got an earful. It will be interesting to see how you boil this all down in your report." The engineers responded that they had just presented the "report." The only additional material they would present would be a written summary of the specific ideas and suggestions developed in the interviews in each department. In surprise, the plant general manager asked, "Aren't you guys going to give us any recommendations on this?" "Sure we'll help," said the team leader, "but why don't you all decide what you want to do? There is no sense in our drawing up lists of projects. How do you want to tackle it? That's the real question."

Then the plant manager took over the meeting. He had been sitting back, letting the engineers carry the ball. He and his managers began to puzzle over an approach. They were obviously pleased to learn that the "experts" didn't really have all the answers. More important, they were impressed with the respect for their judgment implied in the engineers' approach. At the same time, they were taken back a bit. There were no easy answers after all. They would really have to turn the plant around themselves. There was no choice. But how? All the old problems came back to mind. Could they do it?

The first problem was that there were too many ideas to deal with at once. They felt overwhelmed by the sheer number of suggestions and possibilities. Then somebody asked, "Why try to tackle it all at once? Why not begin in only one or two departments?" At this meeting and a few more held during the following week, they developed a plan of attack. Briefly, it consisted of these steps:

1. Establish priority for action. Some of the criteria that might be used are the importance and urgency of accomplishment, the degree to which improvement in a selected area will facilitate improvement in other areas, and the readiness and capacity for action.
2. The second major step is to organize to act.

3. The third major step is to involve supervision. As rapidly as possible to move toward involving supervision in the planning process.
4. The fourth step is to assign the responsibility as agreement is reached on the priority areas where emphasis is to be placed. The plant manager, with the advice of the management group, assigns specific responsibility for action and results to particular individuals and groups.
5. Moving ahead in each area. Once specific assignments are made, a number of independent programs will be designed and moved forward simultaneously.

This effort was to be coordinated by the top managers of the plant. The committee for the purpose of spurring innovations within the plan was called the Operations Improvement Committee. They would help the plant manager organize and manage the innovation program.

## The Formal Assignments

The decision to develop formal written assignments for each department was made for a number of reasons. First, a written assignment would make clear the respective responsibilities of the department superintendent and of the Operations Improvement Committee. Second, by having the superintendents themselves collaborate in the preparation of their own assignments, there would be sufficient opportunity to discuss the issues and to make certain there was consensus on how things were to be done. Finally, putting the assignments in writing represented an important step in helping the managers themselves learn how to organize for improvement. If this program were successful, "improvement" would no longer be a casual responsibility of the plant's managers to be carried out whenever they had time and inclination. It would become a crucial, formal, programmed element of the managerial job.

The following are some excerpts from one assignment:

We are determined to produce a major upgrading of results in Danville during the next year. Your mission is to plan and achieve substantial improvement in your department.

1. *Review and planning: setting objectives.*  It will be the responsibility of your department to bring to the Operations Improvement Committee for review not later than July 15 a plan of action to improve the performance of your department.

   A. *Projects under way.* We suggest that you first review, and include in your report to us, the status of all innovation projects now under way or planned.

   B. *What other innovations are needed or possible?* An "innovation" is anything that contributes directly to results in terms of quality, productivity, waste control, etc. Every phase of Compounding and Press operations should be considered: equipment, maintenance, scheduling, work planning, supervision, operator performance, safety, housekeeping, overtime, absenteeism, etc.

      While the major aim is to show outstanding results next year, do not limit yourselves to large-scale projects or to projects that will take several months to show results. Indeed, it is desirable to include some specific items that can be dealt with quickly. It is also essential that longer-range projects have checkpoints, so that you and we can be sure action is fulfilling plans on schedule.

   C. *How will progress be measured?* Some answer to this question should be a part of each project plan. If present reporting systems don't provide the necessary facts, how could they be obtained? Perhaps in some cases new control systems will be needed. But explore first what could be done by temporary reports, sampling, or other limited measures.

2. *Organizing for innovations.*  Are to have a priority second only to meeting our production requirements. Each member of management must be able to reserve and plan time to work on improvements.

   You are responsible for planning and action. But results will depend on getting the ideas and participation of everyone in your department and from groups whose work affects your department.

   What help will you need? It may be possible to obtain certain kinds of technical help or advice. The engineering-consultant team will be available to work with you.

3. *Engineering survey results attached.*   The engineering-consultant team has put together the suggestions and comments made
   by the managers of your department on ways to improve departmental operations. You may find these suggestions helpful in
   starting your work.

It is interesting to note that a key part of the innovation program
was to stress the process of innovating as an inherent part of *every*
manager's job alongside meeting his day-to-day operating demands
(step 2, above).

The benefits of an innovation program designed to improve a
process or a procedure or to build innovation as part of the managerial job can be multiplied by a certain degree of formalization.
This would include the use of written assignments—as job specifications for the improvement effort—to be followed up by written
plans of action and formal progress reporting. These written assignments should contain the following:

1. *A general statement of the mission.*   This gives the recipient a
   perspective on his job. It should include some background and
   the reasons for the desired result of the project, together with the
   relationship of the task to other improvement goals of the plant.
2. *A clear definition of the assignments.*   Is the recipient only to
   prepare a plan or to submit recommendations? Or is he to carry
   them out as well? Is it a one-shot or a continuing assignment?
3. *Resources and methods available.*   Is the receiver to do the
   work alone, or will he get the help of others or direct others?
4. *Methods of reporting progress.*   How should the recipient report
   back? Formal report? Informal reports? Scheduled presenta-
   tions?
5. *Measures of progress.*   What specific measures of progress can
   be established? What checkpoints and completion dates are to
   be set up?

It is important that assignments and the responsive action plans
be written and that recipients have a major share in preparing their
own assignments. To avoid arousing defensiveness, assignments
should not focus on what is wrong but rather on positive advances
which can be made. Questions should be phrased to lead to action

instead of debate. For example, the question: "Why are short runs padded, resulting in overruns?" can arouse endless discussion. The question: "What can you do to keep short runs short?" is better.

## Groups Take First Steps

Now the departments set to work. After the initial meeting at which the plant manager announced the assignment, each department decided to hold several sessions to design its own improvement program. The following three examples will show how plans were developed in one department.

First, the main function of this department was running one basic process that was adjusted for each of several hundred compounds that were regularly processed. While general operating instructions existed for the basic operation, detailed adjustments of pressure, temperature, and timing for each compound were left to the discretion of the foremen and operators. Because there were so many different compounds, it had always been believed that it would be too costly to prepare operating instructions to cover each one, and, of course, the individual artistry has led to many off-spec. batches. Analysis "revealed" that about 75 percent of the department's production was accounted for by only six of the hundreds of compounds. Moreover, most of the other 25 percent were really just variants of the basic six.

An assignment was drafted for a three-man group to develop operating instructions for *all* compounds, with the advice of the plant's technical experts. They were to develop a plan for doing this within four weeks. Operators and foremen on all shifts were to be invited to help this group develop its plan.

Second, lack of service from the plant's maintenance department was blamed for many of this operating department's problems. One group met with representatives of plant engineering to see if they could get some ideas on how maintenance could be handled more effectively. The maintenance superintendent pulled out, at random, a number of "emergency" and backlog requests from this department. A glance at a few of these and some discussion quickly made clear the fact that about half of the requests were obsolete. Moreover, maintenance—with a three-month backlog—had no way of sorting out the urgent tasks from the relatively unimportant ones.

A brief report back to the head of Compounding and Press resulted in this project assignment: a two-man group was to work with engineering, gather all of the backlog items, sort them out, and prepare the data for analysis by the department's managers as a group. They were then to place priorities on the jobs and return the list to engineering for action. The next step was to be the development of a better system to communicate their needs to maintenance.

Third, in a packaging and bag-filling operation, some important suggestions were made for improving the arrangement of certain machines. But this machinery couldn't be spared for the time necessary for experimentation with new approaches. It was barely off the line long enough for the most urgent maintenance.

In the discussion, two supervisors remembered some old equipment which had been designed to handle one customer's special requirements some years ago. When this contract ran out, the equipment was abandoned because it was not efficient enough to use in regular production. But couldn't it be used as auxiliary to permit experimentation with the main line? Several supervisors were given the job of developing a plan for doing this.

Thus the projects were developed. Eventually the two pilot departments were ready to present their plans.

### Plans Reviewed with Operations Improvement Committee

The review of plans with the committee brought the program to a critical point. The plant had invested plenty of time and energy on the work thus far, but now they would really take the plunge. They would have to make decisions and commitments, and then produce results—and with headquarters peering over their shoulders.

The committee spent considerable time deciding how to review the proposed projects with the two departments. A critical question: How should inadequate proposals be handled? Department managers had put so much thought and time into developing their proposals that they might be discouraged if the Operations Improvement Committee were too critical. But committee members agreed that they had to play it straight. They had to make clear that this was not just a game—they were playing for keeps, and the department managers and supervisors had to realize that.

Some proposals, as expected. were poorly or inadequately developed. They were merely *ideas* ("Someone should . . .") rather than specific plans ("We're going to . . ."). Instead of accepting such suggestions or referring the matter elsewhere for further development, the committee adopted the practice of turning these incomplete proposals back to the department with directives for completion, offering to help them out where necessary. The department groups were not in suspense or cut off from their proposals: they had every opportunity for satisfaction with the final outcome of each, whatever it might be.

In discussing priorities for projects with departments, the committee took into account more than the normal business factors such as probable cost, manpower availability, and probable duration. It also considered the element of readiness—what the managers were able and willing to undertake, the likelihood of a project's success, and the extent to which it would seem to lead to more far-reaching projects.

Thus a proposal from one group that they be authorized to replace a particular section of piping was close to the head of the list. Readiness for action was present. The group had long been irritated by the need for frequent shutdowns in this stage while leads were patched. Materials flow was being slowed down, and it was virtually certain that this replacement would improve the efficiency of the stage. The replacement would provide experience in planning and executing a phased replacement program.

### Projects Launched

Now the task forces set to work. Their planning sessions had provided a solid base for moving into action. But progress was not without its problems. One superintendent revealed some of his feelings toward the innovation project when he burst into the room where two engineers were discussing an improvement problem and wailed, "Let's not have another damn meeting; we've got trouble!" It had taken quite a bit of personal fortitude for this superintendent to put in the necessary time to get the program launched. He had been used to spending 10 or more hours each day on his job just to make sure he hit his production quotas. Now for a number of weeks he had let the foremen run the show while he spent more than half his time in meetings and planning. It was new, unfamiliar, and risky, and the results were yet to be proved. He would have been much more comfortable plunging back into the old routine.

The Operations Improvement Committee, too, made mistakes. For instance, it encouraged one department which came up with 14 major projects to go ahead with all of them. That group floundered badly.

At some of the committee progress reviews with the departmental task forces, the plant manager declared that he was not going to tell the group what to do but then did most of the talking, suggesting projects he thought should be undertaken, how they should be done, and so forth. It took time and some practice before he learned how to use the committee as a management tool and discovered that there were many ideas superior to his own on how to attack many of the problems.

The projects also strained the technical resources of the committee. There were a great variety of projects, some focusing on scheduling, some on personnel, some on machinery. Some were brilliant, some modestly creative. Some were just plain wrong—a sophisticated observer would have advised against trying them. Several of these wrong projects were stopped. Those which were continued and did not produce "results" had at least one good effect: the managers learned from their own failures. A sense of planned action was achieved.

Gradually, the first tangible results began to show up. One morning, about a month after the projects began, the plant manager remarked, "I don't know what's happening. We haven't had any electrical emergencies—or any pipe-fitting emergencies either. It's been this way for three days!" Some units produced record runs on one or two shifts. The gains overall were not spectacular, but they were good enough to spark interest and to make the managers feel they were on the right track.

## Initial Successes Lead to Bolder Steps

As results began showing up in the first departments, the program was extended to other plant departments. Moreover, as improvements in each individual department were produced through the first projects, they inspired new ideas for moving ahead even farther.

Often these more ambitious plans required collaboration among several departments. For example, the maintenance group, aware that the improvement program would put much heavier demands on its resources, began to explore new ways of managing its existing work loads. Its investigations—quite aside from the assignments it was given—showed that 75 to 80 percent of its man-hours were spent on unplanned "emergency" work. Work assignments came in so fast that maintenance foremen did not know where their men were.

It did not take much more investigation to discover that only about one-third of the so-called emergencies belonged in that category. The rest represented an attempt by operating managers to get some attention. The maintenance superintendent set up strict, realistic rules on emergency work. Then he assigned three supervisors on a full-time basis for a few months to sort out the entire maintenance backlog. They were to work closely with the operating managers to move the most urgent projects ahead while a better priority system was developed. It is interesting to note that the basic idea for these steps had been suggested earlier when one of the pilot operating departments took the initiative in approaching maintenance.

The industrial engineers and other technical people who for years had been struggling to be heard in the plant began to be seen as valuable resources. "Sam was really helpful," said one superintendent about an engineer. "He was right there with me during that committee meeting when all the guns were aimed at me." The engineers and consultants began to get phone calls from the department managers—calls for help.

For example, one engineer had repeatedly suggested a major modification on all the machines in a line of 12. Engineering studies indicated this would result in a significant reduction in the cycle time. The project had been considered too risky for the plant and had been repeatedly shelved.

The department head, however, now decided to convert just *one* machine in the line to see what happened. The engineer had never thought of trying it with one machine. That would have seemed foolish, because to him there was no doubt about the outcome. He was 100 percent certain the conversion would work, though he could never prove it. But now, with the engineer's help, the manager did convert one machine and, after this proved successful, had no trouble obtaining approval to convert the rest.

Plant management, sitting as the Operations Improvement Committee, began to assume increasing responsibility for coordinating the overall effort, the initiative for which was centered in each department. As many more requests came for engineering assistance, maintenance help, and other technical support, there was a need to examine and revise overall scheduling, to take a new look at the missions of several departments. Many of the plant's practices came into question and they, in turn, were subjected to the same sort of modest experimentation on a plantwide basis (in maintenance scheduling and dispatching, for example) that the departments were attempting on their levels.

The plans of the production and operating groups began to focus on how to bring the service departments—engineering, accounting, purchasing, and personnel—into the planning to help them achieve their goals. The need was now for collaboration between departments and for such mechanisms as monthly backlog reviews in order to permit the departments to help each other more effectively.

Accordingly, the Operations Improvement Committee quite naturally transformed itself into a *permanent* plant management committee—the Danville Innovation Committee. It became a major organ of management action and a focus for continued change.

## Overall Results

There was now a much closer correlation between the day-to-day aims of departments and plant managers and the performance criteria adopted by Corporate Manufacturing in Chicago. As the plant was able to improve its operations on its own—to reduce its costs and improve its delivery and quality performance—it was able to deal with headquarters management on a new basis. By the end of one year the plant manager had new confidence in himself, and headquarters management began to get new confidence in him and his associates. He had undertaken and succeeded in so much on his own that when he asked for additional help in capital or cost items, headquarters was much more prepared to listen and respond.

This program was eventually extended to the other three plants in this corporation. At last report, the industrial engineers in this company—at both corporate and plant level—were as busy as anybody wants to be in helping the plants design and carry out ambitious innovation programs.

# MANAGING INNOVATION FOR GROWTH AND PROFIT IMPROVEMENT [TWA]*

*"Innovation is the unwillingness to accept things as they are and the initiative to improve them. A new idea becomes useful only when it has pushed aside the barriers of tradition and resistance and becomes fact."* This program is based on this statement.

*What we are concerned with is the process of innovation and how it can be managed: That is, how innovation is planned, directed, and controlled.* Many people regard creativity as synonymous with innovating. To them someone who can generate ideas is creative or innovative. This may be true of creative people but innovating requires much more than coming up with an idea. Innovating involves an ability to get an idea, evaluate its potential profitability, program the installation of the idea and then implement and guide the change that results.

*Innovation is purposeful, planned, profit-oriented change.* In this program we will look at innovating as starting with the creative step and we will stress developing skill in this most important step. Then we will build on the creative skill to plan and evaluate the implementation of the idea as successful change.

In the following pages you will find material to be read in preparation for your participation in this workshop.

* By Ben Miller, Ph.D. Outlined for a two-day Trans World Airlines Management Training Workshop. Adapted and illustrations omitted.

## Creativity

### *The Mental Powers of the Brain*

If you were to divide the human brain into mental functions you would find there are four: perception, reasoning (or judgment), memory, and imagination (or creativity).

*Perception* is our ability to use our senses, the power to observe, absorb, and learn. Our first contact with an object is through the senses and immediately upon contact we trigger a response in the next segment of our mind which attempts to identify and classify this contact.

*Reasoning*—or judgment—is the faculty that sometimes leads us astray. Here a new bit of information is classified and associated with something that is familiar. We recall by association—either through the senses, by a correspondence of time or sequential pattern, by cause and effect, or by use or value. Through reasoning, judgment, and even logic we subconciously alter or distort the information sufficiently so it is no longer strange or foreign but familiar enough so as not to cause alarm or frustration; and in this manner we store it. Occasionally we eliminate or reject it for the simple reason that, try as we may, we cannot fit it into any familiar pattern.

*Memory* is the follow-up function wherein the information influenced by our reasoning is stored. You might liken the memory to vast reference file and the reasoning or judicial function to the file clerk who directs the information be stored in a specific file by whatever cross-reference system it has devised.

*Imagination* or creativity is the fourth function and, for many of us, seems to come in for the least amount of attention. It is this faculty that has the power to draw upon the other three and the ability to trigger recall of the needed thought at the right time. Here again, because of our society, social environment, and education, this function is often compromised to such an extent that imagination or creativity is stifled and the judicial or reasoning element is emphasized. As a result we see things not as they really are but as we want to see them. The amazing fact of this is that the entire process takes place time and again in a matter of a split second. It happens everytime one of the senses is brought into play. The crux of creative thinking is to separate the creative and judicial elements of the mind, suspend judgment, don't drop it—just change the sequence.

### When Doing Any Kind of Thinking the Mind Uses Four Mental Powers

1. *Power to absorb*—The ability to apply attention, to observe. Example: By watching a professional golfer we see and absorb the proper method of holding a golf club.
2. *Power to reason*—The ability to analyze and judge. Example: By using the data on sales performance, a decision can be made as to the quality of that performance.
3. *Power to remember*—The ability to store and recall. Example: Memorizing a marketing plan or procedure.
4. *Power to create*—The ability to visualize and to generate ideas. Example: Designing a door stop after watching the action of the door.

### Judicial versus Creative Thinking for Problem Solving

Judicial type problems have these characteristics:
1. They are purely analytical in nature and exactly stated.
2. Known facts are given.
3. Final result in an answer or decision.

Good judicial thinking is based mainly on experience, precedent, common sense, and facts.

Creative type problems have these characteristics:
1. Problems are stated in broad terms, such as:
   a. What would happen if xxx xxx?
   b. How many ways can you think of doing xxx?
   c. How can we improve xxx?
2. The known facts are usually inadequate for decisions.
3. They involve the use of creative imagination; new ideas for doing something.
4. Final results are ideas.

| *Judicial* | *Four mental powers* | *Creative* |
|---|---|---|
| Define the problem | Absorb | Define the problem |
| Get the facts | Remember | Get the facts |
| Analyze the facts | Reason | Think up ideas |
| Make a decision | Create | Analyze the ideas |
| | | Select the idea(s) |

Sell Decision or Idea(s)
Apply Decision or Idea(s)

It is interesting to note that the steps in the judicial and creative processes are somewhat similar. However, there are notable differences.

1. In the judicial process we are reasoning from a group of known facts, while in the creative process we are working with ideas.
2. In the judicial process we make a decision on a basis of known facts, while in the creative process we select what we *feel* is the best idea for the solution of the problem.
3. The greatest difference between the judicial and creative processes is in step 3 of the creative process "think up ideas."
4. Most problems are like an umbrella—they cover an immense area. If you segment the problem into subproblems or component parts you can solve a subproblem first and the solution you get may point you to the answer to the larger problem.

## The Barriers to Creativity

To improve creativity you must be aware of the barriers to creativity. Our object here is not to discourage you but to make you aware of some of the factors which inhibit creativity. These factors can be classified as perceptual cultural and emotional blocks, habit, and environment.

*Perceptual blocks* include failure to use all senses, failure to investigate the obvious, and inability to isolate and define the problem area. We fail to distinguish between cause and effect. We see things in the same old way and in this fashion are able to withstand the rigors of frustration.

*Cultural blocks* rise out of our desire to conform to adopted patterns of thought or social custom. In our culture most of us desire to be practical above all things and as a result bring judgment into play too soon. We place a great deal of faith in reason and logic and overemphasize competition and our "real" requirements. We have been taught to believe that indulging in fantasy is a waste of time.

*Emotional blocks* come from fear, man's most potent weapon. We are beset by fear of failure, fear of mistakes, fear of supervision, and distrust of colleagues or subordinates. We fear being ridiculed or making fools of ourselves. We have difficulty rejecting workable solutions and searching for better ones. Sometimes our desire to succeed rapidly causes us to refuse to detour in reaching a goal.

*Habit.* We try to solve new problems with old methods. We try to match space age requirements with horse and buggy solutions. We spend a great deal of time and effort in forming habits so that we may react instinctively. Success with a habitual procedure gives us a great tendency to rely on it. This is not to imply that habit forming is useless. We attempt, and rightly so, to form good habits which permit us to perform our requirements with as little thought or effort as possible. This permits us the needed time and energy to resolve the number and variety of problems we face daily.

*Environment.* Man's early environment required our forefathers to develop individual initiative and resourcefulness. Faced by primitive surroundings, they were forced to "think up" or perish. As a result they laid a firm foundation for our present way of life. Our present day environment tends to discourage creative thinking in many ways. We are living in a push-button world where we have experts and specialists to take care of our needs. Easy living can numb creativity. Our managerial environment may contain factors which serve as barriers to development of creative thinking.

*Environmental Barriers to Creative Thinking*

| | | |
|---|---|---|
| Fear of mistakes | Negative thinking | Inadequate incentives |
| Fear of criticism | Routine jobs | Poor communications |

### High Creativity Factors in People

There are five factors present in persons of high creativity. They are: sensitivity, fluency, flexibility, originality, and "imagineering."

*Sensitivity* is the ability to see things as they really are, to recognize that a problem really exists and to be able to clearly identify and define it. Suppose that for the first time two men see a common building brick laid into a wall. The first might simply store the experience with a mental note "Here is small, square, red building brick." He has recorded size, shape, and color. The second man with the tendency to store cross-referenced information could mentally note "Here is a red building brick used in walls. It is approximately 2x4x8 inches and weights about 4 pounds. It is made of fire clay and will not burn. It is wire cut and has holes to give lightness and quick drying." The second man has also recorded size, shape, and color, but in addition, material, chemical characteristics, mechanical characteristics, manufacturing processes, and design characteristics. Whether the next problem be that of designing a translunar vehicle or finding a suitable clothes hanger, the second individual, whose store of knowledge consists of a group of related ideas, is much more likely to form a mental association that will lead to a solution.

*Fluency* is the ability to come up with a large number of ideas in record time. Here, you must be able to suspend or postpone judgment and forget some of the restrictions of the problem until you have a long list of alternate or possible solutions. Man is so strongly motivated to look for the flaws in an idea that he often will forsake 90 percent correctness because of 10 percent wrongness. Ask yourself what were your reactions the last time someone came to you with an idea or the last time you searched for a possible solution. Were they negative or positive reactions?

*Flexibility* means coming up with a great variety of ideas. Even though you are skilled in one area never eliminate other approaches or combinations of approaches just because they are unfamiliar or unknown to you.

*Originality*. A creative person is by habit and mind freer of fears and inhibitions. Through curiosity he is willing to tear down the old and bring in the new. He brings together seemingly unrelated ideas to form new and original ideas. It is curious that we laugh at men who try wild ideas and fail, but accept as normal those men who don't even try.

*"Imagineering"* is letting your imagination soar and then engineering it down to earth. It is thinking about the thing you do, or make, or the service you give, and then deciding how to do, make, or give something measurably better.

### Guides and Attitudes for Creative Thinking

Accept the idea that we have a creative sense and that creativity cannot be taught but that we can be taught to use, and to use to better advantage, the creativity we already possess.

People can force themselves to be deliberately creative. In fact, this drive is one of the most important characteristics of a creatively minded person. In a person or business firm eager to develop, drive is a must.

The more we practice creativity the more we get better and original ideas. Remember that while there aren't any—or at best very few—*new* ideas there are always *better* ideas. One of the most effective ways to generate improved ideas is to look at other ideas for possible combination.

We can stimulate our imagination by the use of questions remembering that broadly there are two types: (a) the judicial question that is capable of one and only one right answer; (b) the creative question that has a multiplicity of answers of varying degrees of acceptability.

Another great spur to imagination is the power of association of ideas. Take any idea as a starting point and see what happens by contrast, by similarity, and by contiguity.

The whole secret of success in creativity lies in the attitude of mind. The attitude is that there is always a better way and the mind is held in a condition of eternal inquiry and creative discontent.

### Ways to Develop Ideas and Become More Creative

The heart of the creative process is the individual. No committee, group, or seminar ever had an idea. All ideas originate in the minds of individuals. Some spurs which can assist in developing individual creativty are discussed below:

1. Make up a list of problems that need to be solved. Refer to this list daily, revise the list frequently.
2. We all produce better when we have a definite goal. A quota to achieve by a certain time sparks us to greater effort.
3. Set a date when the problem must be solved. Deadlines intensify our emotional power. Many creative people are driven to greater accomplishments by a deadline.
4. Make it a part of your daily schedule to talk to people who can give you ideas for the solution of your problems.
5. Set aside a definite time each day for creative thinking, nothing else. Remember you cannot get hot and cold water out of the same faucet at the same time.
6. Set a place for creative thinking but remember that good ideas come almost anyplace; on trains, in planes, in church, on the golf course.
7. Keep a notebook handy and use it. Good ideas sometimes leave as quickly as they come.

On a less formal basis you can take advantage of everyday

activities of all kinds to stimulate creative imagination. Personal contact with interesting and successful people can lead to new ideas. Take advantage of these occasions to empathize, put yourself in his shoes, try to think like he would think. To get the most out of our experiences we need to be curious and to ask questions and to investigate new things. Practice mental gymnastics by changing the existing form of things, rearrange them, substitute for them, expand them, contract them.

Travel is one kind of experience that tends to expand our imagination. Take advantage of accidental events. Many times, years after having taken a trip, ideas are born which would not have come to us if we had not gone somewhere or seen something.

Reading provides another good source of ideas. And while reading, read between the lines. Francis Bacon once said, "Reading maketh a full man." William Lyon recommends the Bible for mental training. Magazines, such as, *Popular Mechanics, Better Homes and Gardens* and the *National Geographic* can serve as a springboard for new ideas.

Writing can do much to develop our imagination. It isn't necessary to write professionally. There are many forms of amateur writing that help. Even letter writing can help, if we will use a little imagination. Hobbies, such as woodworking and metal working in which we think up designs and carry them out tend to make us more creative. The fine arts including music, painting and sculpture all require and stimulate creative imagination, whether you are an observer or particpant.

In summary, for the optimum use of the creative thinking process, rule out all criticism and judicial judgment, welcome and encourage free wheeling orbital ideas and great quantities of ideas. Improve the quantity and the quality of the ideas you stir up by combination and hitchhiking from one to another. Sixteen particular techniques to develop and encourage creative thinking follow:

### Creative Thinking Techniques

1. *Brainstorming:* An intentionally uninhibited individual or group approach. The objective is to produce the greatest possible number of alternative ideas for later evaluation and development.

2. *Reverse Brainstorming:* Sometimes useful prior to a brainstorm

session, it consists of being critical instead of suspending judgment.

   *a*) List all the things wrong with the operation, process, system, or product.

   *b*) Systematically take each flaw uncovered and suggest ways of overcoming it.

3. *Catalog Technique:* Simply listing various and sundry catalogs or other source of printed information as a means of getting ideas that will, in turn, suggest other ideas. May be used in combination with the Forced Relationship Technique.

4. *Check-List Technique:* A system of getting idea-clues or "leads" by checking the items on a prepared list against the problem or subject under consideration. The objective is to obtain a number of general ideas for further follow-up and development into specific form.

5. *Free Association:* A method of stimulating the imagination to some constructive purpose.

   *a*) Jot down a symbol-word, sketch, number, picture—which is related in some key way to some important aspect of the problem or subject under consideration.

   *b*) Jot down another symbol suggested by the first one.

   *c*) Continue until ideas emerge.

The objective is to produce intangible ideas, advertising slogans, designs, names, etc.

6. *Attribute Listing:* A technique used principally for improving tangible things.

   *a*) Choose some object to improve.

   *b*) List the parts of the object.

   *c*) List the essential basic qualities, features, or attributes of the object and its parts.

   *d*) Systematically change or modify the attributes.

The objective is to satisfy better the original purpose of the object, or to fulfill a new need with it.

7. *Forced Relationship:* A method which has essentially the same basic purpose as free association, but which attempts to force association.

   *a*) Isolate the elements of the problem at hand.

   *b*) Find the relationships among these elements (similarities —differences—analogies—cause and effect).

*c*) Record the relationships in organized fashion.

*d*) Analyze the record of relationships to find the patterns or basic ideas present. Develop new ideas from these patterns.

8. *Morphological Analysis:* A comprehensive way to list and examine all of the possible combinations that might be useful in solving some given problem.

   *a*) State your problem as broadly and generally as possible.

   *b*) Define the independent variables present in the problem— as broadly and completely as possible.

   *c*) Enter the variables as the axes of a morphological chart— or make a permutational listing.

   *d*) Select the most promising alternatives and follow them through.

   The objective is to find all of the possible combinations for subsequent testing, verification, modification, evaluation and development.

9. *Input-Output Technique:* A method of solving dynamic system-design problems:

   *a*) Investigate direction (input, resources, etc.)

   *b*) Establish measures for testing.

   *c*) Develop methods.

   *d*) Optimize a structure.

   *e*) Accomplish a structure.

   *f*) Convince others of its value.

   The objective is to produce a number of possible solutions which can then be tested, evaluated and developed.

10. *Synectics:* A structured approach to creative thinking using the following operational mechanisms.

    *a*) Making the strange seem familiar (through analysis, generalization, and model-seeking).

    *b*) Making the familiar seem strange (through personal analogy, direct analogy, and symbolic analogy).

    The objective usually is to produce one best idea and to carry it through to testing, verification, development, and production in final form.

11. *Inspired (Big Dream) Approach:* A "breakthrough" approach which sometimes leads to spectacular advancements.

    *a*) Think the biggest dream possible about something to benefit mankind.

b) Read, study, and think about every subject connected with your big dream, and do so regularly, persistently, continually.

c) Drop down a dream or so, then engineer your dream into reality.

The objective is to make the greatest possible achievement for human benefit.

12. *Edisonian Method:* An approach consisting principally of performing a virtually endless number of trial-and-error experiments. A "last-ditch" approach, to be resorted to only when

a) Other, more systematic methods have completely failed to produce the desired results; and/or

b) One is knowingly and necessarily delving into the unknown, into areas of basic research.

13. *Kepner-Tregoe Method:* A method particularly calculated to isolating or finding the problem and then deciding what to do about it. A systematic outline is made to describe precisely both the problem and what lies outside the problem but is closely related to it in order to find possible causes of the problem and facilitate decision making.

14. *Bionics:* Ask yourself, "How is this done in nature?" Nature's scheme of things is revealed to those who search. (Note: this technique may come into play in synectics when utilizing analogies.)

15. *Value Analysis (or Engineering):* A specialized application of creative problem solving to increase value. It may be defined as an objective, systematic and formalized method of performing a job to achieve only necessary functions at minimum cost. Six questions are evoked concerning each part:

a) What is it?

b) What must it do?

c) What does it do?

d) What did it cost?

e) What else will do the job?

f) What will that cost?

16. *Scientific Method:* Although many scientists today say there is no one "scientific method" the following general approach is by now regarded as traditional and is listed here for comparative purposes.

*a*) Define the problem.
*b*) Analyze the problem.
*c*) Gather data to solve the problem.
*d*) Analyze the data.
*e*) Arrive at solutions.
*f*) Test these solutions.

## Profit Improvement

### Assessing the Profit Improvement Potential of Ideas

1. *Show the importance of profit improvement*
   in meeting external economic pressures of mounting competition for markets.
   in meeting internal pressures for improved management practices in utilizing scarce resources.
2. *Provide the tools for operating a profit improvement program*
   by pointing out important sources for revenue increase.
   by examining practical techniques for achieving improved cost performance.
3. *Stimulate profit improvement through supervisory action*
   by upgrading managerial skills to effect revenue increase and cost reductions.
   by establishing measurement techniques to evaluate supervisory performance in this area of key responsibility.
4. *Focus on increasing productivity through better management of employees*
   by improving the measurement, analysis, and scheduling of work and the work force.
   by optimizing the selection, placement, and development of employees.
   by increasing supervisory and employee motivation through direct and indirect incentives and rewards.
   by measuring effectiveness of employee performance and taking corrective action.
   by promoting idea power of all employees through systematic solicitation of new methods and approaches.
5. *More effectively channel staff services to improved operations*
6. *Make profit improvement a way of life and a crucial part of the company's planning efforts*

by assuring management and employee participation and support.

by improving job security and the conditions of work while improving quality and quantity of output.

### Where to Concentrate Profit Improvement Efforts

REVENUE INCREASE

1. Enter new markets, explore old ones more fully, both passenger and cargo.
2. Develop ideas for increasing share of market.
3. Propose a new customer service.
4. Improve or alter a present service.
5. Develop more effective use of promotion investment.
6. Encourage employees (nonmarketing) to participate in raising revenue.
7. Design programs for increasing efficiency of marketing personnel (higher sales return).
8. Propose improvements in schedule and facilities.
9. Offer ideas for market research and promotion.

COST IMPROVEMENT

1. *Three Main Elements of Cost*
   *a*) Direct labor, overhead (including indirect labor), and materials make up cost elements.
   *b*) Importance of each element varies:
       (1) In marketing, overhead is a major factor of cost.
       (2) In aircraft operation labor cost for flight crews and maintenance personnel is a major cost element.
2. *Analyzing Cost Elements in Each Department*
   *a*) Break down total cost into its major components: direct labor, indirect labor and other overhead costs, and material.
   *b*) Break down each component into specific items of cost.
   *c*) Examine each specific item in terms of:
       (1) How important is it in relation to other items?
       (2) What can be done about it?
       (3) What are the estimated potential savings?
   *d*) On the basis of such an analysis, set up a priority of specific target items for cost reduction.

3. *Suggestions for Supervisory Cost Reduction*
   *a*) Increase worker productivity.
      (1) Improve workplace layout.
      (2) Maintain steady flow of office operations.
      (3) Improve department layout.
      (4) Make sure employees understand job and methods.
      (5) Place employees in jobs that fit their skills.
      (6) Maintain high levels of morale through use of financial and nonfinancial incentives.
      (7) Set up standards to check employee performance.
      (8) Improve manpower scheduling.
      (9) Increase work force flexibility.
   *b*) Better use of materials.
      (1) Devise ways to recover waste products.
      (2) Conserve power.
      (3) Control material usage.
      (4) Improve quality.
   *c*) Improved use and care of equipment.
      (1) Reduce equipment downtime through better maintenance.
      (2) Train personnel in proper care of equipment such as copying machines, typewriters, etc.

### Return on Investment Analysis

Return on investment analysis is a useful tool for a profit improvement program. It helps to evaluate the potential benefits of a proposed idea and thereby ensures a profit-oriented approach towards innovation.

This analysis consists of two parts:
1. The actual calculation of return on investment (RI).
2. The setting of an acceptable rate of return (%) that will be the criteria for determining whether the profit potential warrants implementing the innovation.

The formula for return on investment is illustrated in the accompanying formula chart.

$$\text{RI} = \frac{\text{Earnings}}{\text{Margin}} \frac{\text{(Earnings)}}{\text{(Sales)}} \times \text{Turnover} \frac{\text{(Sales)}}{\text{(Investment)}}$$

Elements of a Comprehensive Profit Improvement Program

| Organizational Level | Objectives | | Measuring Scale | Tools and Techniques | Examples of Factors to Be Measured |
|---|---|---|---|---|---|
| | Revenue Increase | Cost Improvement | | | |
| Top Management and Staff | Decide on: New markets Share of market Investments | Support | Long-range profit Plan (5–10 years) | Mathematical models Simulation Consultants | Share of market Return on investment Break-even analysis Trend analysis |
| Middle Management and Staff | Fulfill profit plan Improve services Increase production Improve schedules and facilities Create new marketing programs | Efficient use of: Men Material Facilities | Operating plan (1-3 years) | PERT Value analysis Learning curve analysis Simulation Work measurement Responsibility accounting Work sampling | Work backlog Back orders Cost of inventory distribution Marketing effectiveness Cost of hiring men Purchasing material Acquiring facilities Research engineering |
| 1st Line Management and Staff | Support | Fulfill operating plan | Budget for current year and next | Work simplification Short interval scheduling (supervision) | Overtime Scrap Tool up time Quality of products Sales efficiency Cost of maintenance services |
| Employees | Support | Support | Methods Procedures Standards | Work simplification (participation) Suggestion program | Production Cost of paperwork Sales quota |

Therefore

$$RI = \frac{\text{Earnings}}{\text{Sales}}$$

For example an investment of $50,000 in organizing a new marketing section results in $25,000 in annual earnings so that

$$RI = \frac{25,000}{50,000} = \underline{\underline{50\%}}$$

### FORMULA CHART
### Relationship of Factors Affecting Return on Investment

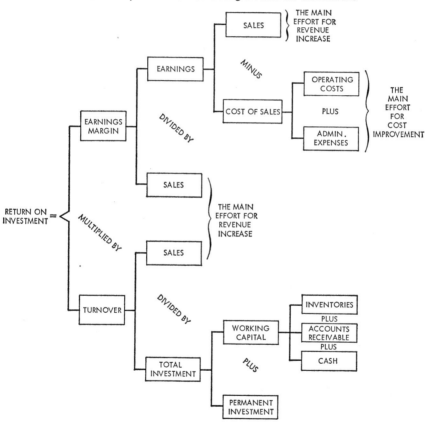

## Finding the Payback Period for an Innovation

There are two steps in the payback approach:

1. Computation of how long it will take the investment to pay for itself, that is, computation of the payback period.

2. Comparison of this payback period with some predetermined standard period in which the investment should pay for itself. If the equipment will pay for itself in less time than the predetermined period, the investment is considered profitable; if not, the investment will be abandoned.

The computation of the payback period can be summarized in a simple formula:

$$P = C/R$$

In which P represents the payback period, C the original cost of the investment (sometimes called the supply price), and R the annual return in dollars expected from the investment. Each of these terms is self explanatory, except R, which calls for some comment. R might represent the savings in direct labor cost resulting from introducing the new machine—this would be the case of a labor-saving investment. It might be the expected profits above variable costs of investment in a new Marketing Program. In any case, R is measured after added variable expenses have been deducted from the *expected added revenue* or the *expected savings in cost*.

A simple illustration may help clarify the approach. Assume that a company is considering investment in Marketing Program. The facts are as follows:

```
Cost of program........................$10,000
Expected life of marketing investment......5 Years
Annual revenue increase..................$ 4,000
Payback criterion........................3 Years
```

The payback period in this case is 2½ years ($10,000 divided by the annual earnings increase of $4,000). Since this is less than the required payback period of 3 years, the investment has satisfied the requirements.

In a similar manner assume that a company is considering investment in a new machine. The facts about the machine are as follows:

```
Cost (supply price).....................$10,000
Expected life............................5 Years
Annual savings in direct labor costs........$ 4,000
Payback criterion........................3 Years
```

The payback period in this case is 2½ years ($10,000 divided by the annual savings of $4,000). Since this is less than the required payback period of 3 years, the investment has satisfied the requirements.

## *Break-Even Analysis*

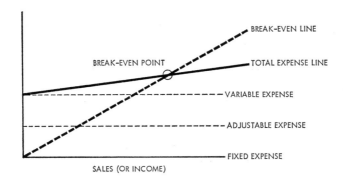

DEFINITION OF TERMS

1. *Fixed Expenses*—are not dependent upon the volume of sales —include property, taxes, insurance, depreciation, etc.
2. *Adjustable Expenses*—do not vary with sales either, but *do* change from time to time at the discretion of mangement. Include sales promotion, number of supervisors, office expenses or anything which management may raise or lower.
3. *Variable Expense*—vary (up or down) directly in proportion to

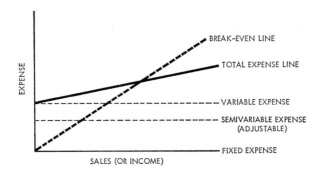

sales and include direct materials, direct labor (usually) and some part of overhead.

4. *Total Expense Line*—shows the total of fixed, adjustable and variable expenses at any specific volume of sales.
5. *Break-Even Line*—sales at any *point* on this line (in dollars) are exactly equal to the expenses.

$$y = a + bx$$
$$y = \text{total expense at any volume of sales}$$
$$a = \text{constant expense (fixed and semivariable)}$$
$$b = \text{slope of variable expense trend to ratio of variable total expense to sales}$$
$$x = \text{volume of sales considered}$$

$$\frac{\text{Variable Expense}}{\text{Sales}} = \text{Expense per Sale}$$

*Example:*

$$\text{Fixed Expense} = 300{,}000$$
$$\text{Semivariable (adjustable)} = 2{,}000{,}000$$
$$.5 = \frac{\text{Variable Expense}}{\text{Sales}} \text{ Ratio}$$

Answer
$$a = 2 + .3 = 2.3 \text{ million}$$
$$b = .5$$
$$y = 2.3 + 5x$$
$$= 2.3 + .5 \text{ } Sales$$

Break-even point is amount of Sales $x$ such that at break-even point $x = y$

$$x = y = 2.3 + .5x$$
$$x = \frac{2.3}{1-.5} = \frac{2.3}{.5} \text{ million}$$
$$x = 4{,}600{,}000 \text{ of sales}$$

Two possible applications include:
1. Break-even point in operating a sales unit.
2. Break-even point in operating an aircraft.

# THE MARTIN COMPANY *

The Martin Company is a manufacturer and distributor of women's foundation products (girdles and brassieres). Its executive offices are located in Philadelphia while its production facilities are in New Bedford, Massachusetts. All told the company employs about 550 people. Martin's sales in 1968 were about $12 million with profits well up in six figures.

The story of how the Martin Company has managed innovation unfolds from an atmosphere of business crisis and personal tragedy to one of dramatic business success and personal satisfaction. The time of crisis and tragedy was 1960 when Bruce Martin took over the reins of the foundation garment firm after the unexpected death of his father who had started the company twenty-five years earlier.

For 1960 the Martin Company showed a slight loss on sales of two million dollars. Moreover, there was clear evidence that the downward trend would continue in succeeding years. The challenge was not only to stop the losses but to develop a new approach that would move Martin towards continued growth in sales and profits. Martin initiated an innovation program destined to overhaul the entire company. One of Bruce Martin's earliest steps was to bring in John Harris to help build the "new" Martin Company.

Before examining innovation at Martin let's review the foundation industry. The industry generates an annual sales volume of $1 billion at the consumer level distributed among some 400 firms.

* Names of Company and personnel are disguised.

243

The largest company in the industry has a market share of only 12 percent with the others falling off sharply to divide the rest. The vast majority of the firms are production oriented and gear their output to the fashion seasons of the year.

Typically, these companies introduce a group of new products each season with the full expectation that 90 percent of them will not survive. Their hope is that the remaining 10 percent which are successes will be enough to assure a profit for the season. The result is that these companies have wide swings in profits and losses from year to year (and season to season). Coupled with this is the excruciating pressure upon production to make available those products that have caught on and to cut back those that have failed. In addition, there is rarely an attempt made to carry a successful product into the next season since a preoccupation with fashion dictates that new products appear in succeeding seasons.

Against this background, the Martin Company embarked upon a program of innovation (planned, purposeful, profit-oriented change) that effected every area of its business. In developing a program to manage innovation Bruce Martin and John Harris concentrated on creating a philosophy and goals for the company, building an organization structure and staffing it with innovative people, establishing a climate that would spur innovation, and initiating projects that would lead to specific administrative and technological innovations.

### Innovation in Philosophy and Goals

Unusual for a company of its size was the Martin Company's determination to completely break away from the fashion oriented approach of its industry. Martin's view of itself was that it was dealing with packaged consumer products that perform a certain function for the consumer and, in the process, serve her wants and needs. It was concluded that any future products developed would be completely divorced from fashion and instead would be offered as a packaged product a la Procter and Gamble. Moreover, rather than have production dominate the company, a more balanced management structure would emphasize the functions of research and development, marketing, and finance as well.

Just as the above philosophy reflects a dramatic break with the foundation industry's traditional approach, Martin set goals that were atypical. Clearly established were targets for growth in sales and profits which were to be achieved on a year round rather than seasonal basis. This was to be achieved with product lines that would be supported by market acceptance and patents which could assure a relatively long shelf life. These goals emphasized an approach to managing innovation that was consistent with that of successful packaged goods companies.

## Innovation in Organization

A major step towards carrying out the philosophy and goals of the Martin Company was the structuring of an organization that was innovative for the foundation garment industry. It involved the creation of new functions as well as staffing them with managers who were enthusiastic in their support for the company's new philosophy and goals. A contrast between the old and new organizations is revealed in comparing the 1960 chart shown in Fig. 1 with the 1968 chart in Fig. 2. What is clear is that Martin moved from a top heavy production structure to one in which research, marketing and finance were given equal emphasis with production.

What is *not* evident from the charts is that the people making up the management team in 1968 were innovative in both spirit and technique.

## Creating the Climate for Innovation

A critical task facing the Martin Company was to make clear to its new management group that the environment in which they would operate would encourage the development of innovations. It was necessary to create a climate that would encourage managers to challenge the status quo, especially as represented by the tradition of a fashion-bound industry.

Managers were expected to depart from tradition, to generate new ideas and to develop projects that would spur company growth and profits. This was supplemented by involving managers in setting targets coupled with handsome recognition for achieving them.

## Developing Projects for Administrative and Technological Innovations

Having marshalled the ingredients for innovation, the Martin Company applied these resources toward the development of specific administrative and technological innovations. In terms of administrative improvements, Martin developed research in basic functions of its products and in the market and consumer it served; developed a systems approach to company operations; designed planning and control procedures for each function; and computerized its operations to generate new and faster data to improve managers' planning and control decisions.

In terms of technological innovations, the company improved its production processes and initiated a product line that would be an expression of its new philosophy and goals. To show how they approached product innovation the development of a current product line will be traced from the inception of the idea (concept) to its introduction to the public. It is important to note that Martin has developed a *process* that is the basis for product innovation and which is to be used to create an endless array of innovations rather than a single fleeting success.

### Innovation of the Won't Twist Girdle

A recount of the development of the Won't Twist product line must start with the team that created it. Not revealed on the organization chart is the existence of a top management innovation project group. This is a standing task force organized to exploit innovative opportunities and consisting of the top management men at Martin. It is interesting to note that the major experience of each of these men before coming to the company, was in an industry dealing with consumer packaged goods and *not* the fashion-bound apparel industry. The project group consists of John Harris, President with heavy experience as an executive with Scott Paper; Doug Burns, General Manager, from International Playtex; Fred Jarman, Vice-President of Marketing, from Standard Brands; and Jim Downes, Vice-President of Sales, from Procter and Gamble.

Let's examine how this innovation project group proceeded to develop the Won't Twist girdle. The emphasis of the group was on thorough research and development to be accompanied by careful testing of the product during key stages. This was followed by careful market testing, promotional campaigns and closely scheduled production. In total, the innovation was managed by planning, organizing and controlling each stage of the Won't Twist development. Fig. 3 shows a chart used to plan and control each phase of the project while Fig. 4 shows a network analysis used in planning and controlling R.&D. at Martin. To indicate the magnitude of the project, Fig. 5 reveals the 58 steps followed by the innovation project group in developing the Won't Twist girdle.

The project group met regularly to coordinate the efforts of R.&D., market research, production, marketing, creative development, and media (the latter two involved in sales promotion and advertising). Another function of the innovation project group was to review evaluations of the project at each state of its evolution to decide on go or no go. The group had to determine whether at any point the project was revealed as unworthy of further consideration and was therefore to be cancelled. On the other hand if profit potential remained strong at each stage of evaluation it was carried to the point of introduction for sale.

In the case of the Won't Twist girdle a testing program carried out by market research revealed outstanding potential at every stage. The first test was that of a consumer reaction to the concept of a girdle that would not roll at the waist. After overwhelming consumer approval of this concept, the Martin Company designed a girdle with a Won't Twist feature and then tested its appearance (show test) and performance (wear test) among thousands of women.

Evaluation of market research tests by the project group led to improvements in the product and with further research the innovation project group became convinced that the Won't Twist girdle had immense profit potential. Market projections were made, sales promotion and production schedules were completed and after two years of preparation the Won't Twist girdle was introduced in the fall of 1969. Indications are that sales will top even optimistic forecasts.

The operations of the innovation project group have already been improved as a result of the experience with the Won't Twist

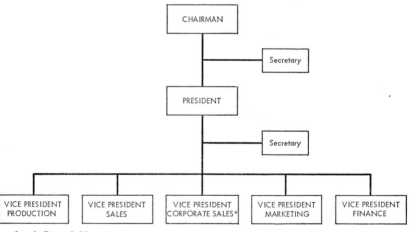

Figure 1

MARTIN COMPANY—1960

Figure 2

MARTIN COMPANY—1968

* and General Manager

project. Greater use of network analysis and quantitative techniques as well as research in human anatomy will be evident in current innovation projects at Martin.

What is interesting about the Martin Company's recent success is that its growth has been achieved entirely through the use of plowed back earnings and short term borrowing. It is Martin's plan to expand in the future by using long term debt and by acquiring

Figure 3

WON'T TWIST DEVELOPMENT SCHEDULE

| Date | Research and Development | Market Research | Production | Marketing | Creative Development | Media |
|---|---|---|---|---|---|---|
| 10/11/68 | | | | Approval final Won't Twist prototype | | |
| 10/14/68 | Basic fittings of Basic 3 sizes | | | | | |
| 10/18/68 | | Release show test on final prototype | | | | |
| 10/21/68 | Release specs & In-process samples | | Begin costing & In-process evaluation | | | |
| 10/31/68 | | Report show test key results | | | | |
| 11/4/68 | Begin indicated design modifica-tions | Report show test reasons | Report costs & In-process evaluations | | | |
| 11/8/68 | Complete revisions & begin full grade | | | Approve final revisions | | |
| 11/18/68 | Release patterns for pilot run | | Begin work on pilot run | | | |

Figure 3—Continued

| Date | Research and Development | Market Research | Production | Marketing | Creative Development | Media |
|---|---|---|---|---|---|---|
| 1/10/69 | | | Send wear-test garments to design | | Agreement to 2 (or 3) creative strategies | |
| 1/13/69 | Begin evaluation of wear test garment | | Pilot run for 6,000 units | | | |
| 1/17/69 | | Release final show & wear test | | | | |
| 1/24/69 | | | | | Present alternative story boards | |
| 1/29/69 | | | | | Approval to produce rough commercial for copy testing | |
| 2/3/69 | | Show keys | | | | |
| 2/10/69 | | Report on show test | | Begin marketing test sell-in | | Agreement to media objective & strategy statement |
| 2/12/69 | | | | | Copy test rough commercial | |
| 2/13/69 | | Report wear test key results | | | | |

| Date | | | | | |
|---|---|---|---|---|---|
| 2/18/69 | Begin final design modifications | | | | |
| 2/24/69 | Report wear test reasons | Begin mkt. test shipments 5,000–6,000 units | Copy test—top line | Agreement to theoretical national plan | |
| 2/26/69 | | Begin national product run if product OK | Approval to produce finished commercial | | |
| 3/3/69 | | | | Agreement to test market media plan | |
| 3/10/69 | | | | Media authorization for test market | |
| 3/11/69 | Release modified & regraded pattern | Begin national production run | | | |
| 3/17/69 | | | Approve corrected answer-print | | |
| 3/24/69 | | | 1st air date test markets | Start advertising 1st air date | |
| June '69 | | | | | National introduction |
| Sept. '69 | | | | National TV break | |

## Figure 4

### NEW PRODUCT DEVELOPMENT PROGRAM
### (Research and Development)

| Basic Development Schedule | Completion Dates | Design Activity |
|---|---|---|
| 1. Design prepares prototype; rough costed; approved by Marketing. | ___ | **Show Test**<br>1. Market Research advises Design of number of products needed for show test. |
| 2. Design completes garments for initial show test. | ___ | 2. Designer prepares products for test and advises Market Research when they will be completed. |
| 3. Market Research distributes show test "key" results. | ___ | 3. Designer keeps on file a duplication of garments being tested and all test numbers recorded on outside of envelope. |
| 4. Market Research distributes show test reasons. | ___ | |
| 5. Design modifies prototype and releases for show test. | ___ | |
| 6. Market Research distributes show test keys. | ___ | |
| 7. Market Research distributes show test reasons. | ___ | |
| 8. Marketing approves prototype design. | ___ | |
| 9. Design sends prototype to Manufacturing for initial costing and evaluation. | ___ | |
| | | **Fittings**<br>1. When show test results are favorable, fitting of basic 34A,B,C,D and basic girdle sizes begin. |
| | | 2. During the fitting time or as soon as possible after show test results are in, designer forwards to Manufacturing a prototype and in process samples for handling and construction evaluation. |
| 10. Design modifies patterns and completes fittings of 34A,B,C,D; or P,S,M,L,XL girdles. | ___ | 3. Designer evaluates all material being used in new product for acceptable production use. Lab testing facilities will be available in the future for a more detailed evaluation and material specifications will be prepared. |

4. When basic fittings are completed, the following is turned over to the Pattern Department:

   a) Master patterns
   b) Approved fitting garments
   c) All information

   needed to complete pattern check. (A form will be available in the future for this purpose.)

5. During the above fittings, the sewing supervisor consults with the designer in the preparation of a product spec.

## PATTERN CHECK

1. Pattern maker refines original master pattern and advises designer of any adjustments needed.

2. Pattern maker prepares hard board patterns for Design Department pattern check and supervises the sewing of basic sizes according to specifications.

3. Pattern maker advises designer when garments are completed and fitted. Pattern checks are compared to approved garments; (designer and pattern maker to be present during fitting) and O.K. for production pattern check.

4. Pattern maker to file master pattern chart and approved garments for fitting reference. Original designer master pattern is to be returned to designer.

5. Pattern maker prepares production pattern check package. This package consists of the following:

   a) Hard board patterns (for cutting)
   b) Manila paper patterns (for costing)
   c) In process samples (sewing operations)
   d) 3 prototypes of 34B or medium
   e) Any new material or accessories not available in production for test
   f) Request for samples (if form is available)

6. Design and Manufacturing will consult and decide if designer presence is required for pattern check.

11. Pattern Department refines patterns, completes initial sewing and material specifications.

# Figure 4—Continued

| Basic Development Schedule | Completion Dates | Design Activity |
|---|---|---|
| | | **PATTERN CHECK/CONSUMER TEST GARMENTS** |
| 12. Manufacturing completes pattern check evaluation and show wear test garments; final costing completed. | _____ | 1. Manufacturing checks all parts for sew matching, advises Design if there are any problems and forwards pattern check consumer test garments to Design Dept. for evaluation. |
| 13. Design evaluates pattern check and show wear test garments. | _____ | 2. Design evaluates test garments by comparing to original approved garments and O.K.'s or rejects for test. |
| 14. Market Research distributes show wear test key results. | _____ | 3. Market Research reports key test results and reasons. Design evaluates results and modifies patterns accordingly for Market wear test. |
| 15. Market Research distributes wear reasons. | _____ | |
| 16. Design evaluates test results and modifies patterns. | _____ | **MARKET & WEAR TEST (PILOT RUN)** |
| | | *Designer and pattern maker follow same procedure as pattern check/consumer test, but grade to all sizes.* |
| | | 1. Designer and pattern maker fit basic and larger sizes for approval for release to Manufacturing. |
| 17. Design grades to all sizes and releases for market test (pilot) run. | _____ | 2. |
| 18. Manufacturing receives dies and starts market test run; Design observes & approves; Production starts. | _____ | 3. Pattern maker prepares all size market/wear test package as follows: |
| 19. Manufacturing completes show/wear preference wear/life test garments and sends to Design. | _____ | a) Revised in process sample |
| | | b) Fit standard garments (basic sizes) |
| 20. Design evaluates garments and approves for all size show/wear preference and wear life tests. | _____ | c) 3 revised prototypes |
| | | d) Hard board patterns all sizes |
| | | e) 2 sets of manilla patterns for costing and dies |
| | | f) Revised temporary product specification |
| | | g) Request for sample form |
| | | 4. Designer checks to make sure product specification is up to date. |

21. Manufacturing completes market test run (ad breaks 4 weeks later).
22. Market Research reports key show/wear preference results.
23. Market Research reports show/wear preference.
24. Design evaluates test results and modifies pattern.
25. Design re-grades modified patterns and releases to Manufacturing.

26. Marketing gives "Go Decision" for national introduction.
27. Design sends permanent specifications and fit standards to Manufacturing.

5. Designer makes trip to Manufacturing to be present for start of test garments. Garments will be fitted from production line.
6. Manufacturing forwards *wear test garments* to designer for evaluation. (Usually 150 garments of various sizes.)
7. As designer O.K.'s wear test garments *Production* continues to complete balance for market test.
8. During the sewing of market test garments, Manufacturing is to send Design 6 each of fitting sizes and three each of all other sizes, for final evaluations before market test release.
9. Market Research reports keys and reasons to Design.
10. Design evaluates results and modifies patterns, if necessary, for full scale production.

FULL-SCALE PRODUCTION

1. Same procedure as market wear test, with the exception that everything is now marked permanent.

QUALITY CONTROL

1. Designer is to receive for evaluation from Manufacturing bi-monthly production garments for a period of three months, and thereafter once a month.
2. A report is to be forwarded to Manufacturing with an explanation of evaluation results.

other companies outside the foundation industry. There is every reason to believe that Martin's rate of growth in sales and profits during the 70's will match its performance of the 60's.

Figure 5

MANAGING THE WON'T TWIST INNOVATION

1. Development schedule
2. Show test (keys)
3. Show test I
4. Meeting
5. Sizing
6. Proposed names
7. Preliminary test market
8. Test market
9. Test market promotion materials
10. Test garments
11. Test markets
12. Test markets
13. Name search
14. Preliminary creative strategy
15. Packaging meeting
16. Test market TV
17. Torso sizing
18. Marketing release—test markets
19. Final creative strategy
20. Changes in development schedule
21. Product evaluation
22. Show test II
23. Copy testing of rough commercials
24. Letter to test market salesmen
25. Wear test II
26. Warrantee set-up
27. Copy testing & production schedule
28. Procedure for test market data collection
29. Name search
30. Development of line extensions
31. TV production estimates on proving grounds commercial
32. Final copy for commercial & storyboard
33. Promotional materials
34. Preliminary marketing release national introduction
35. TV test
36. TV test markets audit
37. Accelerated 1969 forecast
38. Screening of TV commercial
39. TV commercial production time table
40. Final torso breakdown
41. POP material status
42. Evaluation reports
43. Costing on line extensions
44. Test market TV schedule
45. Two-month wear test results
46. Packaging
47. Final marketing release national introduction
48. TV movement report

49. Preliminary marketing release line extensions
50. Product improvement meeting
51. Line extension meeting
52. Schedule for line extensions
53. Addendum to final marketing release—handling of materials
54. Addendum to marketing release—Coop TV break date
55. Fact book—national introduction
56. Copy of weekly movement report
57. Field trip report by agency
58. Evaluation of product

# Notes

# NOTES

## Introduction

1. Peter F. Drucker, *Landmarks of Tomorrow,* Harper, 1957, p. 18.
2. Joseph A. Schumpeter, *Capitalism, Socialism, and Democracy,* Harper, 1942, p. 41.
3. Richard Eells and Clarence Walton, *Conceptual Foundations of Business,* Irwin, 1961, p. 440.
4. Peter F. Drucker, *Practice of Management,* Harper, 1954, p. 69.
5. *Ibid.,* p. 68.
6. Peter F. Drucker, *America's Next Twenty Years,* Harper, 1955, p. 16.
7. Edgar Weinberg, "An Inquiry into the Effects of Automation," *Impact of Automation,* p. 21.
8. *Ibid.*
9. *Ibid.*
10. John Diebold, *Automation,* Von Nostrand, 1953, p. ix.

## Chapter 1

1. James Burnham, *The Managerial Revolution,* p. 82.
2. Robert Presthus, *The Organizational Society,* p. 69.
3. Adolph Berle, *Power Without Property,* Chap. II.
4. Peter F. Drucker, *Practice of Management,* Harper, 1954, pp. 3–4.
5. R. L. Bruckberger, *Image of America,* Viking Press, 1959, p. 207.
6. D. Riesman, with N. Glazer and R. Dem, *The Lonely Crowd,* Doubleday, 1953.
7. "Automation at Volkswagen," *Automation,* February, 1964, p. 73.
8. Michael T. Florinsky, "Automation," *McGraw-Hill Encyclopedia of Russia and the Soviet Union,* p. 49.
9. Jack B. Weiner, "Ford's Road Ahead," *Dun's Review,* August, 1965, p. 69.
10. Max Ways, "The Era of Radical Change," *Fortune,* May, 1964, p. 113.
11. *Ibid.,* p. 216.

## Chapter 2

**1.** "Deadline Near in Rail Rules Dispute," *Business Week,* June 29, 1963, p. 65.
**2.** "RRs Get Green Light to Solve Big Problem," *Newsday,* March 9, 1963.
**3.** "Coast Railroad, Union in Pact Resolving Automation Hassle," *Newsday,* March 18, 1963.
**4.** News Service, "Background on Transportation," Association of American Railroads, #137788, p. 1.

## Chapter 3

**1.** "The Nationalization of U.S. Science," *Fortune,* September, 1964, p. 158.
**2.** "Industry Keeps Pace as R&D Outlays Soar," *Business Week,* July 17, 1965, p. 72.
**3.** "Turnkey Automated Post Office So Far is Turkey," *Business Week,* March 25, 1961, p. 150.
**4.** Arthur Herzog, "Report on a Think Factory," *New York Times Magazine,* November 10, 1963, p. 30.
**5.** "Congress Cuts New Pattern for Cotton," *Business Week,* August 14, 1965, p. 56.
**6.** "Raising the Price for Being Inventive," *Business Week,* July 31, 1965, p. 80.
**7.** U.S. Department of Labor, *Selected Manpower Indicators for States,* Office of Manpower, Automation and Training, Manpower Research, Bulletin #4, November, 1963.
**8.** U.S. Department of Labor, *An Explanation of the Manpower Development and Training Act,* Office of Manpower, Automation and Training, December, 1962.
**9.** *Ibid.,* p. 10.
**10.** "U.S. Hails Easing of Dollar Drain," *Business Week,* August 21, 1965, p. 33.
**11.** *Change, Challenge, Response,* New York State Office for Regional Development, 1964, pp. 8–9.
**12.** "Big Clean Up Begins," *Business Week,* August 14, 1965, p. 25.
**13.** Max Ways, "Antitrust in an Era of Radical Change," *Fortune,* March, 1966, p. 225.

## Chapter 4

**1.** Melvin Anshen and G. L. Bach (eds.), *Management and Corporations, 1985,* McGraw-Hill, 1960, p. 200.
**2.** *Ibid.*
**3.** James R. Bright, *Research Development and Technological Innovation,* Irwin, 1964, p. 12.
**4.** Quoted in Jack B. Weiner, "What's Ahead in Management," *Dun's Review,* January, 1965, p. 32.
**5.** "Why Executives Obsolescence," *Business Week,* November 30, 1963, p. 78.
**6.** Lester J. Weigle, "The Growing Problems of Executive Obsolescence," *Dun's Review,* April, 1964, p. 66.
**7.** Held in Boston, October 29, 1963.
**8.** Anshen and Bach, *op. cit.,* pp. 201–2.
**9.** *Ibid.,* pp. 203–4.
**10.** *Ibid.,* pp. 200–201.

11. "Managing Corporate Technology," *The Executive,* September, 1962, p. 28.

12. *Ibid.,* p. 26. Also, for a six-point program for improving managerial skills for innovation, see "Skill in Initiating Change," *Supervision,* August, 1965, p. 4.

13. "Caught in the Civil Rights Crossfire," *Business Week,* August 7, 1965, p. 102.

14. Jack B. Weiner, "Why Growth Companies Go Wrong," *Dun's Review,* June, 1965, p. 42.

15. In Elizabeth Marting (ed.), *New Products/New Profits,* American Management Association, p. 19.

16. *Ibid.,* p. 31.

17. *Ibid.,* pp. 291–96.

18. Max Ways, "The Era of Radical Change," *Fortune,* May, 1964, p. 215.

19. Peter F. Drucker, *Landmarks of Tomorrow,* Harper, 1957, p. 49.

20. *Manufacturing and the Challenge of Change,* American Management Association, 1962, p. 6.

## Chapter 5

1. Jack B. Weiner, "What Makes a Growth Company," *Dun's Review,* November, 1964, p. 30.

2. James R. Bright, *Research Development and Technological Innovation,* Irwin, 1964.

3. Peter F. Drucker, *Practice of Management,* Harper, 1954, p. 69.

4. Peter F. Drucker, *America's Next Twenty Years,* Harper, 1955, p. 16.

5. Harwood F. Merrill, "Experts Outline Plan for Planning," Management News, AMA, July, 1965, p. 5.

6. *New Product Development,* NICB, 1950.

7. Elizabeth Marting (ed.), *New Products/New Profits,* AMA, 1964.

8. Gerald Fisch, "Line-Staff is Obsolete," *Harvard Business Review,* September–October, 1961.

9. Jay W. Forrester, *Industrial Dynamics,* Wiley, 1961.

10. Irwin A. Rose, "Increasing Productivity Through Job Enlargement," in *Manufacturing and the Challenge of Change,* AMA, 1962, p. 43.

11. Theodore Levitt, *Innovation in Marketing,* McGraw-Hill, 1962, p. 12.

12. Robert W. Ferrell, *Customer Oriented Planning,* AMA, 1964, p. 28.

13. Thomas J. Murray, "Dual Distribution *vs* the Small Retailer," *Dun's Review,* August, 1964, p. 29.

14. Quoted in Jack B. Weiner, "Dis-Organization Man," *Dun's Review,* April, 1964, p. 33.

15. "At the Crucial Points of Decision," *Fortune,* September, 1964, p. 192.

16. John W. Enell and George H. Hess, *Setting Standards for Executive Performance,* AMA, 1960, pp. 15–16.

17. C. Wilson Randle and Willys H. Monroe, "Better Ways to Measure Executive Performance," *Management Methods.*

18. Virgil K. Rowland, *Improving Managerial Performance,* Harper, 1958, pp. 16–17.

19. Frederick Harbison, "Manpower and Innovation: Some Pointers for Management," *Personnel,* AMA, November–December, 1959.

## Chapter 6

1. Peter F. Drucker, *Landmarks of Tomorrow,* Harper, 1957, p. 18.

2. Quoted in Jack B. Weiner, "Dis-Organization Man," *Dun's Review,* April, 1964, p. 33.

**3.** *IBM News,* May 10, 1964, International Business Machines Corporation, New York.

**4.** "Who Do You Promote," *Dun's Review,* 1964, p. 51.

**5.** Weiner, *op. cit.*

**6.** Theodore Levitt, "Creativity is Not Enough," *Harvard Business Review,* May–June, 1963, p. 72.

**7.** Theodore Levitt, "Marketing Myopia," *Harvard Business Review,* July–August, 1960, p. 47.

**8.** Philip H. Abelson, "Creativity in the Sciences," *Science,* June 21, 1963, p. 1271.

**9.** Levitt, "Marketing Myopia," *op. cit.,* p. 54.

## Chapter 7

**1.** Stewart Thompson, *How Companies Plan,* American Management Association, 1962, p. 85.

**2.** Harwood F. Merrill, "Experts Outline Plan for Planning," *Management News,* AMA, July, 1965, p. 5.

**3.** James R. Bright, *Research Development and Technological Innovation,* Irwin, 1964, p. 668.

**4.** Thompson, *op. cit.,* p. 87.

**5.** Merrill, *op. cit.*

**6.** Bright, *op. cit.,* pp. 380–81.

**7.** John S. Harris, "The Product Profile Chart," *Chemical and Engineering News,* April 17, 1961, pp. 110–18.

## Chapter 8

**1.** In Ronald Lippitt *el al., The Dynamics of Planned Change,* 1958, pp. 129–30.

**2.** *Ibid.,* p. 140.

**3.** Harwood F. Merrill, "Experts Outline Plan for Planning," *Management News,* AMA, July, 1965, p. 5.

**4.** Warren Dusenberg, "Applying Advanced Science to Marketing and Ad Plans," *Printers Ink,* September 24, 1965, pp. 15–16.

**5.** Richard G. Canning, *Installing Electronic Data Processing Systems,* Wiley, 1957, p. 130.

## Chapter 9

**1.** D. B. Hertz, "The Management of Innovation," *Management Review,* American Management Association, April, 1965, p. 52.

**2.** Harwood F. Merrill, "Experts Outline Plan for Planning," *Management News,* AMA, July, 1965, p. 5.

**3.** J. A. Schumpeter, *Theory of Economic Development,* Harvard, 1934.

**4.** Joel Dean, *Managerial Economics,* 1951, p. 9.

**5.** *Ibid.*

**6.** See the Du Pont Control Charts in William T. Jerome, III, *Executive Control,* Wiley, 1961, Chap. 13.

**7.** "New Product Development," National Industrial Conference Board, 1950, pp. 20–22.

**8.** "Costing the New Product," in Elizabeth Marting (ed.), *New Products/New Profits,* AMA, 1964, p. 281. Reprinted by permission of the publisher, © 1964 by the American Management Association, Inc.

**9.** Richard G. Canning, *Installing Electronic Data Processing Systems,* Wiley, 1957, pp. 115–16.

**10.** In Marting (ed.), *op. cit.,* p. 297.

## Chapter 11

**1.** *Dun's Review and Modern Industry,* "The Growth Company," October, 1964.

**2.** Quoted in Stewart Thompson, *How Companies Plan,* American Management Association, 1962, p. 119.

**3.** Walter B. Shaffir, "Planning for Change: Organizing for Company-Wide Action," *Management Review,* June, 1965, p. 17.

**4.** Gerald G. Fisch, "New Concepts of Organization in Manufacturing," in *Manufacturing and the Challenge of Change,* AMA, 1962, p. 14.

**5.** D. B. Hertz, "The Management of Innovation," *Management Review,* April, 1965, p. 51.

**6.** Cited in Jack B. Weiner, "The Profit Teams of Management," *Dun's Review,* September, 1964, p. 37.

**7.** Selwyn W. Becker, *The Innovative Organization,* Selected Papers, No. 14, University of Chicago, 1965, p. 10.

**8.** Clyde T. Hardwick and Bernard F. Landuyt, *Administrative Strategy,* Simmons-Boardman, 1961, p. 3.

## Chapter 12

**1.** Paul R. Lawrence, "How to Deal With Resistance to Change," *Harvard Business Review,* May–June, 1954, p. 49.

**2.** Elting E. Morrison, "A Case Study of Innovation," *Engineering and Science,* California Institute of Technology, April, 1950.

**3.** Fritz J. Roethlisberger, *Management and Morale,* Harvard, 1950, p. 61.

**4.** Ben Miller, *Gaining Acceptance for Major Methods Changes,* AMA, 1960, p. 7. Reprinted by permission of the publisher from AMA Research Study No. 44, © 1960 by the American Management Association, Inc.

**5.** Alvin Zander, "Resistance to Change—Its Analysis and Preventions," *Advanced Management,* January, 1950, p. 9.

**6.** *Ibid.*

**7.** James R. Bright, *Research Development and Technological Innovation,* Irwin, 1964, p. 131.

**8.** Zander, *op. cit.*

**9.** *Ibid.*

**10.** Lester Coch and John R. French, "Overcoming Resistance to Change," *Human Relations,* Vol. I, 1948, p. 512.

**11.** *Ibid.,* p. 517.

**12.** Keith Davis, *Human Relations At Work,* McGraw-Hill, 1962, p. 328.

**13.** Lawrence, *op. cit.*

**14.** Morrison, *op. cit.*

**15.** Ben Miller, "Manager—Roadblock to Change?" *Management Review,* April, 1961.

**16.** Lawrence, *op. cit.,* pp. 53–54.

**17.** Miller, *Gaining Acceptance, op. cit.,* pp. 8–10.

**18.** Davis, *op. cit.,* pp. 332–33.

**19.** Robert Saltonstall, *Human Relations in Administration,* McGraw-Hill, 1959, p. 317.

**20.** Bradford B. Boyd, "Skill in Initiating Change," *Supervision,* August, 1965, p. 5.

**21.** Morrison, *op. cit.*

**22.** Lawrence, *op. cit.,* p. 52.

**23.** Zander, *op. cit.,* p. 10.

## Chapter 13

**1.** Cited in "Managing Corporate Technology," *The Executive,* September, 1962, pp. 25–26.

**2.** Floyd C. Mann and Richard Hoffman, *Automation and the Worker,* Henry Holt, 1960, pp. 200–201.

**3.** Goodwin Watson and Edward M. Glasser, "Planning for Change," *Management Review,* November, 1965, p. 40.

**4.** Warren G. Bennis, Kenneth D. Benne, and Robert Chin (eds.), *The Planning of Change,* Holt, 1961, p. 560.

**5.** H. G. Barnett, *Innovation,* McGraw-Hill, 1953, p. 313.

**6.** Alvin Zander, "Resistance to Change—Its Analysis and Prevention," *Advanced Management,* January, 1950, p. 10.

**7.** Dorwin Cartwright, "Achieving Change in People," *Human Relations,* Vol. IV, No. 4, 1951, p. 387.

**8.** Keith Davis, *Human Relations at Work,* McGraw-Hill, 1962, p. 334.

**9.** Mortimer Feinberg, *Effective Psychology for Managers,* Prentice-Hall, 1965.

**10.** Esther R. Becker and Eugene F. Murphy, *The Office in Transition,* Harper, 1957, p. 48.

**11.** Bradford B. Boyd, "Skill in Initiating Change," *Supervision,* August, 1965, pp. 5–6.

**12.** Lester Coch and Rohn R. P. French, "Overcoming Resistance to Change," *Human Relations,* Vol. I, 1948.

**13.** Robert Saltonstall, *Human Relations in Administration,* McGraw-Hill, 1959, p. 320.

**14.** Paul R. Lawrence, "How to Deal With Resistance to Change," *Harvard Business Review,* May–June, 1954, p. 51.

**15.** Chris Argyris, *Personality and Organization,* Harper, 1957, p. 283.

**16.** Douglas McGregor, *The Human Side of Enterprise,* McGraw-Hill, 1960, Chap. 3.

**17.** "Managing Your Manpower," *Dun's Review,* August, 1964, p. 72.

**18.** "When Workers Manage Themselves," *Business Week,* March 20, 1965, p. 93.

**19.** Paul Pigors, *Effective Communication in Industry,* National Association of Manufacturers, 1949, p. 68.

## Chapter 14

**1.** Frederick G. Lesieur, *The Scanlon Plan,* p. 21.

**2.** "Scanlon Plan," *Time,* September 26, 1955 pp. 66, 87.

**3.** *Harold Stieglitz, The Kaiser–Steel Union Sharing Plan,* p. 3.

**4.** John D. Pamfret, "Bridges Defends Dock Contract as Benefiting Coast Unionists," *New York Times,* October 9, 1963.

# Index

# INDEX

269

*This book has been set in 11 point Times Roman, leaded 2 points, and 10 point Times Roman, leaded 3 points. Part titles are in 24 point (small font) Helvetica Regular and Part numbers are in 42 point Helvetica Medium. Chapter numbers are in 14 point Helvetica Regular and chapter titles are in 18 point Helvetica Medium. The size of the type page is 26 x 43⅔ picas.*